PRAISE FOR
QUESTIONNAIRE DESIGN

The difference between useful and useless data can often be traced back to the questionnaire. This book is a great resource, guiding you through the myriad of decisions that face the question writer.
Debrah Harding, Managing Director, The Market Research Society

Whether you are new to questionnaire writing, or looking to fine-tune or update your skills, Ian Brace and Kate Bolton's book is an invaluable, practical, easy to dip-into resource.
Nicole Duckworth, Head of Europe and Global Commercial Excellence, PRS IN VIVO

While technology has moved on, the questionnaire remains the core data source that the insight industry is built on. With more and more people writing questionnaires, it is imperative that books like *Questionnaire Design* exist to make sure that standards persist.
Sam Curtis, CEO, Big Sofa Technologies

A fab book, easily accessible and a treasure trove to dip into. There's an art to writing good questionnaires, and this book shows you how.
Darren Bhattachary, CEO, Basis Social

Designing effective questionnaires is an essential skill for all researchers. Kate Bolton and Ian Brace's guide is practical and easy to read; but most importantly, it will ensure you get trustworthy data and powerful insights.
Vishal Badiani, Regional Creative Strategy Manager, Snapchat

Comprehensive, easy to read and exceptionally practical, I'd recommend this book to anyone wanting to learn more about how to design great questionnaires.
Helen Chesney, Head of Solution, Learning at Kantar

Ian Brace and Kate Bolton have produced the 'must-read' book for anyone working the research and insight industry. Read this and learn from the best.
Simon Wood, Head of Research, BMG Research

Questionnaire writing is one of the most essential parts of the craft, a definite artform that takes time and skill to perfect. This is an absolutely essential read for any budding or established researcher looking to hone their questionnaire design skills and avoid the many pitfalls that exist.
Tom Coombes, Research Director, Boxclever

Fifth Edition

Questionnaire Design

How to plan, structure and write survey material for effective market research

Ian Brace and Kate Bolton

KoganPage

Publisher's note

Every possible effort has been made to ensure that the information contained in this book is accurate at the time of going to press, and the publishers and authors cannot accept responsibility for any errors or omissions, however caused. No responsibility for loss or damage occasioned to any person acting, or refraining from action, as a result of the material in this publication can be accepted by the editor, the publisher, or the author.

First published in Great Britain and the United States in 2004 by Kogan Page Limited
Second edition 2008
Third edition 2013
Fourth edition 2018
Fifth edition 2022

2nd Floor, 45 Gee Street	8 W 38th Street, Suite 902	4737/23 Ansari Road
London	New York, NY 10018	Daryaganj
EC1V 3RS	USA	New Delhi 110002
United Kingdom		India

www.koganpage.com

Kogan Page books are printed on paper from sustainable forests.

ISBNs

Hardback	978 1 3986 0414 8
Paperback	978 1 3986 0412 4
Ebook	978 1 3986 0413 1

British Library Cataloguing-in-Publication Data

A CIP record for this book is available from the British Library.

Typeset by Integra Software Services, Pondicherry
Print production managed by Jellyfish
Printed and bound by CPI Group (UK) Ltd, Croydon CR0 4YY

CONTENTS

Introduction

At times it can seem as if everyone is writing questionnaires. Those wanting answers to questions are varied and diverse. Some are big players, eg multi-national companies needing information to develop commercial strategies, or governments to inform policies. Other instigators of requests are much smaller entities, like a school trying to understand how best to involve parents in their child's education, or individuals such as students collecting evidence for a thesis. New technologies also continue to increase the ways – and immediacy – of delivering a survey request, eg popping up during everyday activities like viewing a website.

Asking questions may be the only way of getting the information that is needed – because it is not available via any other source – or it may be the most feasible way in terms of cost and time. But the information gathered is only as good as the questions that are asked. The question writer faces a wide range of challenges that can undermine the value of the questionnaire. At an overall level, decisions need to be made about what question topics to include and exclude – with pressure to keep the interview as short as possible to encourage participation and hold attention. They need to decide in what order to ask the questions and for each individual question they will need to choose an appropriate question type, select wording, add instructions and consider the visual layout. The decisions they make at every point will have an impact on the answers given.

Many other aspects of survey design have an impact on information quality and usefulness, for example, the sampling approach and the robustness of the analysis. Steps to improve these elements (eg increasing sample size) often have a substantial impact on costs. Better questionnaire writing is a low-cost or no-cost improvement that has major rewards in delivering more accurate answers.

The purpose of this book is to provide some general rules and principles that can be applied to writing any type of questionnaire. The book is written principally with students and practitioners of market research in mind, but it should also be of use to social researchers, political opinion pollsters and anyone else who needs to write a questionnaire.

What is a questionnaire?

A questionnaire collects information through a structured interview in which each respondent is presented with a series of questions according to a prepared and fixed interviewing schedule. Thus, this book will not apply to qualitative research interviews. Although qualitative interviews involve a topic guide, the interview schedule, although prepared, is not fixed. It will, however, apply to the recruitment interview, usually used in qualitative research to identify eligible subjects to participate in later depth interviews or focus groups.

In market research the term 'questionnaire' is used to refer both to those for self-completion by survey participants and also to survey instruments administered by an interviewer – either face-to-face or by telephone. In other disciplines a questionnaire involving an interviewer is often referred to as an 'interview schedule', with the term 'questionnaire' reserved for self-completion. Throughout this book the market research common usage of questionnaire encompassing both self-completion and interviewer-administered surveys is used.

The term 'semi-structured interview' will be avoided as it can mean different things to different people. For some it implies a questionnaire consisting almost entirely of open, verbatim questions with probing instructions. This provides a framework for a degree of consistency between interviews conducted by different interviewers, while providing them with scope for greater exploration than is normally possible. For other people the term simply means a questionnaire that contains open verbatim and closed questions.

When the first edition of this book was written, face-to-face interviewing was still probably the most common form of data collection in commercial and social research. In the intervening years there have been massive changes, with face-to-face interviewing now unusual for most commercial research surveys, and increasingly so in social research wherever a credible online alternative is available. This edition recognizes the primacy of online research in discussion of techniques, but still acknowledges the importance of face-to-face and telephone data collection. Each of these modes has its own opportunities and problems, but the general principles of questionnaire construction and writing apply to all of them.

The role of a questionnaire

The questionnaire provides a standardized interview across all interviewees. It manages the interview flow to ensure that all respondents are asked the questions that are appropriate to them, in the same order and so that questions are asked, or presented, in a consistent way.

Asking the questions in the same way is key to most survey research. If a question were asked differently across respondents, then some may understand the question slightly differently and therefore take different things into account when answering. It would not then be valid to aggregate the answers and, if this were done, could result in misleading interpretations. In some instances wording should be tailored for groups of respondents, to recognize different respondent's vocabulary or knowledge of the topic and therefore to help them understand the question. This can be managed within the questionnaire if there are predetermined and identifiable discrete subgroups of respondents, eg those with regular experience of a service vs new users. They can be directed to a question phrased in the way that is most appropriate for them. It cannot be done on an individual basis, nor if the need is not anticipated. The answers to the question would also need to be analyzed separately for these sub-groups.

Challenges of remote conversations

The questionnaire can be viewed as a medium of remote conversation between researcher and respondent. It is, however, a conversation designed by someone who is not present. It is one of the skills of the questionnaire writer to write questions that have the same meaning to all respondents, regardless of how they are read on the screen or page or how an interviewer might say them.

This remoteness is a major difference between quantitative survey research and most qualitative research. Quantitative researchers must be aware of their remoteness from their subjects and allow for it in all they do. In particular, researchers must not forget that each respondent is a real person – and one who has voluntarily given up their time to take part. There can be a tendency for researchers to see respondents purely as sources of information, and write long, complex and boring questionnaires that fail to treat them with the respect that is due. This leads to a lack of engagement of the respondent with the process and the quality of the data collected consequently suffers. It is one of the key requirements of the questionnaire writer to ensure respondents are engaged and continue to be engaged throughout the interview.

One of the consequences of the remoteness of researcher from respondents is the difficulty that structured questionnaires have in eliciting creative responses. The lack of interaction between researcher and respondents, and the consequent inability to tailor questions to the specific respondent, means that the questionnaire should generally be seen as a reactive medium. It is good at obtaining answers to the questions it asks (although we will see many ways in which it can fail to do even this), but it does not provide answers to questions that are not asked, and it is not a good way of tapping into the creativity of consumers. If that is what is required, qualitative research techniques offer far better solutions.

There are many pitfalls the questionnaire writer has to avoid. Throughout the book, some of the most common errors are illustrated by examples taken from a range of different sources. These demonstrate how easy it can be to depart from best practice or even basic principles and collect data that is meaningless or incapable of interpretation. Minor changes have been made in many cases in order to spare the blushes of those responsible.

Obtaining the best answers

All research only represents a model of the real world. We hope that that model will be as accurate as we can make it. In most cases it is not possible to tell just how accurate it is. The political opinion polls are a rare occasion when the model can be judged against the reality of an election result, and they are not always found to be as accurate as we might hope. In many cases the model developed in opinion polls is as accurate as the researcher would expect, but the expectations of others are often higher. In commercial research, the testing of a model is most likely to occur in sales forecasting, but there are many factors outside of the control of the marketing manager, such as competitor response, which make even that not such a rigorous a test of the model as occurs with political opinion polls.

In most research, though, we are left somewhat blind in determining just how good our model is. This puts the onus on researchers to ensure that the data that they collect is as accurate as it can be in describing the market, the social situation, people's beliefs and attitudes or whatever the model sets out to describe or represent.

And mostly, in surveys, we rely on what people tell us. This is not always accurate, and why should it be? We are usually asking volunteer respondents to give up their time, frequently for no or little reward. We ask them to recall events that to them are often trivial, such as the breakfast cereals that they bought, or the choice of flavours of yoghurt offered in the supermarket. We frequently ask them to analyze and report their emotions and feelings about issues that they have never consciously considered, such as their feelings about different brands of paint. Even if they can recognize their feelings and emotions, can they articulate them? Why should they make any effort to do so? The interview may be taking place on a doorstep, or by telephone, when the respondent's first consideration is where the children are; or they may be irritated because they have been interrupted while watching a favourite TV programme. Or the interview may be taking place in a shopping mall, where the respondents are anxious to complete their shopping and go home. Or it may be taking place online, on a PC where there are distractions, and where the motivation is to get the reward offered by the panel company, or on a mobile device with limited attention paid to it.

As researchers, we have to recognize that we cannot expect to be given perfectly accurate information by our respondents. We must construct and use the questionnaire to help respondents give the best information that they can. And it is not just the respondent's ability or willingness to provide accurate answers that we must consider. Our own instruments are often blunt and it can be hard to assess what is true or accurate, particularly in relation to attitudes and opinions where different surveys can produce seemingly different assessments. This sometimes occurs because of differing objectives but can also be due to differences in the survey instrument itself.

Throughout this book are examples of how question wording, response options and layout can all affect the results obtained. The book sets out to cover how we can help respondents to provide us with their best answers in which we reduce unwanted biases and variations to a minimum or, if we cannot achieve that, to at least make us aware that these biases and variations are likely to exist so that we can have confidence in the model of the world that we present.

Standardized survey approaches

Many market research companies now use standardized (often branded and trade-marked) approaches for some of the more common research requirements, such as advertising tracking, advertising pre-testing, brand positioning and customer satisfaction. These approaches use specified questions or questionnaire formats. Their development is usually driven by the value of building on experience – for example identifying question approaches that have been shown to be good predictors of future behaviour or success. Often databases of norms from across hundreds or thousands of similar studies have been built that help to provide a point of comparison to aid interpretation – but whose validity will be reduced if questions are asked in different ways. Standardizing an approach is also likely to have benefits in terms of cost and time – in project management processes but also by reducing the need for the researcher to determine and decide on the questions to be asked each time. However, using standard techniques does not remove the need for the researcher to be aware of the principles of questionnaire design. Standardized surveys are often written with a particular research universe or product sector in mind and need to be adapted for other populations and product sectors. A technique designed for researching fast-moving consumer goods may need considerable alteration for the financial sector.

Many standardized approaches allow some flexibility for additional questions. Decisions will need to be made about how to ask these and how to assess their value, given that their position in the questionnaire is usually restricted to after the standard questions have been asked. Therefore, designing good questions and understanding what might influence the respondents' answers continues to be a necessary skill.

CASE STUDY   Whisky usage and attitude study

Introduction

At the end of each chapter, we will consider a project that covers information needs typical in commercial research. Chapter by chapter we will look at the issues raised that will affect how we approach the questionnaire. By the end of the book we will have written the complete questionnaire, which can be seen in Appendix 1.

Background and business need

Crianlarich Scotch Whisky (a fictitious brand) is positioned as a brand for the off-trade (ie to be sold through off-licences and supermarkets and drunk principally at home). While it is sold in the on-trade (ie bars, pubs, restaurants) there are no plans to focus on that market. It has recently launched a marketing initiative to consolidate its position in the off-trade. The company is planning an advertising campaign in England and Wales that will run for six months, appearing in a variety of newspapers and magazines and on posters. The aim of the campaign is to confirm Crianlarich's position as a leading off-trade brand.

Crianlarich is sold as a cheaper brand and on the proposition that it is the brand drunk by the Scottish, which is believed to be a key motivator of brand choice in this market, although this has not previously been researched.

The main competition is thought to be Grand Prix (another fictitious brand), which is expected to be advertising at the same time as Crianlarich.

The company wishes to conduct a study that will measure the position of the brand in the market and provide feedback on the success of the advertising campaign.

Key take aways: introduction

- Quantitative research aims to provide a model of the real world.
- The questionnaire manages the collection of information from respondents so that it is valid to aggregate the answers to create this model. It does this by providing a structured and standardized interview.
- The success of a questionnaire in eliciting accurate information is key to the usefulness of that model.
- Unfortunately, there is a lot that can go wrong, not least the challenge of holding the respondents' attention, and asking questions that they can realistically be expected to answer accurately.
- The question writer will need to make many decisions (and compromises), including:
  o what to include (and leave out);
  o order;
  o type of question;
  o exact wording;

o layout;

o instructions.

- As these choices can influence the way the respondent answers, every question writer needs to understand their impact and the steps required to eliminate (or at least reduce) any undesired effects. Users of research data also need to remember these possible limitations when interpreting the outputs.

Defining achievable questionnaire objectives

01

Introduction

The key to almost all the decisions that need to be made by the questionnaire writer is a crystal-clear understanding in the first place of what the questionnaire needs to achieve. Gaining this clarity can sometimes be the hardest challenge of all. Not only will it affect specific decisions about how to structure, order and word questions – but it fundamentally affects whether a question has earned its place in a questionnaire. The questionnaire will be under pressure to be shorter and smarter than ever given the growing number of survey requests that are bombarding our potential respondents.

The questionnaire in the survey process

The questionnaire represents one part of the survey process. However, before any questions can be asked, the sample must be defined, and the sampling method and the data collection medium must be determined. In addition, the overall structural design of the survey must be considered. Typically, decisions on this are driven by thinking ahead to what is necessary, or useful, for interpreting the resulting data. For example, if the survey is measuring the impact of a marketing activity it may be useful to benchmark key measures before the activity starts. In which case the design might involve a pre- and post-wave of interviewing. Or maybe a decision needs to be made about which of two new product recipes should be launched. Should each respondent be asked to test both recipes to give a direct comparison? Would it be better to employ a monadic design where respondents are assigned randomly to one or other product? This would create a more realistic situation but might be harder to interpret as there is no direct comparison. These are all crucial stages in designing a survey that is appropriate to answering the objectives, and although outside the scope of this book, all will have an influence on the way in which the questionnaire is written.

The question writer also needs to plan ahead to what analysis will be most useful. Questions must be included to ensure key analysis sub-groups can be identified (eg age groups, user groups, brand loyal vs repertoire buyers etc). Other questions may be needed to provide the context necessary to understand the key measures: understanding a dog owner's preference for pack size of dog food is likely to be dependent on other variables, such as breed, size, number of dogs, etc.

Questionnaire writing is an integral part of the survey process. How the questionnaire is written affects the other survey processes, and what is to happen in those processes affects how the questionnaire is written.

The objectives of the study

Business objectives and research objectives

It is important to make a distinction between the business/organization objectives that underly the project – and the research objectives that the project (and the questionnaire) will be designed to deliver against.

Business objective: to enter the mobile telecoms market with a pricing package that is attractive to at least 60 per cent of the current contract market.

Research objectives:

- to determine the distribution of the amount that mobile telecoms users who have a contract pay per month;
- to determine how that amount is made up from standing charges, call charges and special offers and discounts;
- to determine level of satisfaction with current supplier;
- to determine the level of price advantage that would be required for them to consider switching supplier.

The business objectives relate to decisions and actions the organization wants to make – whereas the research objectives are articulated in terms of the type and scope of information needed to help make these decisions. In some cases this distinction may seems like a matter of semantics. However, making the difference clear is important in ensuring that end users have a realistic perspective of the role of research. Research in itself doesn't make decisions – research is a tool that enables end users to make better decisions based on the information it generates. Without a clear focused understanding of what the organization is trying to achieve there is a danger that the research objectives will be inappropriately defined – at worst generating information that is irrelevant and useless. A more common problem is that the objectives become too broad. There is limited time in a questionnaire and it will be harder to make decisions about what could be left out. As a consequence the questionnaire is likely to be longer than it needs to be with the resulting risk to data quality, eg through loss of motivation and engagement. Direct actionability of results is also often increased when the questions are focused on specific issues. However, with limited questionnaire space this focus and depth will be compromised if trying to cover too wide a range of issues.

Clarifying the business objectives

It can be harder than it might first seem to ensure that the business objectives underlying the project are clear. Often the question writer is not the end user of the research but is responsible for delivering useful data to other stakeholders in the business. It is important for the question writer to understand from these clients how they intend to use the data. Often the overarching aim is fairly easy to articulate (eg to grow the market share) but it can be harder to think about how to get there. The following may be useful as prompts to help the discussion between the question writer and end user in clarifying the specific need:

- What decisions have already been made?
- How confident are you about the decisions you've already made?
- How did you get to this point?
- What information have you had access to?
- Has any previous research been undertaken?
- What actions are you considering?
- What would you do if you couldn't do any research?
- What's the risk of making a poor decision at this stage?

Study objectives: to determine which of two possible recipes for pasta sauce (A or B) is preferred

At a simplistic level this objective could be answered by asking a sample of the relevant market to taste each of the two recipes and to say which they preferred. However, the first thing to do is to determine what information is required, and that will entail asking questions of the brief. Is it enough to know that x per cent prefer Recipe A and y per cent prefer Recipe B? Do we need to know whether the people who prefer Recipe A differ from those who prefer Recipe B in any way, such as demographic characteristics, the volume of pasta sauce they typically consume, and which brands or recipes they currently use? Can either or both of the recipes be amended following the research to improve their appeal – which would mean that questions about what was liked and disliked about each one should be included? Is it possible to create a new recipe combining some of the characteristics from each of A and B?

Only after the brief has been interrogated in this way can we determine either the final survey design or the information required to address the objective in full.

Translating business objectives into research objectives

Research objectives should not look like a detailed list of all the information needed but more an articulation of the scope of information required to address the business objectives.

The ability of the researcher to translate the business objectives into these research goals is a key skill. In commercial pitches for research projects this can be an important driver of choice for the commissioning company: they would be looking for evidence that the researcher has fully understood the business challenge and has articulated research objectives that they are confident are achievable. A tendency is to overpromise, yet a skilled researcher and question writer will be aware not only of the power of research but also of the limitations. We might need certain information, but we must be realistic about what a respondent is able to answer accurately – even with a well-constructed question.

Be wary of long lists of research objectives, with no clear link to the business objectives, no indication of priority order and measurement language that overpromises. This latter point is a particular watch-out for lower priority objectives; the highest priority objectives should drive the questionnaire design. If compromises are needed (eg in the order in which questions are asked, or in the depth of questioning) then the way the research objectives are expressed should reflect this to manage expectations. It is reasonable to expect the measurement language to be less assertive for lower priority objectives (eg 'to explore' rather than 'to determine').

The ideal situation might appear to be when the researcher receives a brief from the client or end-user that provides both the business objectives and the research objectives. However, even when this occurs the onus should be on the researcher to ensure that the two align and that by delivering against the research objectives the survey will enable the business objectives to be addressed effectively.

Can you get the information from anywhere else?

It is outside the scope of this book to look at overall research design in any detail. However, it's important to recognize that rigorous thinking at the outset is needed about the existence and value of other sources of information, as well as the use of non-questionnaire-based research approaches in collecting some of the information needed.

Too frequently too much expectation is placed on a questionnaire to deliver against all needs, partly due to the attraction of obtaining all the information from a single source. Of course, there can be challenges in aligning data from different sources, and there will inevitably be some gaps and inconsistencies (eg in terminology and definitions used across secondary sources). In addition, spreading the budget too thinly over multiple research approaches can be less effective in the long run as the robustness of each may be compromised. However, we face a reality that questionnaire time is precious: quality is affected by length. Overloading questionnaires can be a false economy and the quality of the resulting learning may be no better – and possibly worse – than integrating insights from a range of sources.

As well as helping to focus the research objectives for the questionnaire survey element, thinking through other sources of information at the outset will also be helpful when it comes to interpreting the data. For example, providing context and points of comparison to help build confidence in emerging conclusions.

Stakeholders in the questionnaire

In designing an effective questionnaire the question writer will need to acknowledge the role and potentially conflicting needs of the different people who will be impacted by it:

- **Clients,** the end users commissioning the study, are the primary stakeholders and want the questionnaire to collect the information that will enable them to address their business issue.

- **Respondents** want a questionnaire that poses them questions they can answer without too much effort, that engages them and maintains their interest, is enjoyable to complete, and does not take up too much of their time.

- **Interviewers,** where used, want a questionnaire that allows them to perform their role well and as easily as possible. They need it to be straightforward to administer, have questions that are easily understood by the respondent and that help to manage the interaction between the two parties in a professional and respectful way.

- **Data processors** want a questionnaire layout that allows for uncomplicated scripting or data entry, and for the straightforward production of data tables or other analyzes that may be required.

- **Researchers** (or questionnaire writers) have to strive to meet all of these people's needs, and to usually do so while working within the parameters of a budget and timing.

The questionnaire writer's job can be summarized, then, as being to write a questionnaire to address the client's issue that collects data as objectively as possible and without irritating or annoying the respondents, while minimizing the likelihood of error occurring at any stage in the data collection and analysis process.

Collecting unbiased and accurate data: summary of problems

While these will be discussed in the context of specific topics throughout this book it is useful to acknowledge the main themes in this opening chapter since they affect what is realistically achievable and may impact how the objectives are defined.

Respondent issues:

- failure of the respondent to understand the question;
- inattention to the interview because of respondent boredom and fatigue;
- desire by the respondent to answer a different question to the one asked;
- inaccuracy of memory regarding behaviour;
- inaccuracy of memory regarding time periods (telescoping);
- respondents wishing to impress;
- respondents not willing to admit their attitudes or behaviour either consciously or subconsciously;
- respondents trying to influence the outcome of the study and giving answers that they believe will lead to a particular conclusion.

The last three respondent issues here are part of a subject known as 'social desirability bias'. Chapter 16 focuses exclusively on this as it is sufficiently important to warrant a chapter of its own.

Questionnaire issues:

- ambiguity in the question;
- order effects between questions;
- order effects within a question;
- inadequate response codes;
- wrong questions asked because of poor routing;
- failure of the questionnaire to record the reply accurately or completely.

Interviewer issues:

- questions asked inaccurately;
- failure to record the reply accurately or completely;
- mistakes made because of boredom and fatigue.

These issues have been long acknowledged in relation to questionnaire writing and an analysis of them can be found in Kalton and Schuman (1982).

CASE STUDY Whisky usage and attitude

The initial request outlined that research was needed to measure the position of the Crianlarich brand in the market and provide feedback on the success of the proposed advertising campaign.

Clarifying the business objectives

Through discussion of the underlying purpose, we confirmed that building sales in England and Wales (rather than Scotland) is central to the client's growth strategy. An important factor influencing the scope of the project was also clarified: ie the focus is on building off-trade sales, where they already have a good retail distribution, rather than through on-trade sales where Crianlarich's presence in bars, pubs and other venues is poor.

The goals of the advertising campaign itself were identified as being to get whisky drinkers to purchase Crianlarich for drinking in home and to position Crianlarich as the brand drunk by the Scottish.

However, through discussions it emerged that the premise of the advertising was suspected rather than known: it was uncertain whether Crianlarich's credentials as the leading Scottish brand would be a key motivator in the rest of the UK. There was also some concern about whether this would be relevant for the most experienced scotch drinkers who were likely to generate the most volume sales – or whether it was more relevant to less frequent scotch drinkers. Greater understanding (through research) of Crianlarich's current position and confidence in the communication strategy was therefore deemed necessary. This would allow the client to make decisions about whether the message and/or the advertising delivering it needed any changes.

Translation into research objectives

From this better understanding of the advertising premise, we agreed the following research objectives:

- to determine the impact of the advertising on awareness of Crianlarich;
- to determine the perceptions of the brand on key product and image dimensions;
- to measure any change in those perceptions over the course of the advertising campaign;
- to determine the importance of the brand's key advertising proposition, that it is a brand drunk by the Scottish;
- to measure all of the above among both light and heavy off-trade scotch whisky drinkers.

Study design

We recognized that it would be difficult for respondents to be able to accurately attribute any change in their perceptions to a specific source (ie to advertising), or even to know whether their perceptions had actually changed. Therefore, we recommended obtaining benchmark measures of the awareness and position of Crianlarich in the market before the launch of the advertising (pre-wave) and again following completion of the campaign (post-wave), to measure changes that may be attributable to the advertising.

The research sample was defined as follows: all adults who have drunk off-trade whisky in the past month and who drink it at least once every three months. We chose this definition as the aim of the advertising is not to convert non-drinkers but to appeal to current scotch drinkers, and we are focusing on understanding the off-trade market. From looking at existing usage data we felt that the time periods used in the definition would allow sub-groups of light and heavy drinkers to be identified.

What respondent limitations and question challenges should we expect?

We can expect to encounter a number of issues with this market:

- Respondents may not always be truthful about the amount of whisky they drink or they may not be able to accurately recall.
- There may be telescoping in the recall, particularly among less frequent whisky drinkers.
- We shall need to distinguish carefully between in-home and out-of-home drinking.
- Brands drunk in bars, pubs, restaurants and other people's homes may not be accurately recalled, or even always known.
- Some respondents may claim to drink more expensive brands than they really do in order to impress.

This is a market with which we know many drinkers are engaged, but nevertheless the risk of fatigue through boredom with the questionnaires is always present.

Other information sources

To help with the interpretation of effectiveness of the advertising we will access published information on advertising spend within this sector.

The client also has extensive previous research among Scottish whisky drinkers. While the focus is on is the English/Welsh drinkers in this project, this existing data source is likely to be useful in building the client's awareness of differences between the markets.

Key take aways: defining achievable questionnaire objectives

- It is important to distinguish between the business objectives that underpin the need for research (ie the decisions that the research will inform) and the research objectives (what the research itself will measure):
  - Research collects information to help better decision making, it doesn't make the decisions.
  - The researcher needs clarity on the decisions the organization wants to be able to ensure the research is focused.
  - Focus is essential as questionnaires need to be short to maximize quality.
- If only the business objectives are provided at the outset, these need to be translated into research objectives: information needs that research can realistically achieve. These must reflect respondent limitations and practical constraints.
- If both business objectives and research objectives are provided the researcher must nonetheless check that they align.
- Identification and consideration of the value of other information sources is vital in ensuring that the questionnaire is focused on gaps and in providing context to help later interpretation.
- Respondents' needs may at times conflict with the client's needs. Similarly, things that make life easier, cheaper or quicker for people involved in the process may not always be advantageous for the end user, or the respondent. The question writer needs to be skilled at making compromises, and in explaining the rationale for their decisions.

Influence of data collection mode on question design
02

Introduction

Questionnaire-based data collection modes can be broadly divided into two categories: self-completion approaches, which include paper, online SMS or IVR (voice recognition), and interviewer administered which will usually be face-to-face or by telephone

Sometimes these approaches are used in combination. For example, interviewers recruiting on-street, administering the screening questions, and then providing a web link to eligible respondents for self-completion later.

Each data collection mode has its own benefits for the question writer, but each also has drawbacks.

Choice of data collection mode

Although the choice of data collection mode has implications for the question writer, the decision on which to employ is usually primarily driven by overall survey design and sample considerations. The lower costs usually associated with self-completion approaches (ie with no interviewer to pay for their time), is often a key consideration. However, this typically needs to be balanced against the difficulties of achieving a representative sample as a high degree of self-selection is common with self-completion studies which may introduce bias, particularly when there is a low response rate. Survey design and sampling are crucial topics, but detailed consideration is outside the scope of this book. Here the focus is on understanding the advantages and limitations that will affect the decisions the question writer faces.

Digitally scripted or non-scripted data collection?

An important factor that overlaps with consideration of the data collection mode is the technology involved in creating the questionnaire and recording answers. For example, will the survey be scripted using survey software with answers digitally recorded? Or will it be non-scripted (typically paper based), requiring later data entry? (This data entry could either be manual or using scanning software.) Whether a survey is scripted or non-scripted also has significant implications for the question writer.

All online self-completion surveys will be digitally scripted and therefore the benefits of using a scripted questionnaire will apply. Online surveys are sometimes referred to as CAWI (computer-aided web interviewing). Paper self-completion questionnaires on the other hand will not be scripted and therefore will share the disadvantages that brings. In contrast, interviewer-administered surveys may be digitally scripted or paper-based and therefore when considering interviewer administered modes the implications for questionnaire design also depend on whether it will be scripted or not.

For face-to-face interviewing the term CAPI (computer-assisted personal interviewing) is commonly used to denote the use of a portable computer that will display a scripted questionnaire on screen for the interviewer. The computers can be either tablet computers with a touch screen or laptop personal computers. Both may have multimedia capabilities. In central locations, desktop personal computers may be used. Personal digital assistants (PDAs) or smartphones can be used in some circumstances where the number of questions is relatively small (Anderson et al, 2011). PDAs have also been used successfully as a self-completion medium.

Computer-assisted telephone interviewing (CATI) brings many of the same advantages of scripting to telephone that CAPI does to face-to-face interviewing.

Benefits of using digital scripting software

For the questionnaire writer, a survey that is digitally scripted presents a number of opportunities in structuring the questionnaire. These include the ability to:

- Rotate or randomize response lists.
- Rotate or randomize questions or repeated question sets.

- Use word substitution in order to customize questions or response lists to the individual respondent, often referred to as 'piping' (using responses given to earlier questions).

- Include real-time edit checks for entry errors or consistency and logic against earlier answers.

- Cope with complex routing. Thus, the next question to be presented to the respondent can be determined by a combination of answers from a number of previous questions.

- Carry out calculations within the interview. For example, an estimate of a household's annual consumption of a grocery product can be calculated. This would be difficult for the respondent to estimate independently, however, they may be able to make more accurate estimates of short-term consumption for each member of the family, from which total household consumption can be calculated. In business-to-business interviewing, volumes of consumption or output can be summed either as a total or within predetermined categories. This information can be used both as inputs to future questions and for question routing.

The combination of being able to make calculations and to randomize response lists has allowed the development of some complex techniques such as adaptive conjoint analysis. This includes an element of instant analysis of responses to determine which and how many questions are then shown. With adaptive conjoint, the responses to questions asked at the beginning of the sequence are used to construct scenarios shown at later questions where the respondent is asked to provide preferences between them.

Even if the routing is not especially complex, the fact that this is handled automatically has benefits for both interviewer-administered and self-completion approaches. In a face-to-face or telephone survey the interviewer's attention can be fully focused on creating a good interviewing relationship or rapport, rather than being distracted by working out what question comes next. In an online self-completion, where motivation to continue or to stay fully engaged may wane if survey mechanics get in the way, the respondent can concentrate on thinking about the questions rather than on navigation so data quality may be improved.

Playing or demonstrating material can also be achieved with some scripted surveys. TV or cinema advertisements can be shown – either to measure recognition or to evaluate content – although the quality with which they are seen will depend on the equipment the respondent is using to view them. Packs can be displayed, and supermarket shelves simulated. This creates opportunities to simulate a presentation, as it would appear in a store, with different numbers of facings for different products, as an attempt to reproduce better the actual in-store choice situation. Three-dimensional pack simulations can be shown and rotated by respondents.

Direct digital inputting of the answers with a scripted questionnaire means that issues resulting from illegibility of the respondent's or interviewer's handwriting are clearly avoided. This is of particular benefit for numerical questions (handwritten 1s can often look like 7s). There may still be some issues with disentangling spelling and typos for verbatim answers, but generally typed verbatims are easier and quicker to decipher than handwritten answers.

A key benefit in terms of data quality is the ability – as mentioned in the previous list – to script real-time edit checks that can lead to fewer errors and reduce the amount of time spent cleaning data. For example, during a numerical question an immediate check could be made to ensure that the number entered falls within a sensible range. This would help to catch gross typing errors (eg typing '77' instead of '7'). Other simple entry checks can also easily be made (eg checking that only one answer is given for questions that require a single coded response), or checking that numbers add up (eg if asking people to reiterate their last 10 purchases across brands). Logical consistency across answers can also be monitored (eg ensuring that brands identified as being in a purchase repertoire have also been coded at an earlier brand-awareness question). These types of checks can help reduce errors caused by misunderstanding the question or to catch the occasional unhelpful respondent giving nonsense answers (this is especially valuable on self-completion questionnaires where there is no interviewer to encourage engagement). Responsibility for deciding what edits are needed typically lies with the question writer even though they might not be the person creating the actual programmed script.

Challenges of using digital scripting software

Generally, if scripting the questionnaire is a feasible option for the question writer, then this route is usually taken due to numerous benefits discussed; most of which are likely to lead to improved data quality over non-scripted/paper versions regardless of the data collection mode. However, there are a few challenges of which the questionnaire writer needs to be aware:

The script for the questionnaire can be harder to check, especially if the capabilities that it offers for tailoring via piping answers and complex routing have been fully utilized. The multiple routes through a questionnaire will each need to be tested to ensure they are working correctly. This can involve extensive script checking of many combinations of possible answers. On a paper, non-scripted questionnaire, whose workings are more transparent, there are likely to be more opportunities to spot problems: whether it is the respondent handwriting a comment, or an interviewer feeding back to the researcher that a particular section always seems to be bypassed by the routing.

If the questionnaire writer has used the opportunity to script real-time edits, they need to be confident that these will catch genuine errors and not simply constrain the data on the basis of their assumptions. For example, setting an allowable range for numerically entered data. If set too tightly then genuine answers outside this range will never be captured and this could lead to erroneous conclusions. Mistakes like this are perhaps most likely when creating questionnaires for multi-country studies where the responses might vary considerably. In this case, a question writer might determine an acceptable range based on their own national frame of reference, without international consideration.

Consideration also needs to be given to whether the intelligence that is scripted in should be forward-driven (ie piped through on the basis of answers to previous questions), or backward-driven (ie an error message triggered by an edit check against an earlier answer). A danger of forward-driven programming is that an early mistake may carry over and dictate what the respondent is exposed to later. For example, an early question on brand awareness could determine which brands are shown to respondents during a subsequent question about purchase habits. Brand lists for awareness questions are often lengthy. If the respondent skim reads the list and misses a relevant brand, it would not feature in the later purchase list. This is a particular risk if they are aware of many brands and feel that they have ticked 'enough' even if their awareness answer is not complete. If no piping was involved and the whole list was shown again, then any inconsistencies in awareness could be back filled on the basis of purchase (which is likely to be more accurate, involving fewer brands and thus not suffering from selection fatigue).

Scripting software often requires an answer to be input at each question before the next question is displayed. This prevents respondents or interviewers missing questions by mistake, or by deliberately speeding through. Therefore a 'don't know' option is usually listed to ensure that everyone is able to select an answer. However, it may be that explicitly offering this as a valid response encourages the use of 'don't knows', which are often reported in higher volumes than in non-scripted surveys (in comparison with 'no answer').

It might be thought that an issue with scripted questionnaires would be the difficulty of recording open-ended verbatim responses with both respondent and interviewer typing speeds being slower than writing speeds. However, experience has shown that while this is undoubtedly an issue for some, the overall level of detail to verbatim question can be maintained.

Self-completion surveys

Advantages of self-completion for the question writer

From a questionnaire design perspective, one of the main advantages of any self-completion form is that respondents have time to consider their answers. They can pause while they think about an issue, go away to check something or look up some information. With little time pressure on them, they can write lengthy and full answers to open questions if they wish to do so. This benefit of time is particularly advantageous if any stimulus material that they are required to read is complex or particularly detailed, such as concepts for financial services or business-to-business research.

Self-completion can also benefit from the absence of an interviewer from the process. This removes a major source of potential bias in the responses and makes it easier for respondents to be honest about sensitive subjects. Self-completion modes can be considered as capturing the unedited voice of the consumer, so that open-ended responses can more revealing. In addition, evidence from Kellner (2004) and Basi (1999) supports the view that because there is no interviewer there is less social desirability bias and the respondents answer more honestly. This means that data on sensitive or polarising questions – where respondents feel a need to appear to be socially acceptable – is likely to represent better how the survey population really feels.

Disadvantages of self-completion for the question writer

A major disadvantage is not having an interviewer on hand to clarify questions or to repair misunderstandings. This reinforces the demands made on the questionnaire writer to make the questionnaire clear, unambiguous and engaging.

   The presence of an interviewer also gives the respondent a reason to continue with an interview that they might otherwise have stopped, or to continue to make an effort even though they might be losing interest. While the quality of answers is likely to be affected by tedium and excess length regardless of data collection mode, the impact is likely to be greater for self-completion surveys. Therefore, there is even greater onus on the question writer to consider how intrinsically interesting the topic is likely to be for the respondent and to see the questionnaire completion experience from the respondents' point of view. While many options for making surveys more engaging will apply to all modes, thinking how to make the questionnaire more visually appealing will be additionally important for self-completion surveys, and the design time and capabilities to do this need to be factored in (see Chapter 11).

   Having time to consider answers – while often an advantage of self-completion surveys – is not always what the questionnaire writer wants. With attitudinal and image questions, it is often the first reaction that is sought, rather than a considered response. An instruction in the question for respondents to give their first reaction cannot be enforced, nor encouraged in the way that an interviewer can, either face-to-face or by telephone.

Online self-completion

There are several different ways of carrying out surveys using the internet. The questionnaire can either be delivered by email or accessed via a web page. The main approaches are summarized by Bradley (1999) as follows:

- **Open web**: a website open to anyone who visits it.
- **Closed web**: respondents are invited to visit a website to complete a questionnaire.
- **Hidden web**: the questionnaire appears to a visitor only when triggered by some mechanism (eg date, visitor number, interest in a specific page). This includes pop-up surveys.
- **Email URL embedded**: a respondent is invited by email to the survey site, and the email contains a URL or web address on which respondents click.
- **Simple email**: an email with questions contained in it.
- **Email attachment**: the questionnaire is sent as an attachment to an email.

The last two of these (the simple email and email attachment) are rarely used in commercial research for a variety of practical reasons. Attachments require respondents to download the questionnaire, complete it and then return it. This requires a lot of cooperation and has been shown to lead to low response rates. Questionnaires embedded within emails can have their layout distorted, depending on the email software with which they are opened. Both of these approaches also suffer from the inability to include complex routing. Most practitioners use questionnaires hosted on a website to which respondents are invited or routed in some way. This book looks only at this dominant form: the web-based online questionnaire.

The invitation to the website or questionnaire can be delivered in a number of ways:

- By link in an email to people on a panel or to a mailing list of customers or people who might qualify for the survey.
- Pop-ups used to direct respondents to the questionnaire while they are visiting another site.
- Invitations can be posted as banner ads on other sites, such as ISP home pages.
- Respondents can be directed to the site following a face-to-face or telephone recruitment interview, or from an online advertisement for respondents (Nunan and Knox, 2011).

Each of these presents different issues regarding how representative of the target population the sample is, in particular where the population contains a significant offline element. These are survey design issues outside the scope of this book and are well covered elsewhere. In addition to internet-based surveys, IVR and SMS self-completion modes are options, but as they usually constrain the survey to a couple of questions they will not be considered separately here. The general principles of question composition will, however, still apply to these modes.

Advantages and disadvantages of online self-completion for the question writer

With scripted self-completion questionnaires, it is possible to control whether the respondent is able to look ahead, or go back and change previous answers. This capability offers the question writer the opportunity to ensure that questions are presented in the sequence that the researcher wants them to be answered. This also means that – in comparison with paper self-completion – it is possible to ask spontaneous questions without the risk of the respondent being influenced by later questions.

Many online studies use respondents who have opted in to panels to take part in research projects. Usually, panellists are rewarded with some kind of incentive system – typically collecting points related to the volume of surveys completed. The panel providers have a variety of quality control procedures to catch rogue respondents, such as 'speeders', who may simply be trying to amass points. From the question writer's perspective it is especially important to ensure that their screening questions successfully disguise the eligibility criteria so that respondents can't work out themselves how to qualify for surveys. At the same time, a panellist may well have several surveys to choose from during the course of a typical week, and so the writer also has to ensure that the initial survey introduction and early questions are immediately engaging.

When designing an internet-based survey it is vital that the question writer considers the likely device on which the survey will be taken. This is usually a mix of computers, mobile phones and tablets, with the proportion of respondents using handheld devices continuing to increase. Smaller screens and portrait orientation place additional constraints on the layout and presentation of questions (see Chapter 10).

Paper self-completion questionnaires

Paper self-completion questionnaires are typically sent by mail to people who qualify or are thought to qualify as eligible for the study. They may be selected from a database, such as the customers of a business or the members of an organization. In many countries the national database of postal addresses is comprehensive and up to date in terms of listing residential properties, and as such using this for postal self-completion surveys potentially provides the most inclusive way of contacting all types of respondents if a nationally representative sample is required. Balanced against this, however, is the typically low response rate, especially if postal return is required with the additional effort this involves. Sometimes postal is used for the means of contact, but with a web link provided so that the actual questionnaire is conducted online. This allows the benefits of a scripted mode to be utilized.

Paper self-completion questionnaires are also extensively used in convenience sampling of specific target populations (eg distributing questionnaires on-site to people attending an event, staying at a hotel or eating in a restaurant).

Advantages and disadvantages of paper self-completion for the question writer

There are few obvious advantages of paper self-completion for the question writer – this approach is usually adopted if it is the most practical solution to reach a specific target audience at a specific location ie by handing out paper questionnaires.

With a paper self-completion questionnaire, it is impossible to stop respondents from reading through all of the questions before responding. Certain questions therefore cannot be included. It is not possible to ask a spontaneous brand-awareness question if the questionnaire includes brand names in any of the other questions.

Where prompt material has been sent to the respondents for their reaction, it is also difficult to retrieve all of it. This can present a security concern if the material is commercially sensitive.

Interviewer-administered questionnaires

Advantages of the interviewer's presence for the question writer

The presence of an interviewer can be a benefit for the question writer for two main reasons. First, the rapport that a skilled interviewer can build with a respondent can create a helpful environment, encouraging thoughtful answers and maintaining momentum throughout the interview. Second, the interviewer is on hand to deal with any issues or queries.

Respondents can be encouraged by the interviewer to provide deeper responses to open questions. At the simplest level, a series of non-directive probes (eg 'what else?') can be used by the interviewer to extract as much information as possible from the respondent. If a bland and unhelpful answer is anticipated, the interviewer can be specifically asked to obtain further clarification. For example, the question, 'Why did you buy the item from that shop in particular?' is likely to get the answer, 'Because it was convenient.' An interviewer can be given an instruction not to accept an answer that only mentions convenience, and the questionnaire will supply the probe: 'What do you mean by convenient?'

Sometimes a question can be unintentionally ambiguous. Although this should have been spotted and corrected before the questionnaire was finalized, it is possible for such questions to slip through. If respondents cannot answer because of an ambiguity, then they are able to ask the interviewer for clarification. Interviewers, though, must be careful not to lead respondents to a particular answer when giving their clarification, and should report back to the researcher that clarification was required.

Interviewers can sometimes spot that respondents have misunderstood the question by the response they give. This may be because of the answer given or because it is inconsistent with previous answers, or simply inconsistent with what the interviewer already knows (or suspects) about the respondent. Such inconsistencies can be challenged, the question repeated, and the response corrected if necessary.

Disadvantages of the interviewer's presence for the question writer

The accuracy of the data can be influenced by the interaction between interviewer and respondent. Although interviewers are instructed to administer the questions exactly as they written it is not uncommon to hear an interviewer change the wording or paraphrase a question. The root fault may lie with the question writer however for creating the situation in which the interviewer feels their actions are necessary to be able to manage and complete the interview, for example:

- The interviewer finds the wording stilted. Anyone who has written a question to be spoken will have sometimes found that – however natural it appears on the page – when spoken aloud it sounds awkward and does not flow. Interviewers may paraphrase accordingly.

- The interviewer may think that the question is too long. One of their aims is to maintain the attention of the respondent, and a long and detailed question with several sub-clauses detracts from that.

- The interviewer may think the question is repetitive, either through repetition within the question, repetition of instructions or descriptions between questions or may think that the question has already been asked. Again, to keep the respondent engaged they may omit what they see as duplication.

- They may not understand the question themselves, or feel that the respondent is unlikely to. With business-to-business interviews, there may be terminology that is completely new to the interviewer who then mispronounces key words or substitutes them with other, more familiar, words. With consumer interviews, overuse of marketing jargon can have the same result. A thorough briefing of the interviewers in the technical terms used and the provision of a glossary of terms that are likely to be used by respondents is worthwhile here. Such a glossary may also be of value to coders and analysts in later stages of the survey process.

If a question is paraphrased, there is a chance that its original meaning (and subsequent response) are changed. The role of the interviewer is to hold a conversation with the respondent that fulfils the aims of the researcher. The question writer must therefore ensure that questions are written in a manner to best achieve this.

Interviewers may record responses inaccurately in a number of ways:

- They may simply mishear the response – this is particularly likely to happen if the interviewer's attention is focused more on the mechanics of applying the interview. Scripted questionnaires reduce these challenges (eg by automatically handling routing to the next question), but interviewer distraction can be a common problem with complex, non-scripted paper-based surveys.

- With open-ended (verbatim) questions, interviewers may not record everything that is said. There is a temptation to paraphrase and précis the response, again to keep the interview flowing and so as not to make the respondent wait while the full response is recorded.

- It is common to provide a list of pre-codes as possible answers to an open question that only the interviewer sees. Their task is to listen to the answer given then scan the list and code the answer that most closely matches. This is open to error. None of the answers may match exactly what the respondent has said. The interviewer then has the choice of taking the one that is closest to the given response, or there is frequently an option to write in verbatim responses that have not been anticipated. There is a strong temptation to make the given response match one of the pre-coded answers, thus inaccurately recording the true response. The pre-coded list may contain similar, but crucially different answers. The onus is on the question writer to ensure that these are carefully grouped to give the interviewer most chance of seeing subtle differences and selecting the right answer.

- A long and tedious interview affects not only the respondent but also the interviewer. Like everybody else, interviewers make mistakes. Responses can be misheard, or a wrong code recorded, and these errors become more frequent if the interviewer is tired of the interview. With a tedious or repetitive questionnaire, the interviewer may feel embarrassed to bore the respondent. The interviewer could then respond by reading through the questions faster, leading to an increase in the number of errors.

The presence of an interviewer is also likely to increase the chance of social desirability bias through respondents wishing to impress or appear polite. This is covered in detail in Chapter 16.

Face-to-face interviewing

In the UK, face-to-face interviewing was the dominant mode of data collection for many years prior to the advent of online surveys. Face-to-face surveys are expensive to conduct compared to online surveys and are therefore mainly used for surveys requiring a representative sample of a population; access to a difficult-to-reach sample; or where there is product or material to be demonstrated (eg car clinics or test kitchens).

In countries where there is a wide geographic spread of the population, such as the United States, face-to-face interviewing has never accounted for the same high proportion of interviews and is mainly limited to mall-intercepts.

Advantages and disadvantages of face-to-face interviewing for the question writer

One clear advantage of using face-to-face interviewers over telephone interviewers is the ability to show prompt cards to respondents. These cards can be used in questions where prompted awareness or recognition of names is required; where respondents are being asked to select their answer from a scale; or where it is desirable to prompt with a list of possible responses.

Social desirability bias is likely to be greatest when the interviewer is physically present, so the question writer needs to consider what steps they can take to reduce this.

Telephone-administered questionnaires

Most of the advantages enjoyed by telephone interviewing over face-to-face are to the benefit of survey design rather than to questionnaire design. There are efficiencies in cost and speed, particularly where the sample is geographically dispersed, or where – as often happens in business-to-business surveys – the respondents are prepared to talk on the telephone but not to have someone visit them.

Advantages and disadvantages of telephone interviewing for the question writer

One advantage for data accuracy is that the telephone as a medium gives more anonymity to the respondents in respect of their relationship to the interviewer. This can help to diminish some of the bias that can occur as a result of respondents trying to impress or save-face in front of interviewers, but not as much as removing the interviewer altogether. It is also the experience of many researchers that respondents are more prepared to discuss sensitive subjects such as health over the telephone, rather than face-to-face with an interviewer. Fuller responses are achieved to open questions, and they are more likely to be honest because the interviewer is not physically present with the respondent. Telephone interviewing thus becomes the medium of choice for interviews where there is a need for an interviewer-administered interview, coupled with a sensitive subject matter.

From the point of view of the questionnaire writer, telephone interviewing has a number of disadvantages. First, it places constraints on questions that involve prompted lists of answers that require the respondent to hear all options before answering. These might include list of reasons or attributes from which selection of the most appropriate is required, or semantic rating scales where each scale point must be understood before answering. These lists must be short and simple enough for the respondent to hold in their heads. For longer lists of response options, or repeated lists such as scales, respondents can be asked to write them down but their compliance and accuracy in doing this is not guaranteed.

> With telephone interviewing, respondents have to remember or write down response lists. Don't make these too long, or they won't be able to remember all the options or bother to write them down.

The inability to show stimulus material such as concepts or advertising is another drawback of telephone interviewing. However, radio adverts or the soundtrack from TV adverts can be played over the telephone as a prompt for recognition. Care must be taken to distinguish responses that arise because of the quality of the recording as heard by the respondent – which can be variable – from those relating to content.

It is possible to mail material to respondents for them to look at before or during the telephone interview. This creates a lengthy and more expensive process. The respondents must be recruited and their agreement obtained in an initial interview. The material then has to be sent, and the main interview can only be carried out once the material has arrived.

It may be desirable for respondents not to see the material before a certain point in the interview. In that case, the initial contact would complete the interview up until that point, when respondents would be asked permission for the researcher to send them material and to call them again to complete the interview. This procedure runs the risk of a high proportion of respondents refusing to be sent 'mystery' material.

With some populations, it is possible to speed up this process. In business-to-business studies, it is more common to email material to respondents. This means that the gap between the first and second parts of the interview can be reduced to minutes. By reducing that period, fewer respondents are lost between the two stages.

Another way of showing material, particularly in business-to-business surveys, is to ask the respondent to log on to a website where the material is displayed. The respondent can log on while the interviewer continues to talk on the telephone. Interviews started on the telephone can be continued online, by asking the respondent to log on to a website that contains the remainder of the questionnaire together with the prompt material.

Comparability of data across collection modes

Reflecting upon the points discussed in this chapter, it is easy to understand why the data collection approach employed could influence the data that is collected. This is clearly a particular issue when seeking to draw comparisons with data collected via different modes.

The distribution of usage of points on rating scales, for example, has been shown to be different between modes, with less extreme positive points reported through online surveys than is found through face-to-face or telephone interviewing. However, Cobanoglu et al (2001) have shown that mean scores for data collected via a web-based questionnaire are the same as for other self-completion methods, postal and fax surveys.

There are many papers that shed some light on these differences but it is difficult to draw simple overarching conclusions given the range of factors and the range of subject matters, target populations, cultures etc. Although adopting the same mode might seem to be the best solution, there can be circumstances in which a multi-modal approach is preferable with sample considerations outweighing the argument for data mode comparability. For example, although online panels might provide the best route for accessing the majority of the sample, older people on an online panel may be less representative of their age group and thus an alternative approach may be needed to better reach them.

CASE STUDY   Whisky usage and attitude

Data collection mode

We must now consider which we are going to use. There are three main considerations:

- Feasibility – can we reach this target audience in the time scale required?
- Cost – what are the relative costs?
- Questionnaire – what are the issues regarding the different types of questionnaire?

Our interest here is principally in the last of these. However, a consideration of the feasibility may help us eliminate some options.

Feasibility

Our target sample are drinkers of whisky. From a recruitment sample of all adults aged 18 or over, we can screen and identify people who qualify.

We can rule out a self-completion paper questionnaire distributed by post because of the lack of control over when it is completed, which is crucial here because timing of each stage must coordinate with the advertising schedule. Response rates would also be a major issue.

We are therefore left with online, face-to-face and telephone data collection to consider.

Questionnaire issues

We must consider what we are likely to encounter when writing the questionnaire and which media are most appropriate.

Five considerations have been identified:

- We shall want to show prompts of the advertising and possibly of the brands to avoid confusion.
- We shall want to ask about how much whisky respondents drink, and their responses could be subject to social desirability bias.
- One of our key questions will be spontaneous brand awareness.
- Lists of brands will need to be randomized between respondents in some questions.
- Because of the need to ask about both in-home and out-of-home drinking, we shall want to rotate the order in which these are asked between respondents.

Table 2.1

Issue to consider	Online	Face-to-face	Telephone
Showing prompts of brands and advertising	Yes	Yes	No
Asking about weight of drinking (minimizing social desirability bias)	Best	Worst	Middle
Spontaneous brand awareness	No	Yes	Yes
Randomized brand lists	Yes	Yes	Yes
Rotating order of questions	Yes	Yes	Yes

With either online or face-to-face we can show prompt material. This is not possible over the telephone.

Face-to-face interviewing suffers the most from social desirability bias, therefore consumption habits reported this way are likely to be the least reliable.

Spontaneous brand awareness will be one of our key questions. In an online questionnaire, respondents will enter this as free text. There could be some confusion between similar brands because of incomplete responses (eg Johnnie Walker Red Label and Johnnie Walker Black Label), which interviewers could be alerted to.

Randomizing and rotating are possible in all modes.

Conclusion

Each of the three modes have potential weaknesses. Telephone interviewing, however, can be ruled out because of the inability to show material given the inclusion of a brand recognition question.

We then have to make a judgement between improving the accuracy of the weight of drinking or avoiding confusion on some of the brand names in the spontaneous awareness question. We prefer to get the sample correct and maximize the accuracy of the amount drunk. In the spontaneous brand awareness data our main interest will be in Crianlarich, which should not suffer from any confusion. The questionnaire writer's recommendation, therefore, is to use an online questionnaire.

Cost issues

Aside from questionnaire considerations, the cost of an online survey using an online access panel will be considerably less than any form of face-to-face interviewing and is likely to be a significant factor in the choice of the data collection mode.

Key take aways: influence of data collection mode on question design

- Choice of data collection mode is usually primarily driven by overall survey and sample design considerations, but the decision will have implications for the question writer. The choice may also affect the way the respondent answers. A consistent data collection approach can aid comparability with other surveys.

- Digitally scripting questionnaire software, whether for online self-completion or for computer-assisted, interviewer-administered surveys, offers many benefits to the question writer:

  o Management of structure and flow allows the respondent or interviewer to focus on the questions rather than navigation.

  o Adaptive question wording creates a more personalized and engaging conversation.

  o Opportunity to build in real-time edits to reduce errors.

- In self-completion questionnaires, the respondent can control the pace and their anonymity can encourage more honest answers, however:

  o The question writer has an even greater responsibility to ensure that the questionnaire works, as there is no interviewer safety-net to catch problems.

  o Particular emphasis must be given towards the respondents' attention span and motivation to complete the questionnaire.

- In interviewer-administered questionnaires, the rapport built between interviewer and respondent can lead to greater depth and thoughtfulness, however:

  o The question writer has to anticipate how the interviewers' presence will influence the respondent.

  o Particular emphasis must be given towards helping the interviewer build a rapport with the respondent so this benefit can be actualized.

Planning a questionnaire 03

Introduction

Writing good questions takes time, so you want to be sure that any question you have spent effort on is absolutely necessary.

You also want to ensure that your eventual questionnaire will be an appropriate length. Even if there were no cost constraints it is in the interest of data quality to keep the interview short so that the respondent's motivation to give considered answers is maintained. The reliability of the data may be affected by the sequence in which the questions unfold, therefore deciding the overall order and flow at an early stage is also important. In subsequent chapters we look at issues affecting the detailed wording, format and layout of individual questions. In this chapter we consider how to create a questionnaire outline that helps you visualize its broad content and structure.

Key steps in an effective process

The detailed processes in questionnaire design are likely to vary depending on the answers to several questions:

- Is the question writer also the end user of the data or an agency researcher?
- Will the questionnaire be digitally scripted or paper-based?
- Is the study limited to a single country, or does it span multiple countries?

Regardless of these variables, there are some common steps that are key for all questionnaires:

Step 1: get clarity on the core purpose and end use

In Chapter 2 we considered the importance of being absolutely clear of the business need underlying the research objectives. Without this clarity it will be difficult to judge what questions are essential and to make the hard decisions about what to leave out.

> You should be able to say out loud the core purpose of a study in a single sentence.

Step 2: consider what else needs to be front-of-mind

There will be a range of other considerations that will guide your design. Think about these before you start on the detail. For example:

- **Data collection mode**: if it's self completion, with no interviewer to clarify, the instructions and layout will need to be especially clear. Will extra effort be needed to make it visually engaging and motivating to complete?

- **Cost and timing**: what length has been budgeted for the study? How much time do you have for questionnaire design?

- **Subject matter**: how inherently interesting is the topic? How hard will you have to work to maintain respondent motivation? Is it a sensitive topic that will need careful introduction?

- **Target respondent**: is the sample definition broad or focused? How much knowledge are they likely to have of the topic? Will there be diverse groups with different experiences that require separate lines of questioning?

- **Other surveys**: is there a need for comparability with other surveys (eg common rating scales)?

Step 3: scope the content

In defining the research objectives, you will already have given some thought to question areas and maybe even specific questions. However, it is important that you give yourself one last chance to think broadly, as after this point every question design decision will be about focus.

Involving other stakeholders – for example, in a questionnaire development workshop – will help to ensure that you look at the issue from different perspectives. Keeping an open mind towards what information could be captured, it can be useful to take each research objective at a time, brainstorming possible dimensions or angles. Think about the broad areas of information first, then once these have been identified consider how that topic could be explored – what are the different components? At this stage don't veto ideas or worry about detailed question wording; the aim is to ensure that you have fully explored possible inputs so that you don't miss a useful angle.

Now start to narrow down – consider each suggestion in turn and evaluate its usefulness:

- Can we broadly predict what the result is likely to be? How confident are we?
- How will knowing that result help in making business decisions?
- What are the results we might expect/not expect? How would each potential result affect the business decision?
- Can we get this information from anywhere else?
- Do we need to know anything else to help us make sense of the answer to this?
- Is it needed to help analyze other questions?

The output from this process will be a focused set of the essential question areas. This step is helpful later in managing last-minute requests for additions to the questionnaire; a common problem that is often the root cause of questionnaires becoming longer than necessary. This way, you will have consciously made decisions about what to leave out and therefore feel more confident in assessing last-minute additions.

Step 4: identify the three to four key questions

By this stage all the questions you've identified can be described as 'useful' rather than just 'interesting'. But even with this reduced set, some questions will be more useful than others. Push yourself to identify the three to four questions that are absolutely critical. This is important for several reasons. Firstly, the reality of the question design process is that you will be up against a deadline; of course you want all questions to be as effective as possible but in particular your key questions need the most attention. Write them first so you don't run out of time. This will also give more time for:

- others to review and check them;
- optimising visuals, layout and instructions.

Secondly, the reliability of the responses to a question is likely to be influenced by its position in the questionnaire; there are order effects related to both motivation and the impact of previous answers on the respondent's mindset. Ideally, we want to protect the key questions by keeping them in a prominent position.

If you're finding it hard to identify only three to four key questions, try putting yourself in this scenario: you get a call from IT, the data file has been corrupted and they've only managed to save the data from four questions – which questions are you hoping they will be? As discussed in Chapter 11, scenario-creation is a useful approach for surveys too!

Step 5: create a questionnaire outline

Considerations affecting order decisions are discussed later in this chapter. There are, however, several useful points to remember when creating an outline:

- Visualize the overall structure – put broad topic areas in order.
- Identify sections that are just asked of certain groups (eg routing to a specific section for users).
- Put questions in a sensible order within each section.
- Show the position of key questions.
- Make decisions about question type (eg rating, spontaneous, prompted, open verbatim etc).
- Set any limits to help manage stakeholder expectations (eg indicating how many brands it will be feasible to include in a list).
- Identify where visual prompts such as brand logos will be required so that you can begin sourcing.
- Estimate the timings for each section.
- Map each question back to the objectives.
- Check the balance of questions and their respective timings against the priority order of objectives.

Timing can be hard to estimate as you haven't written the actual questions yet. Very approximate guidelines per question type are:

- Prompted/closed questions: 15–20 seconds each (3–4 per minute)

- Ratings using the same scale: 8–10 seconds each (6–8 per minute)

- Spontaneous open/verbatims: 30–60 seconds each (1–2 per minute)

Step 6: obtain end-user stakeholder approval for the outline

Ensuring that end-user stakeholders buy-in at this stage will help reduce the number of last-minute requests you receive.

You're now ready to start thinking in detail about the questions.

Considerations for question order

As a rule, it is better to work from the most general topics through to the most specific. Thus, the interview might start with questions about the respondent's behaviour in the market in general, before proceeding through to specific questions about the client's product and finally to a new proposition for the client's product. There are two reasons for this.

First, if the questions on the specific product or brand of interest were asked first, the respondents would be aware of the question writer's interest, and this would bias their answers to the more general market questions that come later. Raising the respondents' consciousness of the product or brand in question will tend to lead to it being over-represented as a response to any questions that follow.

Second, respondents are rarely as interested in the market as are the researcher and client. They may find it difficult to respond immediately to questions about the detail of a particular brand or product. Starting with questions that are more general helps the respondents to ease into the subject, recalling their overall behaviour and how they feel about brands and products before reaching the detailed questions. There are many exceptions to this general rule when there is a good research reason for not starting with the more general questions, but the questionnaire writer should always be prepared to justify the decision.

Of particular importance here is the consideration of where the key questions are placed. Respondents should be allowed to answer a few questions about the topic before any of the key questions. This helps them to get into the mindset of the subject matter to provide more considered answers.

However, key questions should be asked while the respondent is still engaged with the survey, before they get bored and inattentive, and before you inadvertently begin to bias their thinking through the act of asking them questions on a subject that they have not previously given much thought to.

An example of this is found in customer satisfaction surveys. There is often poor correlation between responses obtained from an overall satisfaction question asked at the beginning of a survey and the same question asked towards the end of a survey (Flores, 2007). The author's own experience is that the rating asked later in the questionnaire is invariably lower than the rating asked earlier. In this case, the questionnaire may be measuring two different things that are equally legitimate (Katz, 2006), but this demonstrates how the process of completing the questionnaire changes the responses to a key question.

Questionnaire flow

The questionnaire should flow logically from one subject area to the next. Avoid returning to a topic area previously asked about.

In the example flow chart (see Figure 3.1), the objective is to establish what journey types buses are used for; to determine why the bus or other public transport is preferred to using a car; and to obtain a rating of different types of public transport. People who do not use any form of public transport are not to be asked to respond to the final section. This diagram does not tell us precisely what questions need to be asked. What it determines is how the question areas that the different categories of respondents (bus users, non-bus users who use other forms of public transport, and people who use no public transport) who need to be asked will flow.

Here the key questions come towards the end of the questionnaire. However, the questionnaire is short, so respondents are asked no more than a few minutes into the survey. Additionally, they follow some necessary behavioural questions which determine which version of the key question is asked. The behavioural questions also serve the purpose of attuning the respondent's mindset to the issues of transport. The flow chart also demonstrates that there will be some routing issues. Whether or not the respondent has use of a car appears three times in different paths. Complex routing will

Figure 3.1   Flow chart to plan questionnaire

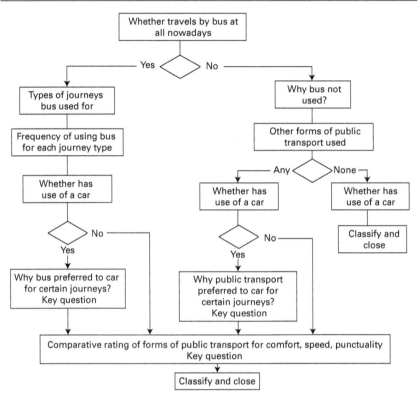

be required if the questionnaire writer decides that this question should appear only once, to facilitate analysis. Alternatively, the same question can appear three times, once in the path of each respondent category. The latter approach is less likely to result in interviewer error if using paper questionnaires, or in routing errors within electronic questionnaires.

The flow chart is a very useful aid in checking the routing in online or other computer-aided questionnaires. Without a chart, it can be difficult to determine whether every route has been correctly defined in the script, and there are many examples of important questions not being asked because of routing errors not picked up in script checking.

> Don't be afraid of complex routing and skipping. It is better than asking questions that don't make sense to the respondent and losing their confidence. However, always check the routing carefully.

Behaviour before attitude

It is generally advisable to start any section of the interview with behavioural questions before going on to ask about attitudes and images. This is in part to allow the respondents to assess their behavioural position and then to explain their behaviour through their attitudes. Behavioural questions are usually easier to answer because they relate to fact and require only recall. If respondents find it difficult to answer behavioural questions, this is usually because the questionnaire writer has been too ambitious in the level of detail expected, and the reliability of the information that is being reported will therefore be in doubt.

If attitudes are asked first there is a danger that respondents will take a position that is not thought-through and/or contradicted by their behaviour. They may subsequently misreport their behaviour in order to justify their attitudes.

Spontaneous before prompted

It may appear obvious, but great care must be taken not to prompt respondents with possible answers before asking questions designed to obtain their spontaneous response. Thus, you cannot ask, 'Which brands of instant coffee can you think of?' if you have already asked, 'Which of the brands of instant coffee on this list do you buy?'

Sometimes it can be virtually impossible to obtain a 'clean' measure of spontaneous brand awareness, particularly where purchase or consumption of a brand is one of the screening criteria for eligibility. This is because respondents will have been exposed to a list of brands in the screening questions. For example, respondents may be recruited based on their brand consumption in order to evaluate a new advertisement. Part of that evaluation may be to show the test advertisement among other ads. For TV ads this would be as part of a clutter reel; for press ads they would be contained within a mock-up of a newspaper or magazine. The test ad will, however, stand out from the rest if the respondents have been sensitized to the brand or the category through the screening questions. To ameliorate this, a series of mock screening questions are sometimes asked that relate to the products and categories shown in the other ads. While this is unlikely to reduce the sensitization of the respondents to the test ad's category, it does raise the level of sensitization so that it is the same for all the ads, thereby cancelling out the differential effect. This type of strategy often needs to be adopted where it is essential that prompting occurs earlier than is desirable.

Prompting also extends to attitudes. A questionnaire may include a series of attitude statements to which respondents are asked to respond. If attitudes on the same subject are to be assessed spontaneously, that must be asked before the attitude statements have been shown or respondents will continue to play back the attitudes with which they have been prompted.

Sensitive sections

If the questionnaire is to include questions of a sensitive nature, they should not be asked at the beginning of the interview, if at all possible.

Normally, these questions should be positioned towards the end of the questionnaire. This is because:

- Having been prepared to divulge information about themselves in earlier questions, it becomes easier for respondents to disclose data that is more sensitive than if asked early in the questionnaire, where they might provoke a termination of the interview.

- If the survey is terminated by the respondent because of the sensitive questions, the researcher will have already captured most of their responses, which may still be usable in analysis.

Where the questionnaire is interviewer-administered, having sensitive questions at the end allows a relationship to be built between interviewer and respondent, so that the respondent is more willing to disclose sensitive information.

If, however, questions are so intrusive as to cause a significant level of offence, the questionnaire writer should consider the ethical position carefully before including them. (See Chapter 15 for what may constitute a sensitive topic.)

Exclusion question

A common though not universal practice is to exclude respondents from research surveys who work in market research, marketing or the client's industry. This will normally be the first question, so that they can be identified and excluded as quickly as possible and neither the respondent's nor the interviewer's time is wasted.

Someone who works in marketing or market research is likely to differ from the general population in terms of patterns of behaviour, particularly in relation to new products, brand awareness and responses to attitudinal questions. People who work in the industry that is the subject of the survey pose not only a threat to the security of the study, but may well have behavioural characteristics that are very different from the rest of the desired sample.

The researcher should decide whether or not to exclude any profession based on the risk posed to the project. A behavioural study of the consumption of bread is unlikely either to reveal any new concepts to respondents or to stimulate the writing of an article. However, a study evaluating a new design for a car is likely to arouse a great deal of interest. This information is not only of value to competitors, but also to sections of the press, so can be highly sought after.

The security question is usually asked as a prompted question, with respondents shown a list of industries and professions. It is advisable to include jobs and professions in addition to those you wish to exclude; this reduces the possibility of a respondent trying to manipulate the outcome. Sometimes respondents will do this unintentionally. Most people's natural inclination is to try to be helpful and answer questions positively. Some people will 'stretch' the eligibility of someone in their household and say that they work in one of the industries or professions, believing that they are being helpful. If the only industries and professions offered are the exclusions, respondents may be eliminated from the study unnecessarily.

Typical exclusion question

- Do you or does anybody in your household work in any of these industries or professions?
  - Accountancy
  - Advertising*
  - Computing or information technology
  - Marketing/market research*
  - Alcoholic drink production or retailing*
  - Banking or insurance
  - Grocery retailing
  - None of these

* Respondent to be excluded from the interview. (Asterisks are not shown on the screen.)

It is not always necessary to exclude anybody at this stage. Where it is important to gain an accurate picture of the ownership of particular items, or how people behave – and there are no security issues – then there is no reason to exclude anybody. This may particularly apply to surveys about social issues.

Screening questions

Following the exclusion question, screening questions come next to identify respondents for eligibility for the survey, depending on whether or not they belong to the research population. In many surveys the researcher only wants to interview people with certain demographic, behavioural or attitudinal characteristics.

Even for broad samples, there will often be quota requirements for various demographics that have to be determined and met before proceeding with the interview. If drawing a sample from a panel, much of this will be known beforehand and the sample can be selected accordingly. Nevertheless, it will often be necessary to ensure that the person completing the questionnaire is the person for whom demographic data is held by the panel owners, and that this information is up to date.

Eligibility criteria can include both behavioural and attitudinal questions, or complex behavioural criteria. The screening questions can take several minutes to administer and seem like an interview in their own right to respondents. Panel members who are being paid for completing a questionnaire can feel cheated if they complete a lengthy screening questionnaire and then receive no reward because they do not qualify for the main survey. A reduced reward may be considered in these instances.

With interviewer-administered questionnaires, lengthy screening also takes up interviewer time, and if paper questionnaires are being used, may lead to errors in the assessment of eligibility. The complexity of the eligibility criteria should be a consideration in the survey design, and kept as simple and as straightforward to administer as possible.

Classification questions

Partly because they can be seen as intrusive, classification questions are normally asked at the end of the questionnaire. They are also positioned here because they are usually disconnected from the subject matter of the interview. Asking them earlier in the interview could disrupt the flow of the key questions. Even though classifications like gender, age, income, final level of education etc may not appear to the respondent to have a relevance they are proven discriminators in many behavioural and attitudinal fields and so are invaluable for cross-analysis purposes.

The researcher should resist the temptation to ask for more classification data than is needed simply because it might be useful for cross-analysis. This is often personal information and respondents do not always understand why it is needed.

What if it is too long?

Macer and Wilson (2013) measured the median acceptable length of an online questionnaire as being 15 minutes. Work by online panel company SSI suggests that average attention span is about 20 minutes for an online survey (Cape, 2015). This author's own work has shown that while around 50 per cent of survey completers rate the experience as 'very enjoyable' when the median completion time is five minutes, this drops to 35 per cent at 15 minutes, and below 30 per cent at 20 minutes. If this is taken as a proxy for engagement, it demonstrates how this falls away at around this questionnaire length, resulting in less attention being given to the questions and to the responses. This can take the form of:

- less time spent on each question;
- fewer responses selected at multiple response questions;
- fewer characters used at open-ended questions;
- the position of sliders left unchanged.

With more surveys being taken on mobile devices this drop off engagement is only likely to increase. Several leading research companies aim for an average survey length of 15 minutes to ensure that attention and engagement is maintained by most respondents throughout the questionnaire.

What can you do?

Given the demand for information, it is often impossible to collect as much as is needed within our target time. There are several routes we can adopt to deal with this:

1 We allow the interview to continue for as long as necessary. If we do this, we must recognize that the quality of the data will decline as the questionnaire goes on and attention and engagement among respondents decreases. We should therefore ensure that our key questions come within the first few minutes and the less important questions thereafter.

2 We break up the information we want into several segments and write a questionnaire for each segment that is of acceptable length. We than conduct a number of parallel surveys, one for each segment of information. To get the full picture this requires having samples that are well matched on key criteria for each of the parallel surveys and then fusing the data across the different samples to create a single data set that contains our full data requirements. This is possible, but the analysis to create the full data set requires specialist skills and can take time.

3 We identify the key questions and then organize the other, lower priority data requirements into modules or chunks with a common theme (eg behavioural questions and attitudinal questions; or holiday travel and business travel). Each module is presented only to a sub-group of the sample, using a random allocation procedure. Each respondent then sees only the key questions and one or two of the modules (depending on how many modules you have), making the survey shorter for them. It is necessary to accept that the modularized data will be based on smaller sample sizes and will therefore be less reliable than the key data.

The third route would generally be the preferred option to deal with data requirements that can't be handled within a single questionnaire of no more than 15 minutes.

When using question modules, select respondents for a module at random – not based on their behaviour – or you will bias the responses within the modules. For example, selecting heavy users of a brand for one module will result in them being under-represented in other modules.

A typical questionnaire structure is shown schematically in Figure 3.2. If all questions were asked of the total sample, the estimated completion time would be 25 minutes. However, four modules have been identified, one that will take seven minutes to complete, and three that will take three minutes each. The questionnaire writer has been able construct three pathways, with each having an estimated completion time of around 15 minutes. Module 4 contains attitudinal data that will be used for creating a segmentation, so this appears in two pathways in order to provide a larger sample size on this data.

Figure 3.2   Modular scheme

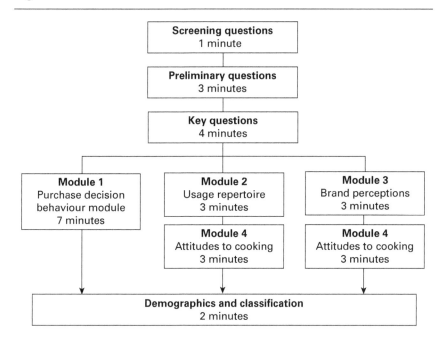

This approach can frequently be used in tracking studies which report the same data on a regular basis. A tracking study of performance for a retailer, for example, might need to report a few top line service-related measures each month for which a sample size of 1,000 is required in order to provide the required level of accuracy. But other measurements may only be reported quarterly – or less often – if they are slow to change. They are unlikely to require a sample size of 3,000 if reported quarterly, or 6,000 if reported bi-annually, so these modules can be rotated between respondents and still provide sufficiently reliable data.

CASE STUDY   Whisky usage and attitude

Planning the questionnaire

Now we must think about what questions we are going to ask and the order in which they are to be presented.

Questionnaire planning

To meet the objectives, the key measures that we need to establish are:

- **Spontaneous brand awareness** of Crianlarich and key competitors. This tells us how 'front-of-mind' the brand is compared to other brands. As one of the objectives of the campaign is to improve awareness, this will be an important measure to compare before and after the campaign.

- **Prompted brand awareness** for Crianlarich and key competitors. This measure relates to how well-known the brand is and tells us how many people in the market have still not heard of it. This is an important measure for new brands in a market, as they establish recognition. For established brands, prompted brand awareness is already likely to be high and so unlikely to change greatly over the course of a single campaign.

- **Brand image perceptions**. These need to be related to the objectives of the campaign, so that we can measure any change in image perceptions over the campaign period. They need to be measured for Crianlarich and five other brands, including several brands that are more expensive. The purpose of measuring so many other brands is so that we can map the market and determine whether or not consumers perceive Crianlarich and Grand Prix – the closest competitor – as a sector distinct from the leading brands. The approaches to be considered are:

  o monadic rating of brands either on semantic differential or Likert (agree-disagree) scales;

  o brand image association.

The brand image association technique is proposed because it is less time-consuming with this number of brands. A rating scale approach would have allowed only three brands to be rated by each respondent – Crianlarich and two competitors. Thus, the competitor brands would have to have been rotated between respondents and measured on a reduced sample size, which we want to avoid.

- Image importance. We could derive the importance of the image dimensions to brand choice by correlation analysis. However, we want to be able to cross-analyze respondents to whom price is an important factor in their choice so as to determine their attitudes to, and level of use of, Crianlarich. A direct approach is therefore to be used. A constant sum allocation of 11 points between two dimensions has been proposed.

Further consideration of the types of questions that have been proposed and a decision as to their use will be returned to when we consider the issues appropriate to them later.

Together these form our key questions. But there is other information that we need to know:

- Behavioural information on the weight of drinking – both on- and off-licence – and whether the respondent is influential in brand choice, is required for analysis purposes. Which brand or brands are bought is also required, for measurement, to see if it changes over the course of the campaign, and for analysis purposes.
- Awareness of Crianlarich advertising needs to be measured at a number of different levels to determine whether or not respondents have seen or have remembered the advertising. How well the advertisement is branded will probably be measured by showing an unbranded ad for Crianlarich and for a competitor as a benchmark, although alternatives will be considered.

At this stage, the estimated length of completion is 15 minutes, so there is no need to chunk up the questionnaire into modules for sub-samples.

The question areas appear in the following order:

- screening questions;
- spontaneous brand awareness;
- spontaneous brands recall seeing advertised;
- prompted brand awareness;
- advertising awareness prompted by brand name;
- advertising source and content recall (where drunk, bought or specified);
- behavioural information – amount drunk;
- importance of image factors in brand choice;
- brand image associations;
- recognition of unbranded ads, with branding question;
- classification data.

Unusually, one of the key questions is asked at the very start of the questionnaire. This is spontaneous brand awareness. This is in part because we must ensure we do not prompt with any brand names before asking this question, but also because what we are trying to replicate here are the brands that come to mind when no thought is given to it, potentially recreating the situation when first entering a supermarket or off-licence as far as we can.

Behavioural questions come before brand image questions to avoid any tendency to distort behaviour in line with image perceptions. Showing advertising material comes last, to avoid influencing responses to the brand image questions.

We can now produce our flow diagram (Figure 3.3). The behavioural questions are quite complex in their routing and a separate sub-routine has been created to show this section in detail. (Figure 3.4).

Figure 3.3   *Overview flow diagram*

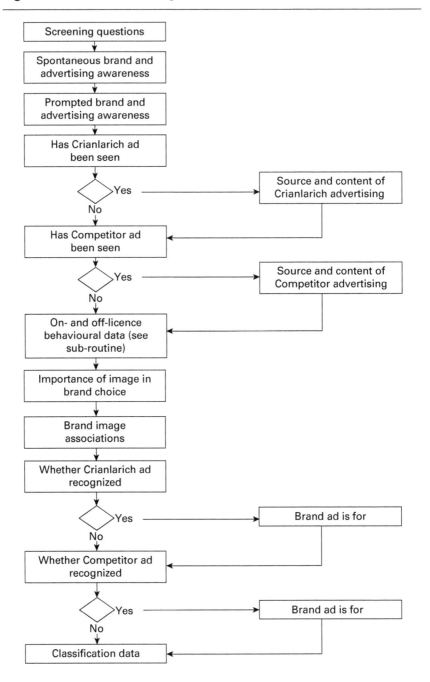

Figure 3.4   Behavioural section sub-routine

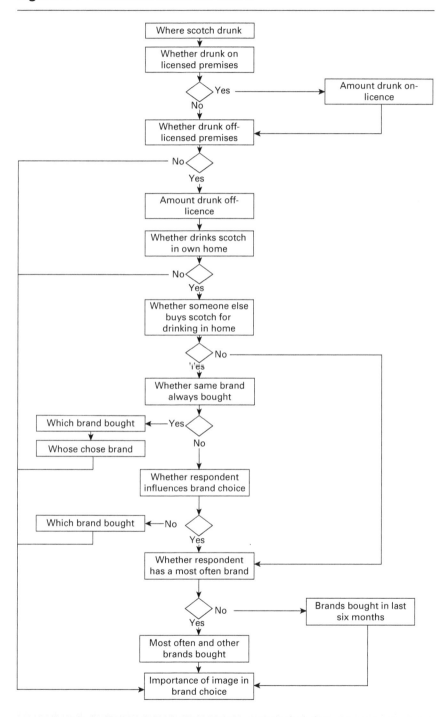

Key take aways: planning a questionnaire

- Writing detailed question wording takes time – make sure you really are ready to start before diving in.
- Get clarity on the core purpose and end use.
- Consider what else needs to be front-of-mind to guide the design.
- Judge how inherently interesting the topic is (ie how hard you will have to work to maintain engagement).
- Scope the content:
  - o Allow yourself one last chance to think broadly about the topic before narrowing. The output from this step will be a focused set of question areas – ones where you have thought ahead to possible outcomes and end use.
  - o By consciously deciding what to leave out, it will be easier to handle inevitable last-minute requests for additions.
- Identify the three to four key questions:
  - o Some questions will always be more important than others.
  - o Give them the best chance of working: positioning them in the interview where quality of response is likely to be highest, and writing them first so you have more time to check them and get others' perspectives.
- Create an outline questionnaire:
  - o Start with the overall structure and question order within sections – identifying routing and any modular sections.
  - o Initial thinking should focus on question types and practical parameters (eg limits on the number of brands or statements used).
  - o Map the outline against objectives – check the balance of content against priority order of objectives.
  - o Estimate the length of the questionnaire – if it is too long, consider modularising lower priority sections/questions to allocate randomly.
- Get end-user stakeholder approval of this outline to reduce last-minute requests for changes.

An overview of question types 04

Introduction

There are a few basic structures underlying the different ways a question can be asked and the answers recorded. The questionnaire writer should understand these as the choice will impact the task required of the respondent – and the data that is produced. This will influence the types of analysis and ultimately the usefulness of the data in addressing the reason for asking the question.

Question types

The first classification is whether the question is:

- **Open or closed**: can the answer come from an infinite, or certainly unknown range of responses, or only from a closed or finite number of possibilities?

Two further classifications (which can overlap with the above) are whether the question is:

- **Prompted or spontaneous**: are possible answer options shown or not?
- **Open-ended or pre-coded**: is the answer recorded verbatim or against a list of possible answers? (A pre-coded list can only be used with a spontaneous question if it is interviewer administered and hidden from the respondent.)

Open and closed questions

An open question is one where the range of possible answers is not suggested in the question and which respondents are often expected to answer in their own words:

- What did you eat for breakfast today?
- How did you travel here?
- What did you like about this product?

Open questions always seek a spontaneous (ie unprompted) response. In conversation, one person trying to start another person talking about a topic would use an open question. An open question may elicit a short answer (eg the respondent recounting the one or two items they had for breakfast), or it may lead respondents to talk at length using their own words in order to give fully their answer (eg in answer to, 'Why do you eat that brand of breakfast cereal more than any other?').

The response format may be open-ended answers recorded verbatim, or with interviewer-administered surveys only, a list of the most commonly given responses may be provided to the interviewer that can be coded. Open pre-coded questions like this require the interviewer to quickly match the response given to one of the codes available. The questionnaire writer must make sure that the code list is clear, comprehensive, unambiguous and easy for the interviewer to navigate.

On the other hand, closed questions tend to bring conversation to a stop. This is because there is a predictable and usually small set of answers that the respondent can give. Any question that simply requires the answer 'yes' or 'no' is a closed question, and not helpful to opening out a conversation. An evening spent with a new acquaintance with both of you asking only closed questions would be very dull indeed.

In a research interview, closed questions also include any question where the respondent is asked to choose from a number of alternative answers. Thus, any prompted question is a closed question. Examples of closed questions are:

- Have you drunk any beer in the last 24 hours?
- Are you aged under 25?
- Which of these brands of tinned meat do you buy most often?
- Which of the phrases on this card best indicates how likely you are to buy this product?

The first two can only be answered 'yes' or 'no', and in the last two the respondent is being asked to choose from a list of possibilities.

Closed, and therefore pre-coded, questions are popular with researchers as processing is cheap. A numeric code can be assigned to each answer beforehand so transformation into the digital format needed for analysis is easy.

A questionnaire that measures behaviour is likely to consist mostly of closed questions ('Which of these brands ...?', 'When did you last ...?', 'How many did you buy?'), whereas one exploring attitudes is likely to have a higher proportion of open questions. From the point of view of maintaining the involvement of the respondent, the interview should consist of a mixture of both types of question (see Figure 4.1).

Spontaneous questions

A spontaneous question is any question for which the respondent is not given a list of possible answers from which to choose. All open-ended questions are by their nature spontaneous, but, as explained earlier, not all spontaneous questions need be open-ended.

Spontaneous questions will be used when the questionnaire writer:

- does not know what the range of responses is likely to be; or

- wants to collect the response in the respondent's own words; or

- wants the respondent to think for themselves without prompting them.

Figure 4.1 Examples of question types

OPEN QUESTIONS CAN APPEAR AS EITHER OPEN-ENDED OR PRE-CODED QUESTIONS		
[OPEN QUESTION]	[OPEN-ENDED]	Why do you prefer Product A to Product B? Please write in your answer in your own words
	[PRE-CODED]	Why do you prefer Product A to Product B? [INTERVIEWER OR RESPONDENT: CODE RESPONSE AGAINST LIST OF ANSWERS PROVIDED OR ENTER 'OTHER ANSWER' VERBATIM]
[CLOSED QUESTION]	[PRE-CODED]	For which of these reasons do you prefer Product A to Product B? Please mark as many reasons on the list below as apply

In interviewer administered questionnaires, where it is possible to use either an open-ended or pre-coded response format for spontaneous questions, the decision depends on whether it is important to record the response verbatim and whether the full range – or at least the majority – of likely responses is known.

One of the difficulties with spontaneous questions is that they often require more effort on the part of the respondent. Their motivation to think carefully and answer fully is often affected by the mode of interview. With self-completion questionnaires it is easier to disengage than when an interviewer is present. Lack of motivation also depends on how interested they are in the subject and how engaging the questionnaire itself is.

Common uses of spontaneous questions

Spontaneous open questions are frequently used in market research to measure awareness, recall and attitudes, for example:

- brand awareness;
- awareness of brands seen advertised;
- recall of brands or products used or bought;
- advertising content recall;
- attitudes towards a product, or activity or situation;
- likes and dislikes of a product or concept.

With spontaneous questions we are trying to determine what is at the forefront of people's minds (ie information they can easily access). We interpret this as *saliency* in the case of awareness of brands, or as *importance* in the case of attitudes. However, spontaneous responses are unlikely to reflect respondents' full awareness or attitudes. When investigating behaviour, spontaneous questions might tell you what behaviours are front-of-mind, but often the aim with these more factual measures is to get a more complete and accurate response so a prompted question is usually favoured.

Spontaneous brand awareness

This would be the result of the following (or similar) questioning: 'Which brands of breakfast cereal have you heard of?' The objective here is to obtain every brand that the respondent can think of from memory, and so probes asking for 'what else?' or 'any more?' will be used extensively in interviewer-administered interviews. The list of possible brands will usually be given as pre-codes on the questionnaire for the interviewer to record responses. Frequently the first brand mentioned will be recorded separately, to give a measure of the one most front or 'top of' mind. A challenge with interpreting saliency measures from spontaneous awareness is that brands may be front-of-mind for many reasons – some positive (eg the most likely to be considered for purchase), some negative (eg a controversial brand, or the subject of recent poor publicity).

If the respondent is able to read-ahead (eg in paper self-completion formats) it will not be possible to obtain spontaneous awareness if any brands are mentioned elsewhere in the questionnaire. With online self-completion this limitation can be overcome if the question writer requests controls to be scripted in to stop forward-reading.

Sometimes we wish to know precisely how respondents refer to a brand, in which case the responses will be recorded verbatim. The researcher can then determine whether it is the brand, sub-brand or variant that is mentioned, or what combination of these. This is particularly used in advertising research where it can be important to know precisely what level of branding is being communicated.

> If you are asking spontaneous brand awareness where there are a number of variants, be clear in the question whether you are looking for just the main brand name or the variants as well.

Spontaneous advertising awareness

When evaluating the effect of an advertising campaign, spontaneous advertising awareness is usually a key measure. Exactly how this is measured, though, differs between researchers.

One way is to ask spontaneous brand awareness first, followed by a spontaneous awareness of brands seen advertised, followed by content recall of the advertising claimed to have been seen. All questions require spontaneous responses; the first two are likely to be pre-coded with a list of brands, and the third question will be open-ended:

- Which brands of breakfast cereal have you heard of?
- Which brands of breakfast cereal have you seen or heard advertising for recently?
- What did the advertising say, or what was it about? (Repeat for all brands for which advertising has been seen.)

An alternative approach is not to ask brand awareness first, but to ask the respondent to recall spontaneously any advertising for any brand in the category:

- Please describe to me any advertising that you have seen recently for a breakfast cereal. What did it say? What was it about? What brand was that for? (This question is then repeated until the respondent can recall no more advertising.)
- Please tell me any other brands of breakfast cereal that you have seen advertising for.

Advocates of the second approach claim this focus of attention on the advertising means it is less affected by a common effect of big brands dominating memory, whether or not they have been advertising.

Spontaneous attitudinal questions

Typical spontaneous attitudinal questions are:

- What, if anything, do you like about ...?
- What, if anything, do you dislike about ...?
- How do you feel about ...?
- Please describe to me your feelings about ...?

The responses to these questions would most likely be recorded verbatim as open-ended answers. This enables the capture of the full range of answers, which may include some that were not anticipated. This also allows the researcher to see the precise language used by respondents to describe their feelings and attitudes.

Preliminary qualitative research may have been carried out to determine the full range of attitudes held on the issue in question. Or the study may be a repeat of a previous one in which the attitudes were explored and so can now be defined. In these cases, summaries of the main attitudes may be pre-coded on interviewer-administered questionnaires to save the time and expense of coding the responses at the analysis stage. With self-completion questionnaires pre-coding is not a possibility if the attitudes are to be expressed completely spontaneously.

If you don't know the terminology that is likely to be used by respondents, or how they might express their views, use an open-ended spontaneous question.

Prompted questions

Most people find it difficult to articulate everything that they know or feel about a subject, or they forget that they know something, or they have given one answer and aren't prepared to make further effort to think of additional answers. Prompting with a set of options tells the researcher what people know or recognize, rather than what is front-of-mind. Prompting also particularly helps people to recall actions and behaviour which might otherwise be overlooked. From the researcher's point of view, it means that they express their answers in the framework desired by the researcher – it may also reduce some of the variability caused by respondent limitations. The order of items in a prompted list can have a significant effect on the response. This is considered further in Chapter 11 (Writing effective questions).

Often, both spontaneous and prompted measures are obtained: prompted inevitably giving higher percentages than spontaneous, but the size of the differences providing an additional perspective that can lead to insight (eg understanding why spontaneous scores are much lower for one brand than for another despite both having similar prompted levels).

Open-ended questions

An open-ended question is an open question where the response is recorded verbatim. An open-ended question is nearly always also an open question (it would be wasteful to record yes/no answers verbatim). Open-ended questions (also known as 'unstructured' or 'free-response') are used when:

- We genuinely cannot predict what the responses might be.
- We want to avoid being presumptuous in any way (ie by assuming that we know what the range of answers is likely to be).
- We want to know the precise phraseology or terminology that people use (eg if we are looking to understand and replicate consumer language in communications).
- We want to quote some verbatim responses in the report or presentation to illustrate something such as the respondent's strength of feeling. In response to the question, 'Why will you not use that company again?', a respondent may write in: 'They were awful. They mucked me about for months, didn't respond to my letters, and when they did they could never get anything right. I shall never use them again.' Had pre-codes been given on the questionnaire this might simply have been recorded as 'poor service'. The verbatim response provides much richer information to the end user of the research.

Common topics for open-ended questions include:

- likes and dislikes of a product, concept, advertisement, etc;
- spontaneous descriptions of product images;
- spontaneous descriptions of the content of advertisements;
- reasons for choice of product/store/service provider;
- why certain actions were taken or not taken;
- what improvements or changes respondents would like to see.

These are all directive questions, aimed at eliciting a specific type of response to a defined issue. In addition, non-directive questions can be asked, such as what – if anything – comes to mind when the respondent is shown a new idea, and whether there is anything else that the respondent wants to say on the subject.

Open-ended questions suffer from several drawbacks:

- Respondents frequently find it difficult both to recognize and to articulate how they feel. This is particularly true of negative feelings, so asking open-ended questions concerning what people dislike about something tends to generate a high level of 'nothing' or 'don't know' responses.
- Without the clues given by an answer list, respondents sometimes misunderstand the question or answer the question that they want to answer, rather than the one on the questionnaire.
- In interviewer-administered surveys they are subject to error in the way and the detail with which the interviewer records the answer.
- Analyzing the responses can be a difficult, time-consuming, and a relatively expensive process.

In addition, some commentators (Peterson, 2000) see verbosity of respondents as a problem with open-ended questions. It is argued that if one respondent says only one thing that he or she likes about a product, but another says six things, the latter respondent will be given six times the weight of the former in the analysis. To even this up, a suggestion is to only count the first response of the more verbose respondent. In practice, steps are usually taken to encourage all respondents to give as much detail as possible by probing.

Probing

With most open questions it is important to extract from respondents as much information as they can provide for a greater depth of understanding (eg the first reason they give for having bought one brand may be the same for all brands and will not discriminate). The first responses given to open questions are often very bland, and non-directional probing is required to try to fill out the answer.

Probing is very different from prompting, and the two must not be confused. In prompting, respondents are given a number of possible answers from which to choose, or are given clues to the answers (eg prompting them with specific examples: 'anything else you liked, for example the appearance or taste?'). Probing makes no suggestions. A typical probe for an interviewer administered questionnaire is:

- What else did you like about the product? [PAUSE. THEN PROBE.]
- What else? [CONTINUE UNTIL NO FURTHER ANSWERS.]

The object here is to keep respondents talking in reply to the initial question in their own words until there is no more that they can or wish to say. They are not led in any direction.

Do not use phrases such as, 'Is there anything else?' as a probe. That form of probe allows or even encourages the respondents to say, 'No, nothing else.' If the probe is, 'What else?' this makes a presumption that there is more that the respondent wants to say and puts the onus on the respondent to indicate that he or she has no more to say. This helps the researcher to obtain the fullest answer rather than helping the respondent to say as little as possible. With self-completion questionnaires, probes in the form of additional instructions can also be used but are likely to be less effective than when interviewer administered. Interestingly the size of the space allowed for the answer has been shown to act as a visual probe, encouraging respondents to keep answering for longer (Christian and Dillman, 2004).

It is occasionally possible to anticipate unhelpful answers and ask for these specific responses to be elaborated.

> 'Because it is convenient' is often given as a reason for a particular behaviour – but is rarely helpful. Include an instruction or follow-up question to find out what 'convenient' means.

Coding

To analyze the responses, a procedure known as 'coding' is used. This can be either done manually or by specialist software. Manual coding first examines a sample of the answers and groups these under commonly occurring themes, usually known as a 'code frame'. If the coder is someone other than the researcher, that list of themes needs to be discussed with the researcher to see whether it meets the latter's needs. The coder may have grouped answers relating to low price and to value for money together as a single theme, but for the researcher it may be useful to identify these as separate distinct issues. The researcher may also be looking to see if specific responses occur that have not arisen in the sample of answers listed. It may be important for the researcher to know that few people mention this, but to be sure that this is the case the theme must be included on the code frame. When the list of themes has been agreed, each theme is allocated a code and all questionnaires are then inspected and coded according to the themes within each respondent's answer.

Manual coding is a slow and labour-intensive activity, particularly when there is a large sample size and the questionnaire contains many open-ended questions. Most research agencies will include a limit to the number of open-ended questions in their quote for a project, because it is such a significant variable in the costing.

There are a number of computerized coding systems available that are increasingly used by research companies (Esuli and Sebastiani, 2010). Word recognition software, using a range of keyword searching or text recognition, text mining and sentiment analysis, has also helped to automate this process. These reduce but do not eliminate the human input required. Responses to open-ended questions can be input to word cloud software producing a visual summary of the most frequent terms used.

Pre-coded questions

Pre-coded open questions

This type of question is only found where there is an interviewer. The respondent does not see the list of possible responses (these are purely an aide to the interviewer and the researcher), and so answer in their own words. The pre-codes may simply be a brand list, or they may be used in order to categorize more complex responses (see Figure 4.2).

This type of question requires the questionnaire writer to second-guess what the range of responses is going to be. It is usually done to save time and the cost of coding open-ended verbatim responses. It might also be used to provide some consistency of response by forcing the open responses into a limited number of options. It is important to provide a space for the interviewer to write in answers that are not covered by the pre-codes. It is

Figure 4.2   Pre-codes used to categorize responses to open questions

Q. Why did you buy that particular brand of mayonnaise?
DO NOT PROMPT

IT'S THE ONE I ALWAYS BUY	1
THE ONLY ONE AVAILABLE	2
THE CHEAPEST	3
ON SPECIAL OFFER	4
THE FLAVOUR I WANTED	5
THE PACK SIZE I WANTED	6
OTHER ANSWER (WRITE IN)	7

unlikely that the questionnaire writer will have thought of every possible response that will be given, and it is not unusual for quite large proportions of the responses to be written in as 'other answers'. However, there is still a danger that interviewers will try to force responses into one of the codes given rather than write in a response that is close to, but does not quite fit, one of the pre-codes.

The richness and illustrative power of the verbatim answer is lost by providing pre-codes, as are any subtle distinctions between responses, but the processing time and cost will be reduced. Consistency with other surveys may also be increased.

Although it was stated earlier that a pre-coded answer format for an open-ended questionnaire is only an option for interviewer-administered questionnaires, there is a variation for online modes. Once the spontaneous response is obtained, a list of pre-determined codes is revealed, and the respondent asked to select the answer they feel most closely corresponds to their verbatim answer. This allows a quick quantitative analysis of the main themes while still retaining the depth of the verbatim answer.

Pre-coded closed questions

Closed questions will tend to be pre-coded. Either a prompt list of possible answers is used or there is a known and finite number of responses that can be given. There are three main types of pre-coded closed questions:

- dichotomous;
- single response;
- multiple response.

Dichotomous questions

The simplest of closed questions are dichotomous questions, which have only two possible answers:

- Have you drunk any beer in the last 24 hours?
  - Yes
  - No

Dichotomous questions such as these are quick to ask and should be easy to respond to, which makes them potentially useful for screening questions.

Single response questions

Frequently the question will offer a number of possible pre-coded responses, but will be seeking only one answer; this is a multiple-choice single-response question. Examples will be:

- Which brand did you buy most recently?
- Which of these types of exercise do you do most often on these days?
- When did you last visit a museum?
- Out of 10, how would you rate this product?

There may be a number of responses which are simply a range of options (eg a brand list or types of exercise), or the responses may form a type of scale (eg a time scale with various options, or a rating scale).

Multiple response questions

Closed questions with more than one possible answer are known as multiple response (or multi-chotomous) questions. Such a question might be:

- Which makes of beer have you drunk in the last month?
- Which of these types of exercise do you do on all these days?

Clearly, there is a finite number of answers; the range of possible answers is predictable; and the question does not require respondents to say anything 'in their own words'. Defining the brands of interest makes this a closed question.

With both single and multiple response questions, you may want to include an 'other answer' response option, with the ability to capture that answer verbatim. For example, if you think a brand list may not be comprehensive or where you are asking about behaviour or attitudes where you cannot predict all possibilities. This then looks like you have created an open question where the respondent can respond in their own words, but the provision of a list of possible responses will inevitably mean that most people will try to fit their answer into one of the responses provided, thus effectively making it closed. See also the issue of satisficing covered in Chapter 9.

'Don't know' responses

Questionnaire writers are often unsure as to whether they should include a 'don't know' response to pre-coded questions.

It can be a legitimate response to many questions where the respondent genuinely does not know the answer, and so a 'don't know' code must be included. For example:

- Which mobile phone service does your partner subscribe to?
- When was your house last repainted?
- From which store was the jar of coffee bought?

With other questions it is not always so clear. These tend to be questions either of opinion, where a likelihood of action is sought, or of recent behaviour – which the respondent could be expected to remember:

- Where in the house would you be most likely to use this air freshener?
- What method of transport did you use to get here today?
- Which brand of tomato soup did you buy most recently?

A concern with including a 'don't know' code is that it may encourage respondents to make less effort to think and if there is any uncertainty – or lack of motivation – to answer 'don't know'. With interviewer-administered questionnaires, it is argued, the inclusion of 'don't know' legitimizes it as a response. If it is not on the questionnaire, the interviewer will be more likely to probe for a response that is on the pre-coded list before writing in that the respondent is unable or unwilling to answer the question. It may be prudent, therefore, to limit the use of 'don't know' categories to those questions where the researcher believes it to be a genuine response.

However, with any survey that is scripted (eg online, CAPI or CATI) the software may require an answer to be inputted before it is possible to move onto the next question. Providing a 'don't know' answer here can avoid ethical difficulties whereby the respondent will be forced to give an answer that they feel does not fit.

From a learning perspective the level of 'don't know' responses can provide important information about the knowledge of respondents and their ability to answer the question. Isolated 'don't know' responses when an answer should logically be expected to be known might identify respondents who have been mis-recruited against desired selection criteria. Widespread responses of this type might indicate that the information asked is beyond the scope of this research universe (eg asking an employee about the profitability of their employers business), or that the question is poorly worded and not understood by many of the respondents. This is generally information worth knowing and should encourage the inclusion of 'don't know' codes on the questionnaire.

CASE STUDY   Whisky usage and attitude

Types of questions

As our usage and attitude study (U&A) is going to be an online self-completion survey, the range of question types available to us is limited.

Open-ended questions: Our principal interest is whether we use open-ended questions or pre-coded questions. Open-ended questions impose additional work on respondents, as well as being more expensive to analyze, so we shall want to keep them to a minimum.

We should consider an open-ended question for spontaneous brand awareness. Our client's brand, Crianlarich, is not a major brand, and we need to see how well drinkers can retrieve the name from their memory without any prompting. As a relatively young brand, much advertising effort will be put into transitioning it from being a brand that is recognized to one that is front-of-mind. Spontaneous brand awareness is therefore a key measure.

Respondents will have to enter the name, so we shall also be able to see how often it is incorrectly spelled, which can inform us about potential difficulties with online searches for the brand:

- Please enter the names of as many brands of whisky as you can think of.

The order in which the brands are entered will be collected and we shall hope to see Crianlarich appear higher in the order over time.

Had the performance of advertising been the main focus of this study, we would have considered including a second open-ended question asking respondents to describe any Crianlarich advertising that they had seen or heard, to get a measure of take-out. However, as that is not our main focus, we shall be content with one open-ended question.

Open questions: There will be a number of questions which could be open questions, in that they do not demand an answer from a finite list. These could include:

- Which brands have you seen advertised?
- On what occasions do you drink whisky?

These could be recorded using an open-ended response format. However, we can anticipate most of the responses that we are likely to get, so an open-ended question, with its additional burden to the respondent and cost to us, is not worthwhile. Instead for both questions we shall present a list of responses.

Although there would be an 'other, write-in' response, respondents will have been prompted by what is on screen. This will give those answers greater salience which will steer respondents to choosing one of those. This means that answers written in under 'other' cannot be compared in the frequency distribution to those that have been prompted. For the advertising awareness question, our preference therefore is to limit the list to the main dozen or so brands, with no 'other' option, because we will not use that information. It also helps us to keep the competitive set for this question constant over time (there will be a 'none of these' option). The question then becomes:

- Which of these have you seen advertised?

For an 'occasions' question, we could not presume to know the complete set of occasions on which people may drink whisky, however we may only be interested in broad categorizations based on locations rather than precise details. Here, we would set out a list of what we believe to be the main ones, but retain the 'other, write in' response. Although this, technically remains an open question, from which we may learn of other emerging locations at which it is being drunk, we must accept that respondents will tend to select answers from the list we have provided. Those lacking motivation are unlikely to spend effort describing 'other' situations. The question therefore becomes:

- Where have you drunk Scotch whisky out of the home in the last week?
  - In a pub/bar with friends

- In a pub/bar on my own
- In a restaurant
- In a club
- Other. Please describe:

Closed questions: The majority of the questions will be closed, with a number of answer options for respondents to select from. For example:

- whether whisky drunk at home, out of home, or both;
- whether respondents specify the brand to be bought.

Both of these questions have a specific set of possible responses.

Key take aways: overview of question types

- The question writer faces several choices when deciding the underlying structure of a question:
  - o Is an open or closed question needed?
  - o Is the response elicited spontaneously or through prompting?
  - o Is the response recorded using an open-ended (verbatim) format or via a pre-coded list?
- Both **spontaneous** and **prompted** questions have several main advantages and disadvantages:

Spontaneous:
  - o respondent-led, front-of-mind thinking;
  - o doesn't constrain answers;
  - o good for exploring how a respondent thinks/behaves;
  - o captures the exact language they use.

However:
  - o Answering usually requires more effort from the respondent and slows the interview.
  - o Quality of answers can be particularly affected by motivation and engagement.

- o When the answers are recorded verbatim an additional analysis process (coding) is needed.
- o Recording against pre-coded lists is only possible if interviewer-administered (hidden from the respondent).

Prompted:

- o can reduce effects of respondent memory and motivation to answer fully;
- o the answer lists can help to clarify the question;
- o usually less effort for the respondent;
- o easier and quicker to turn into aggregated analysis.

However:

- o more knowledge is needed by the question writer (eg developing an appropriate and comprehensive list);
- o more potential for bias introduced by the question writer's suggestions and assumptions;
- o practical challenges with implementation (eg items catching the eye unequally, long lists to read through, etc).

- • Most quantitative questionnaires are mainly comprised of closed, prompted questions using pre-coded answer lists. The number of open spontaneous questions is usually limited to reduce respondent fatigue and for more efficient analysis.

Identifying types of data created by questions

05

Introduction

Data collected by a question can be classified as nominal, ordinal, interval or ratio. The questionnaire writer needs to recognize which type is being collected as this will determine the analysis that can be carried out on that question.

Nominal data

Nominal data is data that is assigned to a discrete category and named (eg male, female; New York, Chicago, Los Angeles; purchaser of pizza, non-purchaser of pizza). A code number will often be assigned to each category and used to record the response and conduct analysis. However, that number is purely arbitrary and implies no value that can be given to the response category; the numbers are given for identification purposes only. Thus, if a sampling point is described as 'urban' and is given a code of 1, and 'rural' is assigned a code of 2, there is no relative value implied between the two categories (Figure 5.1 shows a further example). Some online data capture systems avoid this misunderstanding by recording the variable using its name. For some analysis packages however, such as SPSS, they need to be converted to numeric values to operate certain functions. Respondents are classified into one category or another.

The categories should be exhaustive (ie everybody should fit somewhere) and mutually exclusive (ie there should be no overlap between them). Questions that can be multi-coded – such as brands bought where a respondent may have several brands in their repertoire – also create nominal data. In effect,

Figure 5.1   Assigning code numbers for data recording purposes

Q. Which of these supermarkets in your opinion sells the best-quality fresh vegetables?	
Asda	1
Morrisons	2
Safeway	3
Sainsbury's	4
Somerfield	5
Tesco	6

a respondent is assigned either as a buyer or not for each brand, thus fulfilling the no-overlap criteria.

Analysis of nominal data is limited to frequency counts against each category. It is meaningless to calculate an average across the responses or to carry out any other calculation based on the value of the code assigned to that category.

Ordinal data

Ordinal data is most commonly created by questions that require the respondent to put nominal categories in order according to a criterion contained in the question (ie questions involving 'ranking' or 'comparative' scales). This is often order of preference, as shown in Figure 5.2.

Other questions might include ranking by order of:

- a product characteristic – such as sweetness, consistency and strength;
- frequency of use – such as most used, commonly used and least used;
- recency of use – such as last used and next-to-last used;
- perceived price – such as most expensive to least expensive;
- ease of comprehension – such as easiest to understand to most difficult.

Ranking puts the nominal data into the appropriate order, but tells the researcher nothing about the distance between the points. In the example above, strawberry yoghurt might be liked almost as well as black cherry, with both liked considerably more than blackcurrant. The researcher however cannot deduce this from the data. Nor can the researcher determine whether the last choice (raspberry), is actively disliked and would never be

Figure 5.2   Placing nominal categories in order

Q. Please put the following flavours of yoghurt in the order in which you prefer them, starting with 1 for your first choice through to 5 for your least preferred.

Blackcurrant 3

Black cherry 1

Peach 4

Raspberry 5

Strawberry 2

chosen by this respondent, or whether it is firmly in the repertoire of pre-ferred flavours. It may even be the case that the respondent actually likes none of these five flavours, and the ranking is based on which flavours are least disliked.

Ranking can be useful in forcing differences between brands, products or services, which would not be apparent with rating scales. This is illustrated in Alwin and Krosnick's (1985) experiment in which they assessed 13 at-tributes of children for desirability using both ranking and rating. When the attributes were rated on an importance scale, 12 of the 13 were rated as 'extremely important' by between 24 and 40 per cent of respondents, a span of only 17 percentage points resulting in poor discrimination between them. When ranked as first to third most important the same attributes spanned 3 to 41 per cent, giving much greater discrimination but at the loss of the knowledge that even the least important is extremely important to a quarter of the sample.

The task of ranking can become difficult with a large number of items. Certainly a question tool is needed with an element of interactivity (ie allow-ing the respondent to insert items into the order as they work through them rather than creating their right order first time). Drag-and-drop tools (Figure 5.3) are common for online, or physical cards – one for each item – if face-to-face. With telephone (ie where no visual stimulus is possible) ranking usu-ally needs to be limited to five items or less). However, even if a question tool is used, ranking a large number will still pose a significant cognitive chal-lenge and for many it would also lack realism: they may have a number that they like and a number that they dislike, but have some in between that they have no feelings about. Simply because question tools exist to ensure it is done in a survey does not ensure that meaningful data will be produced.

With a large number of items it is likely that the exact rank positions of items in the middle of the ranking will be less reliable than the rankings at

Figure 5.3 Using drag-and-drop to obtain a ranking for a large number of items

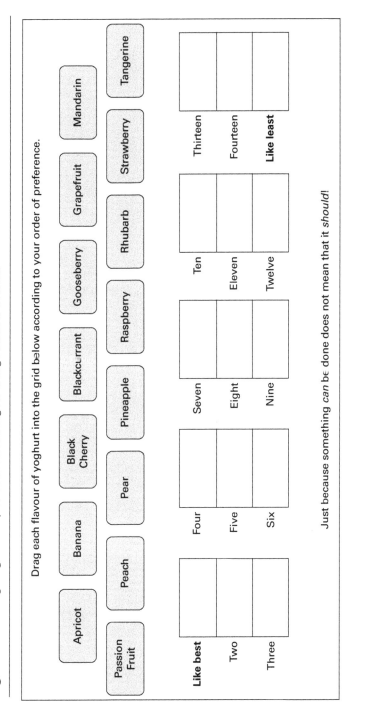

Drag each flavour of yoghurt into the grid below according to your order of preference.

Apricot Banana Black Cherry Blackcurrant Gooseberry Grapefruit Mandarin

Passion Fruit Peach Pear Pineapple Raspberry Rhubarb Strawberry Tangerine

Like best
Two
Three

Four
Five
Six

Seven
Eight
Nine

Ten
Eleven
Twelve

Thirteen
Fourteen
Like least

Just because something *can* be done does not mean that it *should!*

Figure 5.4   Ask top and bottom three

Which of these flavours of yoghurt do you most and least like?			
	Most liked	Second favourite	Third favourite	Three liked least
Apricot	O	O	O	O
Banana	O	O	O	O
Black Cherry	O	O	O	O
Blackcurrant	O	O	O	O
Gooseberry	O	O	O	O
Grapefruit	O	O	O	O
Mandarin	O	O	O	O
Passion Fruit	O	O	O	O
Peach	O	O	O	O
Pear	O	O	O	O
Pineapple	O	O	O	O
Raspberry	O	O	O	O
Rhubarb	O	O	O	O
Strawberry	O	O	O	O
Tangerine	O	O	O	O

either end. Therefore, one option for simplifying the respondent task – and potentially creating data that is more stable – is to just ask respondents to nominate their top three (or some other specified number) and their bottom three; but with no requirement to order the ones in the middle (Figure 5.4).

For the items not ranked in the top or bottom three we then give a notional rank order equal to the mid-point, so that a notional mean score equivalent to average position can be calculated. This is not unrealistic – as respondents will often know what they like and what they dislike – and have a group of items in between about which they have no strong views.

Many approaches to simplification are seen (eg first sorting items into categories such as 'would consider' vs 'would not consider' and then only ranking the 'considered' group).

Interval data

Interval data is created by rating scales that have a numerically equal distance between each point, and an arbitrary zero point (interval scales). The five flavours of yoghurt could be individually rated on a scale from 1 to 10 for how much each is liked, and comparison of scores across the flavours gives the relative strength of the relationships. It is relative because although there is an equal interval between each point, a score of 8 does not necessarily mean that one flavour is preferred twice as much as a flavour scoring 4.

The advantage of the interval scale over the ordinal scale is that the researcher can tell whether an item is liked or disliked (or thought to be too sweet or not, etc.) by its rating. However, if two items are given the same rating it is not possible to assign a rank order (as shown in Figure 5.5). The first respondent has given a different score to each flavour, so that not only can we rank-order that person's preferences, but we can now tell that the person likes black cherry and strawberry more than blackcurrant, while peach and raspberry are not liked. For this person we have both rating and ranking scores. The second respondent, however, likes all five flavours and it is therefore difficult to deduce a meaningful rank order of preference from the interval scale responses.

In practice, the researcher is rarely dealing with data at an individual level but with aggregated data over the whole sample. Interval scales allow mean scores and standard deviations to be calculated across the sample. From these it is often possible to deduce an overall rank order of the items. However, mean scores may still be too close to infer a ranking.

The distribution of the data across the scale should also be examined because the same mean score can be produced by very different distributions. Standard deviations will indicate the extent of polarization of opinion within the sample.

Figure 5.5 Rating on an interval scale

Please give each flavour a mark between 1 and 10 based on how much you like it.

	Respondent 1		Respondent 2	
	Rating 1 to 10	Deduced ranking	Rating 1 to 10	Deduced ranking
Blackcurrant	5	3	9	1=
Black Cherry	9	1	8	3=
Peach	2	4	9	1=
Raspberry	1	5	8	3=
Strawberry	8	2	8	3=

Care must be taken in the interpretation of interval scales. To be an interval scale it must be assumed for analysis purposes that the conceptual distance between each point is constant (ie that when presented with a 10-point scale the respondent allocates the same level of discrimination between scores of 7 and 8 as between scores of 2 and 3, for example). This has been shown to not always the case and is returned to in Chapter 6.

Many scales used in measuring attitude, brand perceptions, customer satisfaction, etc. are semantic rather than numeric, such as Likert scales. They are generally considered to be interval scales, but some caution is needed when interpreting analysis as it can rarely be demonstrated beyond doubt that the conceptual distance between points is constant.

Ratio scales

Ratio scales are a particular type of interval scale. The zero point has a real meaning, such that the ratio between any two scores also has a meaning. Age is a ratio scale, with a 50-year-old person being twice as old as a 25-year-old. Income is another.

This type of scale is also used to ask questions such as:

- Of the last 10 cans of baked beans that you bought, how many were Heinz?

- What proportion of your household income do you spend on your rent or mortgage?

- How long ago did you buy your car?

We might choose to record the responses directly or within categories (as shown in Figure 5.6).

Note that the response categories are not necessarily of equal length. These have been chosen to suit the purposes of the researcher or to reflect the expected distribution of the data. The proportion of income spent on rent or a mortgage could have been recorded as a direct percentage and categorized at the analysis stage. The reason for putting this into bands is that most respondents will not know the answer to the exact percentage point. The length of time since respondents bought their car could be recorded as days, months or years. Few could work out the number of days, however, and only the most recent buyers would easily be able to give the time in months. The researcher here is particularly interested in differences between people who have bought their car relatively recently, so it is most

Figure 5.6   Recording on a ratio scale

Of the last 10 cans of baked beans that you bought, how many were Heinz?	
None	☐
1	☐
2	☐
3	☐
4	☐
5	☐
6	☐
7	☐
8	☐
9	☐
10	☐

What proportion of your household income do you spend on your rent or mortgage?	
0% to 5%	☐
6% to 10%	☐
11% to 15%	☐
16% to 20%	☐
21% to 25%	☐
26% to 30%	☐
31% to 40%	☐
41% to 50%	☐
51% to 60%	☐
61% to 80%	☐
81% or more	☐

How long ago did you buy your car?	
Within the last month	☐
Between one month and three months ago	☐
Longer than three months and up to six months ago	☐
Longer than six months and up to one year ago	☐
Longer than one year and up to two years ago	☐
Longer than two years and up to three years ago	☐
Longer than three years and up to five years ago	☐
Longer than five years and up to ten years ago	☐
Longer ago than ten years	☐

important to be able to distinguish between very recent purchasers (last three months) and less recent purchasers. Think about how the data is to be used and keep the response categories as broad as possible and consistent with that usage. With fewer and broader categories, the levels of guessing and non-response will be reduced, and the reliability of the data improved.

Be aware, however, that changing the scale can alter the way in which people respond. Dillman (2000) quotes a time-based ratio scale where a response category was selected by 69 per cent when it was the lowest option in the scale but which dropped to 23 per cent when the scale was constructed with this same category as the top option. This emphasizes the importance of making the scale appropriate to the anticipated distribution of answers.

The fact that the recording of the data is categorized does not affect the underlying property that there is a relationship between the responses, and the researcher can identify a respondent who buys twice as many cans of Heinz beans, or spends twice as much on their rent or mortgage, or bought a car twice as long ago as another. The accuracy of this calculation is restricted only by the size of the categories used to collect the data.

With allocation of appropriate scores to each point, or average values to each range, we can now calculate mean values and standard deviations for the sample and carry out statistical tests.

> You can tell if it's a ratio scale if you can do meaningful calculations with the data without the result becoming an abstract construct.

Table 5.1 Statistics generated by and uses of each data type

Provides	Nominal	Ordinal	Interval	Ratio
Frequency distribution	X	X	X	X
Mode	X	X	X	X
Median		X	X	X
Mean		X	X	X
Ranking or order		X	X	X
Known distance between values			X	X
Values can be added or subtracted			X	X
Values can be multiplied/divided				X
Points have meaning relative to each other				X

Adapted from My Market Research Methods
www.mymarketresearchmethods.com/types-of-data-nominal-ordinal-interval-ratio/

CASE STUDY   Whisky usage and attitude

Types of data

In designing each question in our whisky U&A study we need to consider whether the type of data it produces is appropriate for our analysis needs.

Nominal data: Many questions will create nominal data. Such questions will include:

- Prompted brand awareness: Which of these brands have you heard of?
- Brands drunk: Which of these do you drink at all nowadays?
- Day of week consumed: On which day or days do you drink whisky?

This nominal data can be used to create analysis categories, including 'aware of Crianlarich/not aware'; 'drinker of Crianlarich/not a drinker'; 'drinker of whisky only at weekends/drink across the week'. We can use the proportion selecting each response to produce descriptive statistics such as hierarchies of awareness or patterns of consumption across the week.

Ordinal data: Asking which brands the respondent drinks may not give us sufficient knowledge, particularly if they have a large repertoire. We will then consider introducing the question:

- Put these brands in order by how often you drink them. Go from the one you drink most often to the one you drink least.

We have now created an ordinal scale, which tells more about their behaviour. We can use this data to produce mean scores and hierarchies of frequency. However, we will not know the difference in frequency of consumption between the most often consumed and the second most consumed brand. This information could be useful in understanding whether the first brand is dominant in the repertoire.

Ratio data: For further understanding of this we could use ratio scales:

- How often do you drink [BRAND]?
- How many glasses of [BRAND] do you drink in a week?

Now we can say that one brand is drunk twice as frequently as another by our sample, or that the volume drunk of one brand is only a third that of the market leader. We can create a rank order between brands, and create means, modes and medians to give further depth of understanding of behaviour.

Interval scale: To help understand the strength of feeling towards each brand in their repertoire – and whether this aligns with behaviour – we could ask respondents to rate the brands they drink:

- Give each brand a score out of 10 for how much you like it.

We could then produce a distribution for each brand of how much it is liked, and provide mean scores to compare position and standard deviations to show how consistently that view is held across the sample.

We may also use interval scales to assess brand perception:

- Rate how much you associate [BRAND] with the following characteristics:
  - Strong heritage
  - Traditional
  - Old-fashioned
  - Good quality

Strongly Agree to Strongly Disagree (5 points).

By calling this an interval scale, we are inferring that the conceptual distance between each point is equal and that it is valid to attribute scores of 1 to 5 to the scale. Not everyone will agree, but if we make this assumption, we could use the scoring to input multivariate techniques such as factor analysis and cluster analysis. This can create segmentations by brand perception and brand maps to visually summarize the inter-relationships.

Key take aways: identifying types of data created by questions

The analysis that can be performed on the responses to a question depends on the type of numeric data that is created:

Nominal:

- Typically produced when numeric codes are assigned to answers simply as a means of identifying the response (eg Male 1, Female 2).
- Analysis is of frequency counts against these numeric codes (ie counts for each answer category).
- It is meaningless to perform mathematical analysis on the number codes themselves.

- This is often the most common type of data from a questionnaire.

Ordinal:

- A numeric ranking is produced by putting nominal categories into an order that has meaning (eg asking respondent to rank brands in order of preference).

- Care must be taken not to overload the respondent with too many items to rank.

- Rankings can help force discrimination but do not tell you anything about the distance between the ranks.

Interval:

- Created by rating scales where the distance between the points is known and equal.

- Typically used to understand strengths and weaknesses across brands but unlike ordinal ranking scales, an individual respondent may give two items the same rating.

- Analysis at the aggregated sample level is via mean scores and standard deviation to understand the distribution across the sample. Sometimes a ranking can be inferred from this.

Ratio:

- Created by scales where the zero point and the distance between points has real meaning (eg frequency).

Creating appropriate rating scales

06

Introduction

Rating scales are a common research tool for investigating a respondent's opinion or attitude. A simple dichotomous question may sometimes be sufficient ('Do you like or dislike this?', 'Do you agree or disagree that...?', 'Is this important or unimportant to you?'). However, frequently this approach might be over simplistic. There are often likely to be degrees of strength of feeling as attitudes and opinions can be complex. Rating scales, with scale points designed to reflect these shades of feeling, can give greater sensitivity to differences between respondents or between items that are being assessed. Rating scales are widely used by questionnaire writers. They provide a straightforward way of asking attitudinal information that is easy and versatile to analyze, and that provides comparability across time. However, there are many different types of rating scales, and there is skill in choosing which is most appropriate for a given task. In this chapter we look at the types of scales and their applications. The measurement of attitudes more generally is discussed in Chapter 8.

Itemized rating scales

The most commonly used approach is the itemized ratings scale. The researcher first develops a number of dimensions (eg attitude statements, product or service attributes, image dimensions, etc). Respondents are then asked to position how they feel about each one using a defined rating scale, usually an interval scale (see Chapter 5) with a range of evenly spaced points.

Figure 6.1 shows two typical examples: the wording on each scale is tailored to be appropriate to the question, and all have five points representing a gradation from positive to negative. They are balanced around a neutral mid-point with equal numbers of positive and negative statements for the respondent to choose from.

Figure 6.1 Some examples of itemized rating scales

How likely are you to use the train for this journey in the near future?

Very likely	O
Quite likely	O
Neither likely nor unlikely	O
Quite unlikely	O
Very unlikely	O
Don't know	O

How effective are the management in this organization?

Highly effective	O
Effective	O
Neither effective nor ineffective	O
Not very effective	O
Not at all effective	O

Being interval data, scores can be allocated to each of the responses to assist in the analysis of responses. The allocated scores are most likely to be from 1 to 5, from the least to the most positive; or from –2 to +2, from the most negative to the most positive with the neutral point as zero.

Think ahead to whether you need to make comparisons with data from elsewhere. Consistency is often the most important factor in rating scale decisions.

Balanced scales

It is usual to balance scales by including equal numbers of positive and negative attitudes. Consider this balanced scale when asking respondents to describe the taste of a product:

Very good

Good

Average

Poor

Very poor

With two positive and two negative statements the respondents are not led in either direction. However, if the scale were as follows, the three positive dimensions would tend to result in a higher number of total positive responses:

Excellent

Very good

Good

Average

Poor

In most circumstances it is important to balance the scale to avoid this bias. However, there are occasions when an unbalanced scale can be justified. Where it is known that the response will be overwhelmingly in one direction, more categories may be given in that direction to achieve better discrimination.

This is often the case when measuring the importance of various aspects of service in customer satisfaction research. Few customers will say that any are unimportant – the customers will be looking for the best service that they can get – and the dimensions about which we ask are the ones that we believe are important anyway. The objective is mainly to distinguish between the most important aspects of service and the less important ones. An unbalanced scale might therefore be used, offering just one unimportant option, but several degrees of importance:

Extremely important

Very important

Important

Neither important nor unimportant

Not important

Here the questionnaire writer is trying to obtain a degree of discrimination between the levels of importance. The visual mid-point is 'important', and the scale implicitly assumes that this will be where the largest number of responses will be placed. The scale could have seven points extending from 'extremely unimportant' to 'extremely important' to preserve the balance, but if we are confident they are unlikely to be used these balancing points simply add visual clutter. They may also provoke a tendency to avoid the extremes when scales become long, thus counteracting the increased sensitivity we are trying to achieve at the top end of the scale.

Unbalanced scales should only be used for a good reason and by researchers who know what the impact is likely to be.

Number of points on the scale

The illustrations in Figure 6.1 show five-point scales, which are probably the most commonly used. A five-point scale gives sufficient discrimination for most purposes and is easily understood by respondents. The size of the scale can be expanded to seven points if greater discrimination is to be attempted. Then the scale points can be written as:

Extremely likely

Very likely

Quite likely

Neither likely nor unlikely

Quite unlikely

Very unlikely

Extremely unlikely

Or:

Excellent

Very good

Good

Neither good nor poor

Poor

Very poor

Extremely poor

There is little agreement as to the optimum number of points on a scale. The only agreement is that it is between 5 and 10 (or 11). Seven is considered the optimal number by many researchers for an item-specific scale (Krosnick and Fabrigar, 1997) but there is a range of opinions on this issue and whether extending the number to 10 or more increases the validity of the data. Numeric alternatives to itemized scales provide more flexibility for more points as there is no need to create appropriate labels for each point. Coelho and Esteves (2007) have demonstrated that a 10-point numeric scale is better than a five-point scale in that it transmits more of the available information, without encouraging response error – the characteristic given by Cox (1980) for assessing the optimum number of points. They hypothesize that, among other things, consumers may be more used these days to giving things scores out of 10 and are able to cope with them better than was the case 20 years ago. However, Revilla, Saris and Krosnick (2014) conclude that five points are the optimum for fully labelled agree-disagree scales.

The questionnaire writer's decision as to the number of points on the scale has to be taken with regard to the degree of discrimination that is sought, the feasibility of creating meaningfully distinct labels for those points, and the ability of respondents to discriminate in that much detail. With telephone interviewing, scales with more than five itemized points are difficult for respondents to remember and therefore numeric alternatives are often preferred. With multi-country surveys the feasibility of creating equally spaced itemized scales in different languages also points towards greater use of numeric scales instead (as discussed later in this Chapter).

'Don't knows' and mid-points

In Figure 6.1, each of the scales is balanced around a neutral mid-point; this is included to allow a response for people who have no strong view either way. However, this point is also frequently used by respondents who want to give a 'don't know' response but are not offered 'don't know' as a response category and do not want, or are unable, to leave the response blank.

The reluctance of respondents to leave a scale blank where they genuinely cannot give an answer has always been an issue with self-completion interviews. Unpublished work from TNS BMRB shows that up to three-quarters of those who choose the mid-point may be using it as a substitute for 'don't know', although this varies by the attribute or attitude asked about. However, 'don't know' codes or boxes are frequently not provided as the questionnaire writer is wary of prompting this as a response – instead wanting to encourage the respondent to commit to a response that, in all likelihood, may reflect an attitude unrecognized at a conscious level. In studies where it would be expected that most people would have a view, for example about crime, it can be argued that they hold a view even if they do not recognize that they do. It is therefore legitimate, it is argued, to force a response in one direction or the other. When the subject is breakfast cereals however, it must be recognized that many people may really have no opinion one way or the other. The response points for a scale without a mid-point might look like this:

Extremely likely

Very likely

Quite likely

Quite unlikely

Very unlikely

Extremely unlikely

Or:

Excellent

Very good

Good

Poor

Very poor

Extremely poor

In an interviewer-administered study It is possible to accept a neutral response that is offered spontaneously by the respondent. However, studies have shown that including a neutral scale position significantly increases the number of neutral responses compared to accepting them spontaneously (Kalton et al, 1980; Presser and Schuman, 1980). This indicates that eliminating the neutral mid-point does increase the commitment of respondents to be either positive or negative. This is supported by Coelho and Esteves (2007), who found that the mid-point was used by respondents who are trying to reduce the effort, and so exaggerated the true mid-point score, and by Saris and Gallhofer (2007) who showed that not providing a neutral mid-point improves both the reliability and the validity of the data.

Further complications to the debate include that non-response to one scale among a battery of scales can raise issues of how to treat the data when using certain data analysis techniques. And a practical consideration is that digital scripting software often does not allow respondents to pass to the next question unless an answer of some kind is provided – reinforcing the need for a 'don't know' code if no mid-point is provided.

Figure 6.2 shows an alternative order to typical scales that places the mid-scale neutral element at the end of the options. In this case the question writer took this decision because of the subject matter, ie advertising. There is a tendency to deny being influenced by advertising. By offering the four statements that acknowledge advertising influence together as a block, the visual impact will be such that respondents will be more prepared to consider that they may indeed be influenced. The questionnaire writer has attempted to offset one bias with another. While this could be taking a risk, in this instance the question writer felt there was good reason for doing so based on their previous experiences.

Figure 6.2   An alternative order for responses

Based on this ad, how likely will you be to purchase this product in the future?

Please select one.

Much more likely to buy it	O
Somewhat more likely to buy it	O
Somewhat less likely to buy it	O
Much less likely to buy it	O
The ad had no effect on my likelihood to buy it	O

In conclusion, since the purpose of using ratings scales (as an alternative to a simple dichotomous 'either/or') is usually to create greater sensitivity to differences, some feel it is at odds with this aim to offer a mid-point that might be used as an opt-out answer. However, mid-points continue to be widely used and the questionnaire writer must decide whether or not including one is appropriate for the particular question and subject matter. Comparability with other data will often have greater import.

Anchor strength

With all semantic scales, the wording of the anchor statement is crucial to the distribution of data that is likely to be achieved. A five-point bi-polar scale that goes from 'extremely satisfied' to 'extremely dissatisfied' is likely to discourage respondents from using the end-points and to concentrate the distribution on the middle three points. If the end-points were 'very satisfied' and 'very dissatisfied', they would be used by more respondents and the data would be more widely distributed across the scale. This can make the data more discriminatory between items. As a general rule, the stronger the anchors, the more points are required on the scale to obtain discrimination.

Likert scale

A form of itemized rating scale developed specifically to measure attitudes is the Likert scale (frequently known as an 'agree/disagree' scale). This was first published by psychologist Rensis Likert in 1932. The technique presents respondents with a series of attitude dimensions (an 'attitude battery'), for each of which they are asked whether (and how strongly) they agree or disagree, using one of a number of positions on a five-point scale (see Figure 6.3). It is increasingly common to find any type of attitudinal rating scale – regardless of the number of points – referred to as a Likert scale. Many DIY online survey providers tend to do this – probably for simplicity. Technically, however, it refers only to this specific scale.

Figure 6.3   Use of the Likert scale

Do you agree or disagree with these attitudes about shopping?

	Disagree strongly	Disagree	Neither agree nor disagree	Agree	Agree strongly
Being a smart shopper is worth the extra time it takes.	❐	❐	❐	❐	❐
Which brands I buy makes little difference to me.	❐	❐	❐	❐	❐
I take advantage of special offers.	❐	❐	❐	❐	❐
I like to try new brands.	❐	❐	❐	❐	❐
I like to shop around and look at displays.	❐	❐	❐	❐	❐

The technique is easy to administer online. It can be presented in a number of ways including radio buttons, slider scales, stars or with a range of other graphical techniques.

With face-to-face interviewer-administered scale batteries, the responses may be shown on a card while the interviewer reads out each of the statements in turn. With telephone interviewing, the respondent may sometimes be asked to remember what the response categories are, but preferably would be asked to write them down.

Responses using the Likert scale can be given scores for each statement, usually from 1 to 5, negative to positive, or –2 to +2. As this is interval data, means and standard deviations can be calculated for each statement.

The full application of the Likert scale is to sum the scores for each respondent to provide an overall attitudinal score for each individual. Likert's intention was that the statements would represent different aspects of the same attitude. The overall score, though, is rarely calculated in commercial research (Albaum, 1997), where the statements usually cover a range of attitudes. The responses to individual statements are of more interest in determining the specific aspects of attitude that drive behaviour and choice in a market, or summations made over small groups of items. The data will tend to be used in principal component or factor analysis, to identify groups of attitudinal statements that have similar response patterns and that could therefore represent underlying attitudinal dimensions. Factor analysis can be used to create a factor score for each respondent on each of the underlying attitudinal dimensions, thereby reducing the data to a small number of individual scores.

There are four interrelated issues that questionnaire writers must be aware of when using Likert scales:

1 order effect;

2 acquiescence;

3 central tendency;

4 pattern answering.

The **order effect** arises from the order in which the response codes are presented. It has been shown (Artingstall, 1978) that there is a bias to the left on a self-completion scale presented horizontally. (Order effects are returned to in Chapter 9.)

Acquiescence is the tendency for respondents to say 'yes' to questions or to agree rather than disagree with statements (Kalton and Schuman, 1982). In Figure 6.3, the negative end of the scale is placed to the left, to be read first. With the 'agree' response to the left, the order effect and acquiescence would compound each other. With the 'disagree' response to the left, there is a possibility of the biases going some way to cancelling out each other. Importantly, it has been shown that acquiescence bias tends to be consistent for individual respondents. If measures can be found to assess the bias for each respondent, then corrections can be made. This, though, can be a complex and time-consuming exercise (Weijters et al, 2010).

Central tendency or extreme response bias is the reluctance of respondents to use extreme positions. Greenleaf (1992) showed that, like acquiescence bias, the extreme response bias is consistent within a respondent's answers. He also showed that it is related to age, income and education, but not to gender. It has been shown (Albaum, 1997) that a two-stage question elicits a higher proportion of extreme responses. This investigation used the question:

For each of the statements listed below, indicate first the extent of your agreement and second how strongly you feel about your agreement.

- A product's price will usually reflect its level of quality.

  Agree – Neither Agree nor Disagree – Disagree

- How strongly do you feel about your response?

  Very Strong – Not Very Strong

The question arises, of course, as to whether the two-stage approach is a better measure of the attitude or whether it creates its own bias towards the extreme points. Albaum et al (2007) explored this issue by correlating reported attitude to actual behaviour in charity giving. The results were not conclusive but suggested that the two-stage approach provides the truer reflection of attitudes.

With a large number of dimensions to be evaluated, this may be too time-consuming for most studies, but the questionnaire writer should be aware of this approach and of the different response patterns it is likely to give. This approach is particularly appropriate for telephone interviewing, where the complete scale cannot be shown.

Pattern answering occurs when a respondent falls into a routine of ticking boxes in a pattern, which might be straight down the page or diagonally across it. It is often a symptom of fatigue or boredom. Some online providers look at the time taken to complete such a page. Speeding through is taken as evidence of pattern answering. The best way to avoid it is to keep the interview interesting and reduce the number of items. Some advocate using both positive and negative statements so the respondent then has to read them or listen to them carefully to understand the polarity and to give consistent answers. However, additional analysis is likely to be needed to identify conflicting answers, and decisions will need to be made about how to deal with that respondent. It is also not always possible to be sure that answers really conflict. Therefore, others favour keeping consistent polarity and accepting the risk of some pattern-answering rather than subjective judgment about whether the respondent is likely to have spotted the reversal or not.

Saris et al (2005) argue that agree/disagree scales are flawed not just because of these issues but because the cognitive process involved for the respondent is more complex and burdensome than with a simpler question asked directly about the specific issue. Such construct-specific questions (Figure 6.4) are also believed to suffer less from acquiescence and order bias. This is supported by unpublished work by TNS BMRB, which looked at a number of constructs where the agree/disagree scale could be replaced by a construct-specific scale. Here it was found that while there were significant differences between the responses to end points on the agree/disagree scale when rotated between respondents, demonstrating order bias, the construct-specific scale showed far more consistency, indicating less bias.

Figure 6.4   Labelled construct-specific scale

Did you find this orange juice:	
Much too sweet	O
A little too sweet	O
About right	O
Not quite sweet enough	O
Not nearly sweet enough	O

It should be noted that the European Social Survey no longer uses a Likert scale for new questions. Nevertheless, it continues to be widely used because it is simple to create.

Semantic differential scale

The semantic differential scale is a bi-polar rating scale. It differs from the Likert scale in that opposite statements of the dimension are placed at the two ends of the scale and respondents are asked to indicate which they most agree with by placing a mark along the scale. This has the advantage that there is then no need for the scale points to be individually identified. Any bias towards agreeing with a statement is avoided, as both ends of the scale have to be considered. The original development of this scale by Osgood (Osgood et al, 1957) recommended the use of seven points on the response scale, and this number continues to be the favourite of researchers (McDaniel and Gates, 1993), although both five-point and three-point scales are used for particular purposes (Oppenheim, 1992).

With semantic differential scales the statements should be kept as short and precise as possible because of the need for the respondent to read and understand fully both ends of the scale. Attitudes can be difficult to express concisely, and it is sometimes hard to find an opposite to ensure that the scale represents a linear progression from one end to the other. For these reasons semantic differential scales are usually better suited to descriptive dimensions.

Care must be taken to ensure that the two statements determine the dimension that the researcher requires. The opposite of 'modern' might be 'old-fashioned' or it might be 'traditional'. The opposite of 'sweet' might be 'savoury' or 'sour' or 'bitter'. This forces the questionnaire writer to consider exactly what the dimension is that is to be measured. This gives the semantic differential scale an advantage over the Likert scale where disagreeing with 'the brand is modern' could mean that the brand is seen as either old-fashioned or traditional, and the researcher does not know which.

Figure 6.5 comes from an advertising study, taken from a face-to-face questionnaire where the interviewer would read out much of the text. Online, this would be much simpler (as shown in Figure 6.6). The format is so simple and familiar to respondents that it may not be necessary to explain or label the scale points. Note the difficulty that the questionnaire writer has

Figure 6.5 Example of a semantic differential scale (Interviewer-administered)

Below are pairs of statements. Each one may or may not apply to the advertisement that you have just seen. Please read each pair and indicate which of the statements you agree applies to the ad by ticking one box for each pair of statements.

For example, if you agree strongly that the advertisement was 'mundane', you would tick the box closest to that statement, but if you only agreed slightly, then you should tick a box further away from the statement.

Example

Fascinating ☐ ☐ ☐ ☐ ☐ ☑ ☐ Mundane

Please complete the remaining items according to how you feel about the ad:

Boring	☐	☐	☐	☐	☐	☐	☐	Interesting
Important	☐	☐	☐	☐	☐	☐	☐	Unimportant
Relevant	☐	☐	☐	☐	☐	☐	☐	Irrelevant
Exciting	☐	☐	☐	☐	☐	☐	☐	Unexciting
Unappealing	☐	☐	☐	☐	☐	☐	☐	Appealing
Involving	☐	☐	☐	☐	☐	☐	☐	Uninvolving
Means nothing	☐	☐	☐	☐	☐	☐	☐	Means a lot to me

Scale items taken from Zaichkowsky (1999).

in achieving exact opposites in the first pair of statements. The ad may be worth remembering because it contains useful information, but that does not necessarily mean that it is not also easily forgettable. The questionnaire writer could have included both of the pairs: 'worth remembering – not worth remembering' and 'easy to forget – difficult to forget' but has chosen to force a decision between two statements that are not strictly opposites in order not to have to extend the number of pairs asked about.

Figure 6.6   Example of a semantic differential scale (online self-completion).

How did you feel about this ad?

For each pair of statements click closest to the one that best describes how you felt about it

Worth remembering	O	O	O	O	O	O Easy to forget
Difficult to relate to	O	O	O	O	O	O Easy to relate to
Lively, exciting or fun	O	O	O	O	O	O Dull
Ordinary or boring	O	O	O	O	O	O Clever or imaginative
Helps to make the brand different to others	O	O	O	O	O	O Does not make the brand any different to others
Makes me less interested in the brand	O	O	O	O	O	O Makes me more interested in the brand

Note that the questionnaire writer alternated positive and negative ends of the scale between statements to help catch the flatliners. But dimensions three and four contain potential ambiguities.

Numeric scales

A simple form of scaling is to ask respondents to award a score (eg 'out of 5', 'out of 10' or even 'out of 100'). The end points of the scale should be semantically anchored to avoid misunderstanding. It should also be made clear whether the bottom point is 0 or 1 (Figure 6.7).

- Please give us a score out of ten for how well we performed today – where 10 is good and 1 is poor.

In practice, whether a 10-point scale starts at 0 or 1 makes little difference to the distribution of the responses. To have 0 as the lowest point on the scale as is generally preferred in case there is any ambiguity as to the direction of the scale as it gives a more explicit mid-point (5). The recommended scale for the widely used Net Promoter Score (NPS) is 0 to 10 (Reicheld, 2003).

Numeric scales (Figure 6.7) are simpler to design than itemized scales where the exact language used for each scale point needs to be considered. Therefore, they are attractive for multi-country studies to avoid challenges with consistent translations. When a telephone interviewer is administering the questions, the scale can easily be understood by the respondent without the need to re-member or write down the scale point options. They take up little space which can be important for modes where this is limited (eg on a mobile phone screen).

Figure 6.7   A numeric scale question

Give *The Gingerbread Store* marks out of 100 on each of the following: 100 would mean 'perfect' and 0 'dreadful'.

The layout [   ]

Helpfulness of staff [   ]

Attractiveness of store [   ]

However, interpretation is not always straightforward (eg in determining how people feel in absolute terms: how good is a 7 out of 10?) but where com-parisons are made with previous scores or benchmarks it works well. The re-searcher must also remember that this is an interval scale and not a ratio scale. A score of 8 out of 10 does not mean that something is twice as good or twice as important as a score of 4. Numeric scales are not appropriate for indicating choice between two brands, because the more positive associations implicit in the higher score would bias response towards that option. Finally, a question-naire with a large number of numeric scales can start to feel quite clinical or abstract with the risk of the respondent becoming disengaged.

Figure 6.8   Advantages and disadvantages of main types

Itemized Rating Scale

When to use: When absolute knowledge is required.

Advantage: Precision of response, for both respondent and analyst.

Disadvantages: Scale point wordings often differ between items, requiring separate questions (except Likert scale).

Semantic Differential

When to use: When making comparisons between items.

Advantages: End points understood.
No need to find gradations of meaning for the scale.

Disadvantages: Requires precision in finding opposites.
We cannot know what the points on the scale actually mean.

Numeric

When to use: When comparing with a database or over time

Advantages: Simple to administer.
Simple to understand.

Disadvantage: Lack of consistency of interpretation by respondents.

Stapel scale

Named after Jan Stapel, in the Stapel scale the dimension or descriptor is placed at the centre of a scale that ranges from −5 to +5. Respondents indicate whether they agree positively or negatively with the statement, and how strongly, by selecting one of the points on the scale (see Figure 6.9). Thus, it is a form of numeric scale with both positive and negative scores.

Figure 6.9   A Stapel scale

Please indicate how accurately you feel each of the following words and phrases describes the Gingerbread Store. Select a positive number for the phrases you think describe the store accurately. The more accurately you think it describes it, the larger the number you should choose. Select a minus number for the phrases you think do not describe it accurately. The less accurately you think the phrase describes the store, the larger the negative number you should choose.

The Gingerbread Store

+5	+5	+5
+4	+4	+4
+3	+3	+3
+2	+2	+2
+1	+1	+1
is well laid out	has helpful staff	is attractive
−1	−1	−1
−2	−2	−2
−3	−3	−3
−4	−4	−4
−5	−5	−5

The advantage of this type of scale and other numeric scales over semantic differential scales is that it is not necessary to find an accurate opposite to each dimension to ensure bi-polarity. The data can, however, be analyzed in the same way as semantic differentials, and the scale, with 10 points, has the potential to provide greater discrimination than a five-point scale. By having no centre point, these scales also avoid the issue of whether or not there should be an odd or even number of points on the scale.

Online, this is relatively simple to administer, (Figure 6.10). A slider scale replaces the numbered points and a semantic label indicates the end points. The use of it is very intuitive, and a large amount of text is done away with.

With face-to-face or telephone interviewing, however, they are not widely used as they are thought to be confusing for respondents.

Figure 6.10   An online Stapel scale

How would you describe Gingerbread Store?

| Disagree strongly | Is well laid out ▼ | Agree strongly |

| Staff are helpful |
| Disagree strongly _____▼_____ | Agree strongly |

| Is attractive |
| Disagree strongly _____▼_____ | Agree strongly |

Graphic scales

A graphic scale is one presented to the respondents visually so that they can select a position on it that best represents their desired response. In its most basic form it looks like a slider bi-polar scale with fixed points verbally anchored at either end. Here, in Figure 6.11, it is used to replace the radio buttons in a semantic differential scale.

Figure 6.11   Semantic differential slider scale

How would you describe this ad?

Worth remembering	▼	Easy to forget
Difficult to relate to	▼	Involving or easy to relate to
Lively, exciting or fun	▼	Dull
Ordinary or boring	▼	Clever or imaginative

The distance from the end points of the respondent's marks is measured to provide the score for each attitudinal dimension. Essentially this is a continuously rated semantic differential scale, which provides a greater degree of precision and avoids the issue of numbers of points on the scale. It is a simple way of measuring attitudes and image perceptions but it is usually only practical online.

Although the data collected is continuous, the measurements will be assigned to categories and treated as interval data for analysis purposes. It is possible to have a large number of very small intervals. Some online DIY survey providers offer a choice of whether it is treated as 0 to 5, 0 to 10, 0 to 100 or whatever length scale in between that you wish. These points can often be displayed to the respondent if desired, which effectively then turn this into a numeric scale. The researcher must decide at what level the apparent accuracy of the data becomes spurious. That will depend on the length of the line used, the accuracy with which respondents are able to place the cursor, and the degree of accuracy with which respondents are likely to have tried to place the cursor.

With some software, it is possible to place several cursors or brand logos, on the same scale on screen (see Chapter 11) so that the respondent can position them relative to each other.

We have already seen the slider scale in use as a Stapel scale (Figure 6.10). In a specific application, it can be used for new product development to rate products on specific constructs or attributes (Figure 6.12). Here a consistent centre point descriptor has been added, and the scoring will go from –50 to +50.

Figure 6.12   Semantic slider with mid-point

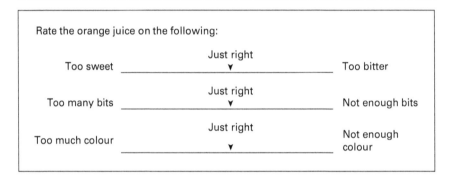

Compare this to the same question shown in Figure 6.4. While the slider scale is better at allowing product developers to see how much they need to adjust their product to meet expectations than would be case with a numeric scale, the labelling of the points in Figure 6.4 may provide a better indication of what the scores actually mean.

> Use fully labelled construct-specific scales for key questions (as this type of scale is easier to interpret) and slider scales (which just have the end-points labelled) for quick reads on lower priority measures.

Visual analogue scales (VAS), require the respondent to place a mark or indicator at a point on the line joining two end points. They thus appear similar to slider scales, but are less frequently found in online surveys than slider scales. They are rarely offered by the online DIY survey providers. This is despite the fact that they require fewer actions by the respondent (point and click, as opposed to grab, move and release) and so should reduce the load on respondents, particularly where there are a number of scales to be answered.

It has been shown (Thomas et al, 2007) that in online surveys, respondents found visual analogue scales as easy to complete as scales using fixed points denoted by radio buttons, and that they felt that VAS scales conveyed their responses with greater accuracy than with a numeric box entry. This view was supported by Cape (2009) with regard to slider scales. Cape also showed that respondents found the slider scale approach more interesting than the radio buttons, a finding supported by others (Roster, Luciano and Albaum, 2015).

Slider scales are popular in online surveys because of their simplicity, but care needs to be taken with them. There may be issues with software compatibility which means that they do not always display properly. There is evidence (Funke, 2016) that they are less easy to cope with on mobile phones and negatively affect completion rates.

Pictorial scales

In many instances, it is desirable to avoid using semantic scales in favour of pictorial representations:

- where the target population is children who are unable to relate their responses to verbal descriptors;
- where there are cultural differences between sub-groups of the target population that may mean that they interpret descriptors differently;
- with multi-country studies where translation of descriptors may alter shades of meaning;
- where there is a low level of literacy in the target population.

A common solution to this is the use of smiley or smiling face scales. A range of smiles and down-turned mouths is used to indicate that the respondent agrees (or is happy) with the statement or disagrees (or is unhappy) with the statement (see Figure 6.13).

Figure 6.13   Smiley scale

Comparative scaling techniques

Paired comparisons

With paired comparisons, respondents are asked to choose between two items based on the appropriate criterion (eg that one is more important than the other, or preferred to the other). This can be repeated with a number of pairs chosen from a set of items, such that every item is compared against every other item (see Figure 6.14). Summing the choices made provides an evaluation of importance or preference across all of the items. The task is often easier and quicker for respondents than being asked to rank-order a list of items, because the individual judgements to be made are simpler. By careful rotation of the pairs, some of the order bias inherent in showing lists can be avoided.

Figure 6.14 Paired comparison

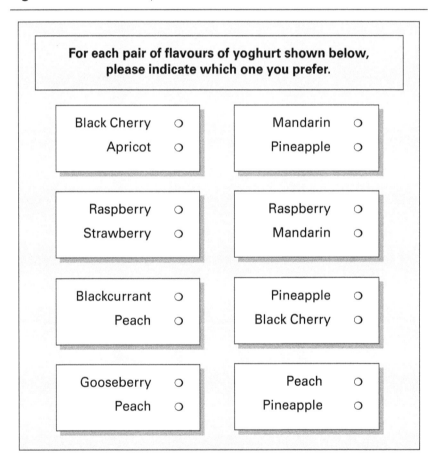

The disadvantage of this technique is that it is limited to a relatively small number of items. With just six items, 15 pairs are required if each is to be assessed against every other, and the number of pairs required increases geometrically. With 190 possible pairs from a list of 20 items, clearly no respondent can be shown all of them. A balanced design of the pairs shown to each respondent can provide sufficient information for the rank order of each item to be inferred.

Constant sum

With a constant sum technique, respondents are asked to allocate a fixed number of points between a set of options to indicate relative importance or relative preference. The number of points given to each option reflects the magnitude of the importance, from which we can also deduce the rank order of the options for each respondent (see Figure 6.15). Some respondents are likely to have problems with a constant sum question, as it requires some effort and mental agility on their part, both to think simultaneously across all of the items and to do the mental arithmetic.

Figure 6.15 Constant sum technique

Following is a list of items that might or might not be important to you when choosing a new car. Allocate 100 points across these five items according to how important they are to you when choosing a new car.

The engine size	☐
The colour	☐
Manual or automatic gearbox	☐
Quality of the radio/CD player	☐
Country of manufacture	☐

100

It is easier online, where the scores allocated can be automatically summed and the respondent not allowed to move on until exactly 100 points have been allocated. However, the need to make simultaneous comparisons between a number of different items still remains. As the number of items increases, it becomes more difficult to think through and to mentally keep a running total of the scores, so this works best where a running total can be displayed.

Another way of asking this is to use a constant sum approach combined with paired comparisons. In another example, the task for respondents had been reduced to making comparisons between 10 pairs of items. Dealing with pairs is usually easier for respondents to manage. Respondents are asked to allocate 11 points between each pair. An odd number has been chosen so that the two items in any pair cannot be given the same number of points; this forces a distinction between them. Had the respondents been asked to allot 10 points per pair, this would have allowed items in a pair to be given equal weight of five points each. This technique can be used equally well for comparing preferences for products, when forcing even small distinctions can be important to the researcher.

Item sorting

When the number of objects is large, say more than 30, then a prior sorting approach can help make a ranking task manageable. Online, the respondent is asked to sort the items into a number of categories. These might be levelled by importance from 'very important' to 'not at all important'. This can be done using a drag-and-drop technique. The following screens show the items that have been put into a category, and the respondent is asked to rank order them. This is repeated for each category. In face-to face interviews a similar process is followed with each item presented on a card.

In this way, the combination of rating and ranking can produce an item scoring system that provides good discrimination across a large number of items.

Q sort

A similar approach designed for larger numbers of attributes (eg 100) is Q sorting.

The objects are sorted by respondents into a number of categories, usually 11 or 12, representing the degrees on the scale, such as appeal or interest in purchase. Respondents may be instructed to place a specific number of objects on each point of the scale so that they are distributed approximately according to a normal distribution. They are asked to put a few objects at the extremes of the scale, with increasing numbers towards the middle of the scale. Objects placed in the two extreme positions can then be rank-ordered by the respondent for increased discrimination.

Using just five scale points and 10 attributes, Chrzan and Golovashkina (2006) showed that the Q sort technique produced results that were better than several other techniques in terms of discrimination and prediction, and was quicker to administer than most. This technique is primarily suited to face-to-face interviewing.

CASE STUDY   Whisky usage and attitude

Rating scales

At Q23, we need to ask the relative importance of whisky attributes when considering which brand to buy. The attributes we have are:

- depth of colour;
- smoothness of taste;

- familiarity with brand;
- distinctiveness from other brands;
- tradition associated with brand.

There are a number of ways in which we might consider asking this:

- Rating of attribute for importance. This, however, is likely to give poor discrimination because most things will be rated as important.
- Ranking of attributes. This will tell us how important each is relative to another, but not how much more important. We will know the order of importance, but not the distance between them.
- Item sort or Q sort are not appropriate because of the relatively fewer number of attributes.

We settle on using paired comparison of attributes, rotating the attributes to cover all pairs. With five attributes, this gives 10 pairs. By obtaining points allocated to each pair, the total number of points achieved by an attribute will indicate its overall importance to the respondent.

The next decision is to how to make the comparisons. We could ask respondents:

- to allocate points between each pair, eg 'Please allocate 11 points between the two attributes.' This requires quite a lot of cognitive effort from the respondents;
- to use a bi-polar slider scale to indicate the relative importance of each of the two attributes. This is simple for respondents and can be translated into a points allocation.

We decide to use the bi-polar scale. There are ten pairs which is manageable. The order of showing the pairs is randomized (Figure 6.16).

Figure 6.16   Q23 Comparative importance rating

How important are the following to you when choosing a whisky to buy?
For each pair of statements move the cursor to indicate how much one is more important than the other.

Depth of colour	▼	Smoothness of the taste
Smoothness of taste	▼	Distinct from other brands
How familiar you are with it	▼	Has lots of tradition
Distinct from other brands	▼	How familiar you are with it
Has lots of tradition	▼	Depth of colour
Depth of colour	▼	How familiar you are with it
Distinct from other brands	▼	Depth of colour
Has lots of tradition	▼	Smoothness of taste
Smoothness of taste	▼	How familiar you are with it
Has lots of tradition	▼	Distinct from other brands

Key take aways: creating appropriate rating scales

- Ratings scales allow degrees of sentiment to be expressed and therefore offer greater sensitivity when measuring opinion or attitudes than simple either/or questions.
- The question designer will have to make a number of decisions:
  - Word scales? Numbers? Pictures? A mix?
  - How many scale points are required?
  - Is a mid-point needed?
  - Is a 'don't know' response needed?
  - Can the scale be unbalanced, or should it have equal positive and negative points?
- There are very few clear cut 'rules' when it comes to making these decisions, as the most appropriate choice is likely to depend on many factors including the subject matter, objectives, data collection mode and exactly who we are interviewing.
- The most practical advice is for the question writer to think ahead to how they will interpret the results. Having a point of comparison is often important to put the results into context. Therefore, consistency with scales used elsewhere can often be the driving factor outweighing decisions that would tailor a scale more specifically to a situation.

Asking about behaviour 07

Introduction

Many of the questions that we ask about behaviour rely on the ability and willingness of the respondent to recall accurately what has occurred, often some time ago. Memory, though, is notoriously unreliable regarding past behaviour. It is invariably more accurate for respondents to record their behaviour as it happens, using a diary or similar technique. However, the cost or feasibility of that type of approach often rules it out, and the behavioural data collected in most studies is behaviour as reported by memory.

In addition to these memory challenges, questions about behaviour can be susceptible to acquiescence bias. This manifests itself in a tendency to agree that they have done or own something if asked a direct question (eg 'have you bought a mobile phone in the last six months?'). Other pressures may also be at play (eg fear of appearing to lack social status by not owning the item).

Asking recalled behaviour

The accuracy of recall will depend on many factors, including the recency and significance to the individual of the behaviour in question. Most people will be able to name the bank they use but will be less reliable about which brand of tinned tuna they last bought. They could probably describe in some detail the process of buying a car undertaken some months previously but struggle to tell you how they decided to buy that particular tuna brand on that last occasion. Frequently what is reported is an impression of behaviour, the respondents' beliefs about what they do, rather than an accurate recording of what they have done. Tourangeau et al (2000) list the following reasons for memory failure by respondents to surveys:

- Respondents may not have taken in the critical information in the first place.
- They may be unwilling to go through the work of retrieving it.
- Even if they do try, they may retrieve only partial information about the event and, as a result, fail to report it.
- They may recall false information about the event, including incorrect inferences they have incorporated into their stored memory of the event.
- They may be unable to recall the event itself, but only generic information about events of that type.

Researchers are generally aware that recall information can be unreliable. However, what is sometimes overlooked is the bias introduced into the responses by the final source of memory failure listed above. When respondents generalize about types of events they will tend to report not only what they believe that they do, but also what they believe that they do most of the time. Even if what they say is accurate, minority behaviour will tend to be under-reported.

> When writing a recall question, ask yourself how far back you can accurately recall a similar event or purchase, and keep your time scale within that. Do not be tempted to go further back in an attempt to get more data points; you will only increase the unreliability of the data.

Inaccuracy of memory regarding time periods (telescoping)

Particularly notorious is the accuracy of memory related to time. Respondents will tend to report that an event occurred more recently than it actually did. Researchers and psychologists have long been aware of this phenomenon. The first important theory of telescoping was proposed by Sudman and Bradburn (1973), who wrote:

'There are two kinds of memory error that sometimes operate in opposite directions. The first is forgetting an episode entirely. The second kind of error is compression (telescoping) where the event is remembered as occurring more recently than it did.'

Thus, when asked to recall events that occurred in the last three months, respondents will tend to include events that occurred in what feels like the last three months (which is usually a longer period). Additional events are therefore 'imported' into that period and mistakenly reported (forward telescoping). In contrast, other events are forgotten or thought to have occurred longer ago than they really did (backward telescoping) and are therefore not reported. The extent to which telescoping occurs will depend on the importance of the event to the respondent and the time period asked about.

A technique that can help is 'bounding', where the respondent is given clear landmarks to which they find it easier to relate time periods. Public holidays and birthdays often provide such landmarks. A survey in the middle of the year that is concerned with behaviour in the previous six months might ask what the respondent has done 'in the last six months (that is, since Christmas)'. Respondents find it easier to fix the date on which they did something as before or after Christmas than whether it was within the last six months. Unfortunately, there are few landmark dates common to everybody that suit the reference period for the questionnaire writer, but if one can be found it will improve the accuracy of the data collected.

Another suggestion (Tourangeau et al, 2000) suitable for interviewer-administered surveys is to extend the number of words in the question beyond what is absolutely necessary in order to give the respondent more time to think before they feel obliged to provide an answer. This may be particularly helpful with telephone interviewing, where silences can be awkward and the respondent may avoid them by answering before they have fully thought it through.

Figure 7.1 Recall period should be appropriate to the importance of the event – some suggestions

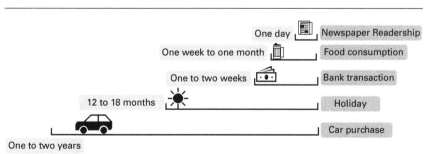

Last week or typical week

When asking respondents to recall behaviour, the question writer has to decide whether to ask what was done in the last week (or relevant time period), or what was done in a typical week.

Answering for a typical week is cognitively more complex because the respondent has to determine what is a typical week, whether such a thing exists, and if not, how to construct something that is typical by taking into account behaviour over a longer time (Chang and Krosnick, 2003). Thus, the typical week response may stretch back over a longer time period than a week, which we know is likely to be less accurate. In their studies Chang and Krosnick (2003) actually found that predictive validity of 'typical week' data was greater than 'last week' data, but concluded that this may have been because they were asking about media usage, which tends to be regular. In categories with more variable behaviour patterns, last week is likely to be more accurate.

Another difference between the two measures is that a typical week will tend to underestimate minority behaviours. Thus, if most weeks you shop at Supermarket A multiple times, but last week you shopped at Supermarket B, your 'typical week' response will be Supermarket A. In aggregate you may get the correct picture if all stores are used in roughly the same proportions. However, if most people in the sample only use Supermarket B occasionally, then usage of that store will be underestimated by this question. If your objective is to determine levels of usage of different brands, asking about behaviour in the last week is likely to provide more accurate data than asking about a typical week. However, if your objective is to use this information for analysis purposes to determine brand loyalty or brand perceptions, you may want to know the respondent's majority behaviour, and the typical week question will give you that.

A more detailed approach to gaining the individual level of brand behaviour is to ask about the last 10 purchases of brands or products in the category. This tells us about both the respondents' majority and minority behaviour. Care must be taken, though, to ensure that it is reasonable to expect respondents to be able to remember the last 10 occasions. Where a purchase is made only once a fortnight, such as is typical for car fuel purchases, then the last 10 may stretch back nearly six months and will not be accurately recalled. Conversely, where a behaviour is frequent, the last 10 may not be sufficient to adequately represent all the minority behaviour where that represents less than 10 per cent of occasions. The questionnaire writer must take into account these considerations and arrive at the optimum question for the market/product concerned. Where this is well-matched this approach has been shown to provide accurate data that mirrors brand shares.

Recalling and recording numeric values

When asking respondents to remember how many times they have done/bought something or the price they paid, the level of detail requested needs to be as precise as is necessary to meet the research objectives without demanding more detail than respondents can accurately give. Sometimes it is possible to record precise values (eg the number of times the respondent has visited a pub or bar in the past week), but frequently we do not want to record that level of detail, and nor can respondents be expected to undergo the cognitive effort to retrieve it. In this case, the answers will be recorded in value bands.

Constructing ranges

If it is reasonable to expect a respondent to be able to recall an exact value it should be recorded as an absolute number as this gives greater precision, and also flexibility with analysis. However, when it is not realistic to expect respondents to remember exact values we can present respondents with ranges of values within which they are more likely to be able to provide a response.

In Figure 7.2, in answer to a question about the cost of a holiday, the questionnaire writer has determined that bands of £200 are sufficiently accurate to meet the demands of the study. Bands of £50 would have given the researcher greater accuracy in calculating the average cost of a holiday and in making comparisons between sub-groups, but might have been difficult for respondents to recall precisely. This could have led to an increase in the proportion of 'don't know' responses.

The pre-coded response categories must be meaningful to both respondent and researcher if the first is to be able to answer and the second to interpret.

Figure 7.2   Determining the level of detail

Q. What was the cost of your holiday, per person?

Up to £200	O
£201 to £400	O
£401 to £600	O
£601 to £800	O
£801 to £1,000	O
£1,001 to MORE	O

When constructing the ranges, ensure that they are mutually exclusive and do not overlap (as shown in Figure 7.3) which is a common error.

> Keep ranges as broad as you can within your data needs. Small ranges will lead to more 'don't know' responses, more guesses, and less reliable data.

The ranges should usually be constructed such that the most popular values occur in the middle of the ranges. For example, if the question is, 'How much did you pay for the paperback novel that you are currently reading?', we know that most answers, if accurately given, will be £x.99. However, it would not be unusual to see the following ranges given for this question:

Under £4.99

£5 to £5.99

£6 to £6.99

£7 to £7.99

£8 to £8.99

£9 or more

This can cause loss of accuracy. A book costing £6.99 would be reported as costing precisely that by some respondents. Other respondents will round it up to £7, and the response will be recorded in the category above the one it should be in. Other respondents may say 'about £7', leaving the interviewer unsure as to where it should be coded. Equally as important in the analysis of this data, we may want to produce an average price paid. Having collected the data in these ranges, we would normally allocate the value of the mid-point of each range to calculate the average. However, if nearly all of the actual values are at the top end of each range, the calculated average price paid will be around 50 pence below what it should be.

Figure 7.3 Duplications in the values

Q. On average, how much do you pay for these text alerts, per text?

Free of charge	O
1–5 p	O
5–10 p	O
11–15 p	O
16–20 p	O
21–25 p	O
26–30 p	O
31–35 p	O
36–40 p	O
41–45 p	O
46–50 p	O
50–75 p	O
75 p – £1	O
More than £1	O
Don't know	O

In this case, the duplications at 5, 50 and 75 pence were all spotted by the agency's checking procedures before the questionnaire went live. It is because this type of error is so easy to make that most agencies have strict checking procedures.

Other markets where prices tend to cluster around price points, such as televisions which tend to have prices around £299, £399 and so on, can suffer from this effect. The average price could then be around £50 below what they should be if the wrong banding is used.

Don't know

In the context of behavioural questions 'don't know' is frequently a legitimate answer if a respondent cannot remember or is unsure. Sometimes respondents can be encouraged to provide an approximate answer if they can't remember an amount or a period of time, which is sufficient for the purpose of the researcher. Showing ranges, as discussed above, means that the respondent does not have to be precise and it is less effort to recall the approximate range than the exact amount, so reducing the likelihood of a 'don't know' response.

Offering a 'don't know' option can be contentious, and can be thought to provide an easy option for lazy respondents and speedsters; this issue is returned to in Chapter 10. With behavioural questions there is likely to be less cognitive effort in retrieving the answer than in attitudinal questions and it is therefore less likely that a 'don't know' answer will be selected to avoid having to make that effort. Without a 'don't know' option, there is the danger of forcing respondents to select answers that do not accurately reflect their behaviour, which can cause inconsistencies and difficulties in analysis.

Question order

With any questionnaire there is the likelihood that the order in which the questions are asked will affect how people respond. If behavioural patterns are established early in the questionnaire then later answers to attitudinal questions may be given to justify the behaviour. Thus, if a particular brand is regularly bought, then in later questions the respondent is likely to say that the brand is of high quality or good value to justify their loyalty to it. However, the alternative is to ask attitudinal questions first, with the consequence that behaviour may be misreported to justify the stated attitudes. A respondent may then claim to buy a brand more often than they really do because in the attitudinal questions they had said how good it is. Ultimately, the judgement of the question writer is needed as to the compromise required against the priority objectives of the survey.

Behavioural screening question

If qualifying for the sample is related to behaviour or ownership there will be a need for behavioural questions to appear very early in the questionnaire. Early questions should be straightforward for the respondent to answer and allow them to ease into the subject. If for any reason they are not straightforward and cause the respondent to work hard to provide the answer, this will increase the likelihood of an early termination of the interview, so efforts should be made to make them as simple as possible. But we must take care to disguise our interest to avoid acquiescence bias in that question and bias in later questions that will arise because we have disclosed what we are really interested in.

Disguised questions

Rather than asking a direct question (eg 'Have you bought a wide-screen television in the last six months?'). A less biased version of the question, which contains a number of blind responses to disguise our interest, is given in Figure 7.4.

Figure 7.4 Questions with blind responses

Which, if any, of these have you bought in the last six months.
This is either for yourself or for someone else.

TELEPHONE
TELEVISION
DIGITAL RADIO
DVD PLAYER
MICROWAVE OVEN
NONE OF THESE

(IF BOUGHT TELEVISION IN PAST SIX MONTHS, GO TO NEXT QUESTION.)

Was the television you bought...?
PLASMA SCREEN
HIGH DEFINITION
FLAT SCREEN
WIDE SCREEN
SURROUND SOUND
DOLBY SOUND
NONE OF THESE

The blind responses, in which we have no interest, should be designed to give most people the opportunity to provide a positive answer. If the real interest is to identify people who own a minority or niche product, more popular products should also be included to allow as many as possible to give a positive answer and remove pressure from them to overclaim purchase or ownership of the minority product.

Funnelling questions

The questions in Figure 7.4 provide a simple form of funnelling. Much more complex pieces of information can often be broken down into a series of disguised choice questions that funnel respondents to the precise informa-tion sought.

If we want to find out how many people have bought packs of four cherry yogurts in the last seven days, it would be dangerous to ask: 'Have you bought any four-packs of cherry flavoured yogurt in the last seven days?'

The cognitive task being asked of respondents is too great, as they are asked to process four pieces of information:

1 product type;

2 pack type;

3 flavour;

4 time period.

Many respondents simply won't bother, while among others the risk of acquiescence bias is high. The resulting sample is unlikely to be an accurate reflection of the desired research population. This should be broken into a series of smaller tasks, with the researcher's interest disguised at each stage, as shown in Figure 7.5. In a face-to-face interview each of the response options would be presented on a show card; online they would appear on screen.

Figure 7.5 Funnelling questions

Which, if any, of these have you bought in the last seven days?

CRÈME FRAICHE
PLAIN YOGHURT
FLAVOURED YOGHURT
SOURED CREAM
COTTAGE CHEESE
NONE OF THESE

(IF FLAVOURED YOGHURT BOUGHT)

What types of pack were the flavoured yoghurts in?

INDIVIDUAL POTS
PACK OF FOUR – SAME FLAVOUR PACK OF FOUR – MIXED FLAVOURS
PACK OF SIX – SAME FLAVOUR PACK OF SIX – MIXED FLAVOURS
OTHER

(IF PACK OF FOUR – SAME FLAVOUR)

What flavour were they?

BANANA
CHERRY
CHOCOLATE
MANGO
PEACH
RASPBERRY
RHUBARB
STRAWBERRY
STRAWBERRY AND RASPBERRY
GARDEN FRUITS
FRUIT (OTHER/UNSPECIFIED)
OTHER
DON'T KNOW/CAN'T REMEMBER

The cognitive process for the respondent is broken down into simple steps rather than having to cope with several pieces of information in the one question. Additional information is also picked up along the way. When the questioning is through a single question, we can only determine the penetration of the defined group. By breaking the questions down we can also determine the penetration of past seven-day yogurt purchasers. This is information that could be checked against other sources to establish the accuracy of the sample, or it may be new information.

CASE STUDY   Whisky usage and attitude

Behavioural questions

Disguised questions: We need to make use of a number of disguised questions which include blind responses to ensure that we get the sample that we want.

The first disguised question is intended to exclude anyone who works in the drinks trade, or has someone in their immediate family who does. They will not be typical consumers, with different levels of awareness of brands and potentially different levels of access to buying whisky. Such people will distort the sample. We also want to exclude people who work in advertising or marketing for similar reasons. We do not wish to alert respondents to our interest or have people saying that they are in the drinks trade because they think that is what is expected. We therefore present them with a range of options, most of which are blinds, but allow them to give an answer:

- Do you or any of your family work in the following industries?
  - Accountancy
  - Advertising
  - Information technology
  - Marketing
  - Production or retailing of alcoholic drinks
  - Production or retailing of soft/fizzy drinks
  - Banking or insurance
  - Grocery retailing
  - None of these

In the second of these questions, to identify Scotch whisky drinkers, we again present a list of items in which we are not interested in order to hide those in which we are:

- Which of these have you drunk in the last three months?
    - Ale
    - Lager
    - Stout
    - Gin
    - Vodka
    - Scotch whisky
    - Irish whiskey
    - White wine
    - Red wine
    - None of these

Funnelling questions: We shall need a short funnelling sequence to identify our research sample, which is people who drink whisky at least every three months. The question above identifies those who have drunk scotch in the last three months, but we need to exclude any who do not drink at least once every three months (ie the occasion recalled was a very isolated one). Our funnel, then, consists of the question above and a second question:

- How often do you drink Scotch whisky?
    - Most days
    - At least once a week
    - At least once a month
    - At least once every three months
    - At least once every six months
    - Less often than every six months

We can then exclude anyone who does not normally drink Scotch whisky at least every three months.

Behaviour recall: The screening and funnelling questions above are impressionistic, in that we cannot expect all respondents to know precisely when they last drank whisky or how often they drink it, particularly if they are less frequent drinkers. However, when we ask detailed questions about behaviour, we need to reduce the time scale to something that is more easily and accurately recalled. Now we switch to a time frame of one week. This shorter time frame should exclude the worst issues of telescoping or memory loss. Note that this will exclude many less frequent (lighter) drinkers of whisky who will not have drunk in the last week, so our sample size will be reduced. However, we know that the profile of whisky drinkers is skewed to heavier drinkers (ie lighter drinkers are a minority), so the improvement in the quality of the data by this change outweighs the loss caused by the smaller sample size. (We shall also have to weight the data by frequency of drinking if we want to return the profile of the sample to that of all three-monthly whisky drinkers for these questions. Again, though, we judge that the improvement in recall will outweigh the loss of accuracy caused by weighting.)

We also need to decide whether we are going to ask about behaviour in a typical week or in the last week. For this we need to consider whether there are any abnormalities in our fieldwork period that might distort data relating to the 'last week', such as Christmas, New Year or a major televised sporting event.

There will be several questions about recent consumption, such as:

- How many glasses of whisky did you drink in the home in the last seven days?

This could be in your own home or someone else's.

A glass is the equivalent of a single measure.

We have used the term 'in the home' rather than 'off-licence' which may be the technically correct term but may not be so easily understood by all respondents. Note the clarification that we need to give about what we mean by 'the home' and what constitutes 'a glass'. When we ask about 'on-licence' consumption we shall need similar clarification of what we mean.

Key take aways: asking about behaviour

- Questions about recall of behaviour have to be written using judgment about what it is realistic for a respondent to remember:
  - over what time period;
  - in what level of detail.

- Even when an appropriate time period/level of detail is used there are further challenges:
  - Acquiescence bias – often seen if a respondent is asked a direct question about whether they have done or own something. Disguise your interest by including other items (blinds) in a list – especially at early screening questions.
  - Recall reflects what respondents think they did – how important or interesting something was can influence their memory.
- In constructing questions about behaviour, reduce the cognitive effort involved:
  - by breaking questions into simpler steps and funnelling down;
  - by focusing on a specific occasion (eg the last time);
  - using response bands for recall of numeric values (eg how many times or amount spent).

Measuring satisfaction, image and attitudes

08

Introduction

For many topics, the survey may be the first time that they have expressed how they feel, be it about the service they received on a train, their perceived images of brands of tomato ketchup or attitudes to their country's overseas aid policy. The possibility that respondents may have never thought about or articulated the perceptions and emotions that we wish to capture, makes them more difficult to measure than behavioural data.

Customer satisfaction

In today's climate of customer service, you may be asked to complete a customer satisfaction survey in a hotel, after purchasing an item or following any number of other activities. They may vary from short one-sided cards left for the customer to complete, to in-depth studies conducted later online or by telephone. Most of them use rating scales.

Rating scales

Scales provide a helpful tool as they give the customer a relatively easy way of assessing the service across different items. For the researcher analyzing the results, the interval nature of the data can produce mean scores that facilitate comparison across items. Further analysis is also possible through correlation or regression analyses using other data eg against measures of behaviour.

Unfortunately, there are many poor examples of their application. Figure 8.1 shows the first part of a survey card left in a hotel room. The questionnaire continued with 53 attributes in total to be rated on this scale and 12 other questions. It contained no instructions other than to define the points of the scale. This example likely resulted in a low response rate – and minimal engagement even among those who did complete it.

Figure 8.1   Part of a hotel guest satisfaction questionnaire

1 = Excellent 2 = Very Good 3 = Good 4 = Fair 5 = Poor					
Cleanliness of your guest room upon entering	1	2	3	4	5
Cleanliness and servicing of your room during your stay	1	2	3	4	5
Overall cleanliness of bathroom	1	2	3	4	5
Cleanliness of bathtub and tiles	1	2	3	4	5
Condition of duvet cover	1	2	3	4	5
Overall guest room quality	1	2	3	4	5
Overall maintenance and upkeep	1	2	3	4	5
Condition of grounds	1	2	3	4	5
Condition of the lobby area	1	2	3	4	5
Condition of the lounge and restaurants	1	2	3	4	5
Functionality of guest room	1	2	3	4	5

It is very common for 10- or 11-point numeric scales to be used, particularly when measuring likelihood to recommend the service or product in the future. Net Promoter Score (NPS) (Reicheld, 2003) is widely used in many markets.

The typical NPS question

On a scale of 0-to-10, how likely is it that you would recommend [organization, product, or service] to a friend or colleague?

The scale runs from 0 (not at all likely) to 10 (extremely likely).

- **Promoters** are designated as customers giving a score of 9 or 10. Typically, they would be loyal, satisfied customers.

- **Passives** are identified as those giving a score of 7 or 8. They might be considered satisfied with the service but not enthusiastic enough to be seen as promoters.

- **Detractors** give low scores between 0 to 6. These are dissatisfied customers unlikely to buy/use again. They may even actively discourage others.

The Net Promoter Score is usually calculated by **subtracting the percentage of detractors** from the **percentage of promoters**.

For example, if 10% of respondents are detractors, 30% are passives and 60% are promoters, the NPS score would be 60-10 = 50. This score can then be compared against any benchmarks that are available to the researcher.

Ratings of performance allow us to track any changes over time, but how does the reported performance relate to expectations? A rating of 'very good' may be wonderful news for a two-star hotel but a poor score for a five-star hotel where everything is expected to be 'excellent'. Do customers bear that in mind when completing customer satisfaction questionnaires? Would the same level of service be rated as 'excellent' in the two-star hotel but 'poor' in the five-star hotel because expectations are different? Nor can it be assumed that these factors will remain constant over time. The ratings may start to decline despite the level of service remaining constant because a new competitor has entered the market with an improved service that has changed customers' expectations.

The questionnaire writer therefore needs to consider other scales as well. A scale may be devised to monitor performance relative to expectations. One such scale might be:

- much better than I expected;
- better than expected;
- as expected;
- worse than expected;
- much worse than expected.

Achieving a high score on this scale would demonstrate both that customers are delighted with the level of service, which they did not expect, and that there is possible over-delivery that could be cut back.

In some circumstances meeting customers' needs rather than their expectations may be more appropriate. For instance:

- The level of service was:
  - A lot more than I needed;
  - A little more than I needed;
  - Exactly what was needed;
  - A little less than I needed;
  - A lot less than I needed.

The provision of hotel services – for example, the swimming pool, the trouser press or the range of restaurants – may have been excellent and may have been what was expected from a five-star hotel, but was more than was needed by the client, who will go elsewhere next time where they can get what they need for a lower price.

In the example in Figure 8.2, the questionnaire writer has chosen to assess the performance of the internet banking website but, with the second attribute in the first block, has included an attribute relating to the needs of the customer, rather than the specific performance of the site. Note that this uses an agree-disagree scale to assess the first three attributes and a scale running from excellent to poor for the next four. Because these are both five-point scales, the temptation for the researcher would be to make direct comparisons between the two blocks of attributes. That, however, assumes that an answer of 'strongly agree' 'that the design of the site is clear and appealing' equates to the design and clarity of the site being excellent. This may not always be the case and how the data will be interpreted must be considered at the time of writing the questionnaire.

As we saw in Chapter 5, replacing the agree-disagree scale with an item-specific question would be likely to improve the reliability of the data. Such a question might be:

- How did you find using the service today?
  - Very easy
  - Easy
  - Neither easy nor difficult
  - Difficult
  - Very difficult

Figure 8.2 Assessing the absolute performance of an internet banking website

First Birmingham Bank Internet Banking – customer feedback survey

0%	25%	50%	75%	100%

Based on your experience today, **to what extent do you agree or disagree** with the following statements?

	Strongly agree	Slightly agree	Neither agree nor disagree	Slightly disagree	Strongly disagree	Don't know
I found the service easy to use	○	○	○	○	○	○
The First Birmingham Internet Banking site did everything I wanted it to	○	○	○	○	○	○
The design of the site is clear and appealing	○	○	○	○	○	○

How would you rate the First Birmingham Internet Banking website on the following?

	Excellent	Very good	Good	Fair	Poor	Don't know
Information being easy to understand	○	○	○	○	○	○
Ease of finding information	○	○	○	○	○	○
Availability of service	○	○	○	○	○	○
Account statements	○	○	○	○	○	○

Previous   Continue

Clearly, however, replacing each item with an individual question such as this will take up more space, in this case more screens, and may raise issues regarding the comparability of responses to the items if the individual response scales are not carefully matched. This is an issue that the questionnaire writer has to consider and find the appropriate balance.

A further task for the questionnaire writer is to determine the number and level of detail of the items to be assessed. In customer satisfaction research the items are frequently defined by operational factors, such as the cleanliness of a room, or a call centre operator's ability to answer questions, or clarity of use of the website. They should be:

- to a level of detail that is realistic to expect the respondent to be able to answer;
- expressed succinctly, simply, and unambiguously;
- limited to a number that it is reasonable to maintain motivation.

In the hotel example illustrated earlier (Figure 8.1) the items requiring rating are not always clear. What does 'functionality of guest room' actually mean? Different respondents are likely to interpret it differently. This appears to be a list of items compiled by someone involved in the hotel's operations with no reference to a researcher.

Brand image

A common objective with brand and communication studies is to measure the perceptions that people hold of the main brands, how they compare and how they might occupy different positions in customers' minds, either as having functional differences or differences in emotional positioning.

Rating scales

With a scalar approach, each brand is evaluated on a number of dimensions defined as the key dimensions that discriminate between brands. Each brand is evaluated monadically across the dimensions, thus the question set is repeated for each brand with the order of brands rotated or randomized. This is important to balance the influence of how ratings given to one brand affect the way respondents rate following brands. How they rate the first brand on, say, 'quality', sets a benchmark for all subsequent brands. A slightly generous rating for the first brand, even though respondents think it might only be of average quality, requires increasingly positive ratings for any subsequent brands thought to be of better quality. Respondents are only asked to evaluate brands that they are aware of from a preceding or earlier prompted brand-awareness question.

Figure 8.3 is typical of the self-completion question to evaluate brand image using an agree-disagree scale. Note that this is technically not a Likert

Figure 8.3   Brand image evaluation

What do you think of The Fluffy Chick Store on the following?					
	Disagree strongly	Disagree	Neither agree nor disagree	Agree	Agree strongly
Is high quality	O	O	O	O	O
Has excellent service	O	O	O	O	O
Is a modern store	O	O	O	O	O
A good range of stock	O	O	O	O	O
Is competitively priced	O	O	O	O	O

scale. As we are not measuring attitude but perception, there is no necessarily positive or negative position for each dimension, only different brand positionings. The individual respondent scores cannot be summed to provide an overall attitude score.

The questions in Figure 8.3 could equally have been posed as a bi-polar semantic differential scale. Care then must be taken in defining the pairs of statements so that they have truly opposite meanings. For example, is 'traditional' the opposite of 'modern' – or should it be 'old-fashioned'?

The scalar approaches to measuring brand image provide strong interval data that can be used in a variety of ways, including the calculation of mean scores and standard deviations and the analytical techniques such as correlation, regression, and factor analyses. They do, though, suffer from two drawbacks. First, because they are completed monadically it is difficult for respondents to reference brands against each other. As discussed earlier, respondents may rate a brand for a particular attribute, only to find that for following brands they have not left themselves sufficient space on the scale to properly express the differences that they perceive between them.

The second disadvantage is that they can take a long time for respondents to complete. A list of 20 attributes for each of six brands requires respondents to complete 120 scales if they are aware of all six brands. At an estimated 15 seconds for each attribute for the first brand, and 10 seconds for subsequent brands, this can take over 20 minutes to complete. This adds to the potential fatigue and boredom of the respondents; encourages straightlining or pattern answering, and adds to the length of the interview and the cost of the study.

Attribute association

An alternative approach (Figure 8.4) is the brand-attribute association grid (also known as the 'pick-any' or 'check-all' technique). Here respondents are shown a list of brands and asked to say which brand or brands they associate with each of a series of image attributes. This is quicker because respondents only have to go through the list of attributes once. They also do not have to make such complex decisions about how well each brand performs on each attribute, only that it applies or that it does not.

Brands of which they are not aware will usually not be nominated as possessing any of the characteristics. Some respondents may nominate brands that they have previously said they are unaware of to have certain characteristics (particularly for attributes such as 'not well known') but these can be identified at the analysis stage. If respondents really are responding with an image of a brand they are hearing of for the first time, that can tell the researcher a great deal about the image attributes of the name alone. Another advantage is that respondents can assess the full set of brands together. This makes it easier for them to make comparisons between brands and determine that an attribute is or is not associated with one brand rather than another.

A task for the questionnaire writer is to determine the attributes that are to be measured. Product attributes are often very specific and easily identified (eg modern, value for money, effective). Brand positioning or image attributes may be less tangible but are often well defined within the brand positioning statement.

Disadvantages

One possible issue with this technique is that it is relatively easy for respondents to go through the question quickly without considering every brand presented. It has been shown (Smyth et al, 2006; Stern et al, 2012) that compared with a forced choice question where the respondent has to say for each attribute whether he or she associates each brand with it, as would be necessary in a telephone interview, this technique gives fewer positive associations for each brand.

A further disadvantage of attributing image statements in this way is the loss of the degree of discrimination that would have been obtained had scales been used. It may be found, for example, that most respondents think that all brands possess certain attributes, whereas a scalar approach would have shown variation in the strength with which each brand is seen to possess them.

Improving discrimination

The level of discrimination can be increased by including opposite expressions of an attribute. Both 'high quality' and 'poor quality'; 'for younger people' and 'not for younger people' could be asked. Note that 'for older people' is not necessarily the opposite of 'for younger people', as the brand could be seen to be for both. This doubles the number of attribute statements that need to be included. It effectively creates a three-point scale, with each brand nominated either for the point at each end of the scale, or not mentioned at all, which can be taken as the mid-point of the scale. The relationship of the association between the two end-points is sometimes referred to as the 'quality of the brand image', and the extent to which the brand is associated at all with the dimension as 'the strength of the brand image'.

An alternative way to increase discrimination is to ask which brand (or brands) respondents would choose if they were looking for one that possessed the attribute. Respondents then tend to nominate only brands that are strongly associated in their minds with the attribute. This reduces the number of brands associated with each attribute and demonstrates 'ownership' of attributes more clearly.

Reference set

The levels of association recorded are not absolute but are relative to the number of brands asked about, the actual brands in the set and the attributes used. The brands included in the set act as the reference set against which each brand is judged. The choice of which and how many brands are included is thus an important decision. Should the number of brands or choice set change over time, on repeat studies or tracking studies, there is a danger that comparability will be lost. A study may, for example, ask respondents to associate brands from a set of five airlines. If the number of

Figure 8.4 Brand-attribute association grid

I am now going to read out a number of words and phrases that have been used to describe different brands of whisky. For each one I would like you to tell me to which, if any, of the brands on this card (SHOW CARD) you think it applies. Each phrase could apply to any number of the brands, all of them or none of them.

READ OUT

	Brand A	Brand B	Brand C	Brand D	Brand E	None of them
High quality	1	1	1	1	1	1
Traditional	2	2	2	2	2	2
For younger people	3	3	3	3	3	3
For older people	4	4	4	4	4	4
A fun brand	5	5	5	5	5	5
A modern brand	6	6	6	6	6	6
To be taken seriously	7	7	7	7	7	7

airlines was to be increased to six in a later study, then we should expect to see the levels of association for all brands decrease. This is because the average number of brands associated with each attribute tends to remain reasonably constant, so that with more brands the average number per brand decreases.

Had one of the attributes been 'innovative' and the new brand introduced been Virgin Atlantic – a brand known for its innovation – then a substantial change in association for the remaining brands should be expected on this attribute. The frame of reference on this attribute will have changed. A similar change on this attribute would have been expected had Virgin Atlantic been substituted for another brand in the set, so that the total number remained the same.

An attribute should not be included without very good reason if the brand set does not include the brand that has the strongest associations with the attribute. The false conclusion that a brand performs strongly on that attribute could easily be arrived at, because it only does so in the context of worse performing brands.

Some researchers seek to reduce the cognitive workload on respondents by only including brands of which they are aware; or possibly only brands that appear in their consideration set; or using only attributes that are important to the respondent. Using 'adaptive sets' requires careful analysis as the reference set has, in effect, been changed.

Binary measurement

While the brand-attribute association or 'pick-any' technique remains the most popular and common way to assess brand image in commercial research, doubts have been raised as to the stability of the data. Experience with commercial research studies shows that in aggregate the data is sufficiently stable over time in tracking studies to be usable, but experimental work has shown that individual respondents change their responses between interviews and there is little replication (Rungie et al, 2005). Dolnicar et al (2012) showed that fewer than half of the brand-attribute associations made in a survey were repeated by the same respondents in a second survey four weeks later. This may raise doubts about the accuracy of any analyses that link these findings to individual respondent characteristics, such as demographic or product usage data.

Far greater stability was found by using a binary technique where the respondent was required to say for each brand whether it was thought to possess the attribute or not.

It has been shown (Dolnicar et al, 2011) that binary questions can be substituted for multi-category scales and:

- be answered more quickly;
- be seen as less onerous;
- provide equal reliability;
- lead to the same conclusions.

Some shades of intermediate opinion are inevitably lost, but these are frequently ignored in the analysis. Others (Anderson et al, 2011) have shown that in street interviewing with pictorial prompts, binary questions took over one second more to answer than did a 0 to 10 scale. Clearly the context of the interview and the nature of the alternatives both need to be taken into account, but unless the shades of opinion are specifically required for analysis, binary questions should be considered as an alternative to multi-category scales.

Attitudes

Probably the most common way to measure attitudes is to use rating scales, whether it is to measure attitudes to products, social issues or lifestyles. Formulating the attributes or statements used to measure attitudes can be a more difficult task than coming up with dimensions to rate performance or brand image. Attitudes can be less tangible.

Respondents may also never have considered the issues that they are being asked about. They may therefore be more open to influence from the question wording or the inferences that they draw from the statements.

Achieving balance

Balance in attitudinal questions is generally achieved by presenting all aspects of the dimension as being equally acceptable. This is important because there is a tendency for people to agree with any proposition that is put to them.

There may be two aspects to the question: 'Do you think that voting in general elections should be made compulsory or not made compulsory?' Or there may be more than two: 'Do you think that women are better suited to bring up children than men, or that men are better suited than women, or that both are equally suited?' The unbalanced version of these questions would be: 'Do you think that voting in general elections should be made compulsory? (Yes/No)' and, 'Do you think that women are better suited than men to bring up children? (Yes/No)'.

These unbalanced versions are likely to lead to a higher proportion of the sample agreeing than would have chosen that option from the balanced questions. The evidence for acquiescence is strong. Schuman and Presser (1981) demonstrated it by asking the balanced and unbalanced version of the same question on the roles of men and women in politics in four separate surveys. The unbalanced version produced agreement with the proposition of between 44 and 48 per cent across the four surveys. The same proposition was chosen by between 33 and 39 per cent where the balanced question was used – the use of the unbalanced form added in the region of 10 percentage points.

Differences of such magnitude were not found with other topics, so acquiescence would seem to vary between subjects and possibly between individual items within a topic. Questionnaire writers rarely have the luxury of being able to test each topic and item to determine whether or not it is likely to be susceptible to acquiescence. It is therefore good practice to treat all questions as if they are, and to write the question in a balanced format. However, Schaeffer et al (2005) compared a fully balanced question with a minimally balanced question by replacing the full description of the alternative by 'is not':

Full balance:

- As it conducts the war on terrorism, do you think the United States government is doing enough to protect the rights of American citizens, or do you think the government is not doing enough to protect the rights of American citizens?

Minimal balance:

- As it conducts the war on terrorism, do you think the United States government is or is not doing enough to protect the rights of American citizens?

Both questions found identical results, suggesting that repeating the proposition in its negative form is not necessary as long as a negative option is offered.

Showing your position

Whether or not the question is balanced, expression of the attitude must not lead the respondents to a particular point of view. A hypothetical example of such a question is:

- Homeless people in our cities are a major problem and deter people from coming here. Do you think that the state should support homeless people or not?

The position of the question writer is quite clear. Only one aspect of the issue of homelessness has been highlighted, and this would be likely to lead respondents to a particular answer. The questions could as easily have been put as:

- Some people find themselves without a home through no fault of their own, and then find it difficult to get back into work. Do you think the state should support homeless people or not?

The actual question is the same, but the information given to 'assist' the respondent in coming to an answer is biased in the opposite direction and is likely to lead to the opposite response from the first version.

> When considering a 'don't know' option, ask yourself if everyone should have a view or attitude, even subconsciously, that you want to get out of them, or is it possible that they really do not know.

With complex subjects such as this, the question writer has the choice of presenting all the pertinent issues as fairly and as equably as possible, or to ask the respondent to base their answer on what they already know about the subject:

- From what you know about the issue of homelessness, are you in favour of or against the state supporting homeless people?

The extent of the wording change does not need to be as drastic as in this example in order to change the response. Schuman and Presser (1981) showed that a relatively small addition of a few words can change the response. In 1974 they asked the question:

- If a situation like Vietnam were to develop in another part of the world, do you think the United States should or should not send troops?

To this question, 18 per cent answered that the United States should send troops. When the five words 'to stop a communist takeover' were added to the question, that proportion increased to 36 per cent. Similar increases were seen when the experiment was repeated in 1976 and again in 1978.

The additional words clearly led to a significant proportion of respondents assessing their position differently because they highlighted one particular aspect of the issue being asked about. It is unlikely that most market research questionnaires explore such emotive issues, but the example clearly serves to show how small additions to the question can change the response, and the care that must be taken with wording the question. Just a few words can alter the tenor of the question or crystallize an attitude that was previously only vaguely held. Question writers should be constantly asking themselves whether the inclusion of particular words or phrases helps the respondent, or in fact alter the basic question.

Evidence of acquiescence bias was reported by the UK Scottish Affairs Committee of the House of Commons. They reported a polling experiment conducted by Lord Ashcroft prior to the Scottish Independence Referendum of 2014. This considered three versions of the possible question shown in Figure 8.5 with the results of the test surveys.

This experiment demonstrated two effects:

- The inclusion of the words 'do you agree' created a small but significant shift towards the proposition.

- Showing both sides of the proposition led to a significant shift away from the proposition posed on its own in the first and second versions.

The conclusion from this is that showing only one side of the issue leads to an acquiescence bias with a significant proportion agreeing with it in the absence of an alternative. The alternative should therefore always be provided.

Figure 8.5   Test of possible Scottish independence referendum questions

Q. A Do you agree that Scotland should be an independent country?	
Yes	41%
No	59%
Q. B Should Scotland be an independent country?	
Yes	39%
No	61%
Q. C Should Scotland:	
Become an independent country, or	33%
Remain part of the United Kingdom	67%

The House of Commons Scottish Affairs Committee; The Referendum on Separation for Scotland: Do you agree this is a biased question? Eighth Report of Session 2010–12. 26 April 2012.

QA was the question used in the Scottish independence referendum of 2014. For the 2016 referendum on whether the UK should stay in or leave the European Union, a question using the format of QC was used.

The case for piloting the questionnaire (see Chapter 15) is clear and should allow for alternative versions of attitudinal questions to be examined and tested whenever there is any uncertainty over them. The extent to which responses are changed by an additional phrase or a small change in wording may depend on whether the opinion had already been formed in the mind of the respondent prior to the question being asked, and how strongly that opinion is held.

The dimensions

Determining the attributes to measure

No matter which scale is used the crucial factor to get right is the wording of the items against which the attitude is to be measured. As with all questionnaire research, if the item is not measured it cannot be analyzed, and if important attributes are not included then the analysis could be totally misleading.

If there is no existing set of attitude or attribute dimensions that have been proven to represent the issues in the market under consideration, they will need to be developed. Ideally the dimensions should be developed through a preliminary stage of qualitative research, designed specifically to determine the range of emotions, attitudes and perceptions that exist and that are relevant to the study and its objectives. This stage can also be used to develop some preliminary hypotheses about attitudinal segments that might exist in the market, which the quantitative survey can then test.

If it is not possible to carry out a preliminary stage, the dimensions must be collated from elsewhere. Previous studies in the same area are the best place to start, even if they were not designed to meet precisely the same objectives. Sometimes, though, it comes down to experience and discussion with stakeholders. This approach has several risks:

- New attitudes that have not yet been identified may be omitted, leading to a continuation of the existing perceptions of the market, rather than providing new insight.
- Something important may be overlooked completely.

- The wording used may not be that used by the respondents.
- In the absence of any information as to what is and is not important, there will be a tendency to produce too many dimensions in an attempt to ensure that everything is covered.

To counter this last point, it is not unusual to conduct a preliminary survey that concentrates principally on the large set of attitude dimensions that have been initially generated. Most other questions are omitted from this questionnaire to make it manageable for the respondents. However, care must be taken not to alter the context of the attitude question by omitting preceding questions such as those about the respondent's behaviour in relation to the topic. Techniques such as principal component or factor analysis are then used to reduce a large battery of attitude dimensions to a smaller, more manageable set that can be included in the questionnaire. There is a danger here, though, that small differences in attitude dimensions – ones that were specifically introduced because they are important – get excluded because the purpose of the factor analysis is to produce broader, underlying attitude dimensions. Therefore, a further review of the dimensions is sensible to reinstate those of particular importance, or showing particular nuances of difference.

There are sources such as the *Handbook of Marketing Scales* (Bearden and Netermeyer, 1999) that provide lists of dimensions for a range of different attitudinal subject areas that have been used in published studies. They are a useful starting point for someone compiling an attitude battery or can be used when looking for standardized wording or checking that the compiler has not overlooked an important dimension.

Number of attributes

The size of the statement battery is something that the researcher should consider carefully. Clearly there must be a sufficient number of statements to address adequately all of the attitudes under consideration. If possible, there should be several statements for each attitudinal dimension to enable the researcher to cross-check responses for consistency within respondents. The number of statements before fatigue sets in will vary according to the level of interest of the respondent in the subject – over 30 is likely to be too much for anyone regardless of topic.

If, despite all attempts to reduce the number of statements, it is not possible to cover the required attitudinal dimensions without producing a formidable battery of statements, it can sometimes be possible to split the statements into two batteries that are located at different points in the questionnaire. The statements should be split so that the two batteries cover different sets of underlying attitudinal dimensions, and this should be explained in the introduction to the question. Without this explanation, there is a danger that, when presented with the second battery, respondents will believe they are being asked the same questions again and will not take sufficient care. Nevertheless, with a battery of statements of any size it is inevitable that some respondent fatigue will set in. Statements at the beginning of the battery will be given more careful consideration than those towards the end (this issue is discussed further in Chapter 9).

With a lot of statements, consider grouping them by topic. Randomize the order of showing the groups.

If you use groups of statements, by showing one group per page this can reduce the visual impact on the screen. Avoid having more than four pages, though, as it then becomes repetitious and respondents get bored.

Indirect techniques

The difficulty that people have in recognizing – let alone accurately articulating – their emotions and feelings about brands has led to a number of techniques that approach the issue indirectly. For example, instead of asking respondents to associate image dimensions with brands, techniques have been established that associate the brand with picture stimuli, which in turn are established as having certain emotional associations. The respondents' feelings about the brand can then be evaluated, even if they do not consciously recognize those feelings. As Penn (2016) put it:

> The fact is, direct questions measure what they can measure and miss what they cannot; we often measure what people can and will tell us rather than what they can't and won't tell us. What we capture is often thought through or deliberative, while what we miss is emotional and implicit.

Most of the techniques of this type, however, are proprietary and have a specified set of questions and are therefore outside the scope of this book.

Pictorial techniques

Many of the indirect techniques use pictorial stimuli either to convey a personality type or emotion with which respondents are asked to associate needs or brands, or to help the respondents to express how they feel in a way that would be difficult for them to do verbally. Great care must be taken with such techniques so that respondents do not identify with something in the picture that was not intended by the question writer. If depictions of people are used there may be unintended associations with age, gender or other personal characteristics and not what was intended.

Because of the difficulty that people have in identifying, acknowledging, and articulating emotions, pictorial techniques have been developed to evaluate people's emotional response to advertising. Respondents are shown depictions of emotions and asked a series of questions, such as which best represents how they felt as they watched the advertisement. This type of approach relies on a theoretical framework that encompasses the full range of emotions, and that defines the emotions to be depicted.

Figure 8.6   Pictorial representation of emotions

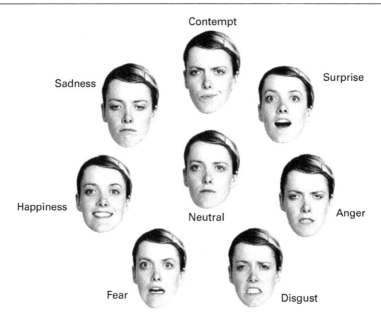

©System1 Research 2006

One of the most successful of these techniques has been System1 Research's proprietary FaceTrace (Wood, 2007), which uses photographs of a face to present seven key emotions, together with a neutral face. This approach uses a single, deliberately androgynous face to avoid the problems of introducing the response effects mentioned above. To successfully achieve these depictions, the appropriate questions and their interpretation requires considerable work and validation. It is difficult to achieve this in the context of writing a single questionnaire and expert advice should be sought.

Implicit Association Test

For some years researchers have been turning to neuroscience to provide indirect techniques to measure issues such as emotion and non-verbal communication (Zaltman, 1997). This has included using eye-scanning techniques, fMRI scans and electroencephalogram (EEG) scans (Hubert and Kenning, 2008). Some, such as eye-tracking, are now used in research, and while the belief is that they are often more robust than traditional research

Figure 8.7   Example screens from a typical Implicit Association Test

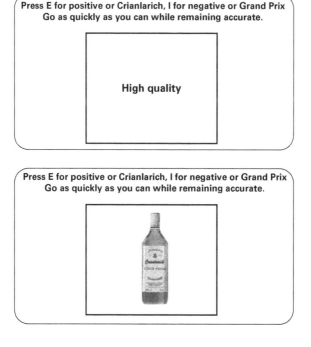

methods, all tend to suffer from small sample sizes (Plassman et al, 2015). These techniques do not involve what the survey researcher would understand as a questionnaire, so further discussion of them is outside of the scope of this book.

One technique, though, has emerged as useful and can be used within the context of the traditional survey – the Implicit Association Test. This is a technique that captures reaction times to a predetermined set of stimuli that can be translated into implicit attitudes.

It takes the form of a task in which respondents are asked to sort items into categories as quickly and accurately as possible. The categories are presented in two configurations, and the difference in response times between the two configurations indicates patterns of association. This in turn reflects implicit attitudes (Gregg et al, 2013). It is described as a valuable and valid measure of implicit consumer cognitions and should sit alongside other information as an explanatory factor for behaviour, choice or judgement (Brunel et al, 2004). It can be incorporated into a questionnaire and administered online or with CAPI.

A number of market research companies now offer this as part of their portfolio of techniques, using it for packaging concept and execution; product concept testing; advertising and communications; and brand perception.

CASE STUDY   Whisky usage and attitude

Attitude and image

There are two areas in which we want to measure attitudes in our questionnaire:

1 Q23, the importance of factors in choice of brand (which we determined in Chapter 6).

2 Q24, brand image perceptions.

For Q24 we want to be able to assess the perceived brand images for Crianlarich and five other brands that we believe to be the competitive set on eight dimensions. The dimensions have been derived from qualitative research which produced a long list of dimensions which discriminate in the market, followed by a pilot exercise to reduce the list to those that maximized discrimination between brands. They mirror the attributes asked about at Q23, so that we can relate the perception on a dimension to how important that is in brand choice. Our options are:

- To rate each brand on each dimension independently, using a rating scale.

- To use a 'pick any' brand-attribute association grid.

To rate each brand individually on each dimension requires 40 evaluations, five brands and eight dimensions. Coming relatively late in the questionnaire we assess that this might be too long a task to maintain the engagement of the respondents. We could reduce the size of the task by not asking about brands the respondent has not heard of, but awareness of brands is high in this market. We could reduce it by not asking about brands the respondent would not consider buying, but this would be likely to remove the more negative ratings, increasing the overall ratings for each brand and reducing discrimination. It would also mean that we could not see why brands were rejected from the consideration set.

Our preferred option, therefore, is to use a 'pick any' brand-attribute association grid, which includes all six brands. It will also include a 'none of these' response option. Without this, some respondents may pick a brand because they think that each line should have at least one response, when they would rather say that the attribute applied to none of the brands presented.

To ensure that respondents are thinking about the brands that we want them to, we might consider using pack shots to identify the brands. This would be a mistake. The packs contain clues as to the desired brand positions which would influence responses. It would become in part a measure of pack communication rather than brand perception.

Figure 8.8   Q24 Brand-attribute association

Which brand or brands do you associate with each of these statements?

	Bells	Crianlarich	Famous Grouse	Grand Prix	Teachers	Whyte & Mackay	None of these
Has a strong heritage	O	O	O	O	O	O	O
Is traditional	O	O	O	O	O	O	O
Is old-fashioned	O	O	O	O	O	O	O
Is different to others	O	O	O	O	O	O	O
Is a cheaper brand	O	O	O	O	O	O	O
Is a more expensive brand	O	O	O	O	O	O	O
A favourite of the Scots	O	O	O	O	O	O	O
A brand I like	O	O	O	O	O	O	O

Key take aways: measuring satisfaction, image and attitudes

- The central challenge for capturing feelings and emotions in these areas is that the respondent may have never thought about or articulated them to themselves before.
- These are also typically multi-faceted topics, difficult to distill down to a few dimensions.
- Ratings scales provide the key tool for measurement across all three areas, but particular care must be taken when creating the dimensions to be rated to:
    - ensure unambiguous, respondent-centric language;
    - keep to a level of detail that is realistic to expect the respondent to consider;
    - limit the number of dimensions to avoid fatigue.
- When measuring brand image an association rather than rating approach is often chosen as it is more efficient and less draining for the respondent. Results are relative, however, to the brands and dimensions included, so the question writer needs to choose these carefully.
- A particular challenge when measuring attitudes is to ensure that dimensions are balanced, offering all sides of the issue to avoid leading the respondent or encouraging acquiescence bias through a tendency to want to agree.

Writing effective questions 09

Introduction

Previous chapters have considered the choice of question type and highlighted issues and limitations that affect how people answer questions. In this chapter we focus on how the writer creates the questions themselves and some of the practical choices influencing how the questions are implemented, including:

- language, words and phrases;
- determining response options;
- order of response options and possible bias;
- use of pictorial prompts;
- influence of preceding questions.

First, though, this box lists some of the main points of guidance for question writing which will be addressed in this and following chapters.

Key dos and don'ts for writing questions

- Avoid ambiguity. Everyone should understand it in the same way and as you meant it to be understood.
- Don't ask two questions in one. (eg 'Was the waiter friendly *and* efficient?')
- Avoid double negatives. (eg 'Do you agree or disagree that X is *not* good value for money.')
- Use simple, everyday language. (eg 'How *often* do you...' not 'How *frequently* do you...')

- Don't use jargon or technical terms. (eg 'What do you think of this *idea*?' not 'What do you think of this *concept*?')
- Keep any explanations of terms separate so the question is still clear.
- Have options for all possible responses – include 'other' to catch minority responses.
- Make sure response options don't overlap and that differences between similar items are clear.
- Is one answer required or can the respondent choose several? Make this obvious.
- Avoid list items drawing the eye more than others simply by being different. (eg longer or shorter terms.)
- Use manageable time frames for memory recall.
- Match the level of detail with what will feel sensible and relevant to the respondent.
- Avoid questions where the answer could be 'it depends'.
- Make the thinking task as simple as possible – no maths!
- Don't make the respondent feel ignorant.
- Don't make the respondent feel they are different from other people.
- Don't ask leading questions that suggest there is a right answer – balance with all sides of the issue.
- Consider whether you are revealing too early what you are most interested in. (eg response options that focus on one issue more than others.)
- Consider the frame of reference set by previous questions.
- Don't vary terms unnecessarily – keep consistency across questions and highlight any deliberate change of focus.

Use of language

We have said earlier that a role of the questionnaire is to manage, at scale, a conversation between the researcher and respondents. In a normal conversation, however, the two parties involved draw on knowledge of each other in choosing their words to convey the meaning they want. This is known as 'audience design'. For example, how you might phrase a question for your grandmother might be different from how you phrase it for your friend. The answer they give may also be tailored to reflect what they know about your motivations for asking the question. In a questionnaire however, the questions cannot be framed for individual respondents.

In normal conversations there is also the opportunity to check that each party has understood what the other has said and that is has entered their common ground. This grounding can come from a simple acknowledgement (such as 'uh-huh' or 'ok'); from a request for further explanation; or from clarification volunteered by the questioner if it is clear that they have not been understood. With self-completion questionnaires this grounding inter-action is not possible. Where an interviewer is involved, some level of grounding might be feasible, however, to avoid introducing bias interview-ers are deliberately restricted in the type of clarification they can give. Often, all the interviewer can do is to repeat the question or give a general indica-tion of the level of detail that a question is aiming for. They are trained to avoid elaboration of individual words. Apart from potentially introducing bias, the interviewers themselves may not understand precisely what is meant and pass on their misinterpretation to respondents.

Writing questionnaires is about helping respondents give the best infor-mation that they can. Questions should be clear and unambiguous so that they are understood in a common way by all. They should be phrased in everyday language to which the respondents can relate, and in ways that reflect their normal thought processes so that the answers they give are real-istic. Because technical terms are often the everyday language of the commissioners of the study, they do not always appreciate that others out-side their industry or profession might not understand them or might under-stand something different by them. Sometimes technical terms are used to describe something, or to differentiate between objects or services, with far greater subtlety than the non-specialist can appreciate. To most motorists a petrol pump is a petrol pump, and they would not distinguish between a 'high line fast flow' and a 'grouped hose blender'. Researchers must ask themselves if it is necessary for the respondent to be able to distinguish be-tween them in the interview. If it is, then the differences must be clearly explained, if possible, without reference to the technical terminology.

The respondent should be put at ease by the tone of the questions and not feel challenged or irritated by the words and phrases used. Respondents who become alienated or fatigued will decide to stop the interview or will make little effort to respond accurately.

Minority language versions

Clearly if a questionnaire is to be used in several countries there will be a need to translate it into different languages. Chapter 17 looks at the issues of designing for multi-country projects in more detail, however even within one country translation may be needed if the sample is likely to include people who speak a language other than the majority language; or whose command of that language is unlikely to be sufficiently good to be able to complete an interview in it. By denying sections of the survey population the opportunity to participate in the study, the questionnaire writer is effectively disenfranchising them from influencing the findings.

This is most likely to be a concern in studies commissioned by the public sector. In the UK, many government studies require questionnaire versions in Welsh, Urdu and Hindi among other languages, and in the United States a Spanish-language version is often required.

The relevance of minority-language speakers to the study will naturally vary by the subject of the study and the degree of accuracy required in the data. For a study of housing conditions, it is likely to be important that recently arrived immigrant communities are represented in the sample.

For most commercial studies the difference that a small number of non-majority language-speaking consumers make to key conclusions from the research is likely to be small, particularly in comparison to the variation caused by sampling error, non-response rates and even interviewer error.

Avoiding ambiguity

Ambiguity is a major challenge for the question writer in choosing the exact words and phrases to use.

While some respondents may see the ambiguity and make a decision on which way to answer, others may not see it and understand it in a way that was not intended. Either way, the researcher using the data does not know the basis on which the respondent has answered.

Ambiguity is not always easy to spot. It is not always possible to anticipate every respondent's circumstances, and a question that may not be ambiguous to most respondents may, because of their circumstances, contain an ambiguity for a few. For example, 'How many bedrooms are there in your property?' is likely to be a simple question for most people. But what is meant by a bedroom? If someone has a study that doubles as an occasional spare bedroom, should that be included?

In most instances this level of ambiguity will not be a major issue. Where the number of bedrooms is collected as classification data to provide a cross-analysis of data by approximate size of house, then this degree of ambiguity may be acceptable to the researchers. Where this information is central to the data collected, say in a study of housing conditions, then the ambiguity must be addressed (eg possibly expanding the question to ask the number of rooms currently used as bedrooms, the number occasionally used as bedrooms and the number that could be used as bedrooms).

Online self-completion vs interviewer surveys

In an online survey the priority is to keep the reading task as succinct as possible to maintain motivation. Researchers who conduct pilots to understand how respondents are completing their questionnaires soon realize that often the question itself only receives a glance – and then the attention drops to the answer options. Therefore, practical guidelines include:

- Keep question wording as short as possible – 10–12 words maximum if you can.
- Keep key words at the beginning of the question.
- Use response codes as part of the question. (eg 'Have you heard of… [response list]?')
- Remove padding. (eg 'Which of the following…')
- Use pleasantries sparingly.

For interviewer surveys the key difference is that the wording used should also help the interviewer build rapport with the respondent. Questions should not be overly wordy, but if they are too succinct the interview can begin to feel like an interrogation. Therefore, there can be slightly more preamble to questions and more pleasantries.

Determining the response options

A quantitative questionnaire will rely largely on questions that involve pre-coded response options rather than verbatim/open-ended inputs. These pre-codes therefore determine what data is collected, so if they have insufficient accuracy or are incomplete, then data will be lost that may be important to answering the objectives. In many instances the response options needed will be obvious (eg simple 'yes/no' pre-codes), but in others care must be taken to ensure that they are:

- as precise as necessary;
- meaningful – making sense to the respondent and being useful to the researcher;
- mutually exclusive and distinct so there is no ambiguity about which is chosen;
- complete – with 'other' being provided to record minority responses.

If there are a lot of 'other' answers written in, the question would have been better recorded as an open-ended one.

Failure to record the reply accurately or completely

The response to the question, 'do you like eating pizza?' sounds as if it should be a simple 'yes' or 'no', but respondents may wish to qualify the answer depending on whether it is home-made or shop-bought; by the toppings or the occasion. If they are unable to do so, an answer of 'don't know' may be recorded. Whatever is recorded is not the complete response.

It is common to see a question establishing behaviour patterns given the possible answers:

- More than once a week
- Once a week
- Once a month
- Once every three months
- Less often than once every three months

The question could have been: 'How often do you visit the cinema?' How would someone who went to the cinema twice in the last week and not at all in the three months before that respond? They would have to judge which is the least inaccurate response.

The alternatives – allowing for all possible responses – could become complicated, both to understand and to analyze. A judgement is needed as to whether this type of situation is likely to occur for the majority; in which case an alternative approach needs to be found, or for a very small minority; in which case the inaccuracy may need to be accepted as a compromise.

Order bias

If the question involves prompted response options, whether on screen or read out by an interviewer, the order they are presented can have a significant effect on the responses recorded. Such bias can occur with:

- scalar responses (eg rating scales or frequency scales);
- any list from which responses are chosen;
- batteries of attitude or image dimensions.

The questionnaire writer must consider how to minimize the order bias for each of these.

Scalar responses

Primacy and recency effects

Artingstall (1978) showed that when respondents are given a scale (eg a rating or frequency scale) in face-to-face interviewing they are significantly more likely to choose the first response offered than the last. This is known as the 'primacy effect'. Thus, if the positive end of a scale is always presented first a more favourable result will be found than if the negative end of the scale is always first. The finding held true for any length of scale (by an increase of about 8 per cent in positive responses) and was independent from the demographic profile of the respondents.

What this and other work shows is that the order of presentation has an effect. It does not say which order gives the best representation of the truth. However, it underlines the need to be consistent in the order in which scales are shown if comparisons are to be made between studies. One approach to dealing with the bias is to rotate the order of presentation between two halves of the sample. This does not remove the bias but at least has the effect of averaging it.

In new product development research, it is not uncommon always to have the negative response presented first on scales rating the concept or the product. This then gives the least favourable response pattern, thereby providing a tougher test for the new product and ensuring that any positive reaction to the idea of the product is not overstated.

When visual prompts are used, respondents notice and process the possible responses in the order that they are presented (Artingstall, 1978). Where prompts are read out (as in telephone interviewing), a recency effect is more marked, as respondents remember better the last option or last few options they have been given. This effect has been demonstrated by Schwarz et al (1991). With telephone interviewing, therefore, a recency effect should be expected, unless respondents are asked to write down the scale for reference before answering the question.

Response lists

As shown in Figure 9.1, showing a list of alternative responses is a common form of prompting to make respondents choose from a fixed set of options.

Figure 9.1   List of alternative responses

	Thinking about the advertisement that you have just seen, which of these would you say describes it? You can mention as many or as few phrases as you wish.
A	It was difficult to understand
B	It made me more interested in visiting the store
C	I found it irritating
D	It's not right for this type of product
E	I quickly got bored with it
F	I did not like the people in it
G	It said something relevant to me
H	I will remember it
I	It improved my opinion of the store
J	It told me something new about the store
K	It was aimed at me
L	I enjoyed watching it
M	None of these

The respondent is expected to read through all of the options and select those that apply. In this question, respondents can choose as many statements as they feel are appropriate, making this a multiple response question. In other questions, they may be asked to choose one option making it a single response question. The convention is that responses in single response questions are collected by radio buttons on screen, and multiple response questions by boxes as shown in Figure 9.2.

Figure 9.2 Single and multiple responses

Single Response	Multiple response
Which flavour of yoghurt are you most likely to buy?	Which other flavours are you likely to buy?
Apricot O	Apricot ☐
Black cherry O	Black cherry ☐
Blackcurrant O	Blackcurrant ☐
Gooseberry O	Gooseberry ☐
Mandarin O	Mandarin ☐
Peach O	Peach ☐
Pineapple O	Pineapple ☐
Raspberry O	Raspberry ☐
Strawberry O	Strawberry ☐
None of these O	None of these ☐

Primacy and recency effects

As with scales, primacy effects should be expected with response lists. The effects have been demonstrated by Schwarz et al (1991), even where there are a small number of possible responses, down to three or even two if they are sufficiently complex to dissuade respondents from making an effort to process the possible answers in full. In a longer list of 13 items, Krosnick and Alwin (1987) demonstrated increased selection of the first three on the list. Duffy (2003) confirms the existence of primacy effects and adds that a significant minority read the list from the bottom. This would suggest that a recency effect can also be expected, as it is in telephone surveys.

Indeed, both primacy and recency effects have been demonstrated by Ring (1975). He showed that with a list of 18 items there is a bias in favour of choosing responses in the first six and the last four positions. The implication is that those in the middle of the list either are not read at all by some respondents or are not processed as possible responses to the same extent.

Where a list is of such a size, then reversing the order and presenting one order to half of the sample and the reverse order to the other half does not adequately address the problem. Ring's experiments showed that with a list of 18 items, the first 14 should be reversed and the last four reversed. This asymmetrical split better balances the bias across the items than simply reversing them.

In practice, however, a simpler approach is usually taken that just randomizes the order of presentation between respondents. This does not eliminate bias but spreads it across the statements more evenly.

Satisficing

Some people, when buying items such as a washing machine or car, will spend a great deal of time researching which of the available models best meets their needs and requirements. Other people will buy one that satisfactorily meets their minimum needs and requirements, and are not interested in investing the time to research all of the available models to determine which is marginally better. The latter approach is known as 'satisficing'

Satisficers will exhibit this behaviour in answering questionnaires when presented with a list of statements from which to choose a response. They will read it until they find an adequate answer that they feel reasonably reflects their view, rather than reading or listening to all of the statements to find the answer that best reflects their view. This is another source of order bias, which will tend to reinforce the primacy effect.

Satisficing is likely to increase with interview fatigue as respondents stop making the effort to answer to the best of their ability. Researchers using online panels should also be aware that Toepoel et al (2008) found that experienced respondents – as are found on access panels – tend to be subject to satisficing more than inexperienced respondents, probably as part of a strategy to complete the survey as quickly as possible.

Satisficing is likely to be more prevalent with telephone than with face-to-face interviewing (Holbrook et al, 2003).

Batteries of statements

Fatigue effect

Where there is a large battery of either image or attitude statements, each of which is to be answered according to a scale, there is a real danger of respondent fatigue. This can occur both with self-completion batteries and where the interviewer reads them out. The precise point at which respondent fatigue is likely to set in will vary with the level of interest that each respondent has in the subject. However, it should be anticipated that, where there are more than about 10-15 statements, later statements are likely to suffer from inattention and pattern responding. To alleviate this type of bias, the presentation of the statements should be rotated between respondents. Online or with CAPI, statements can often be presented in random order, or in rotation in a number of different sequences.

As mentioned in Chapter 8, statements can be broken into topic groups with just one group shown per screen. Once the respondent gets to the fifth such screen, however, they are likely to think that it is becoming repetitive. Get the balance right between reducing the impact of too many words on the screen and keeping the number of screens down to no more than four.

Statement clarification

The order in which statements are presented to respondents can sometimes be used to clarify their meanings. If there is a degree of ambiguity in a statement that would require a complex explanation, a preceding statement that deals with the alternative meaning can clarify what the questionnaire writer is seeking. For example:

- How would you rate the station for the facilities at the station?

On its own, it could be unclear to respondents whether car parking should be considered as one of the facilities at the station. If, however, this statement is preceded by one about car parking:

- How would you rate the station for...
  - *Facilities for car parking*
  - Other facilities and services at the station

Respondents can safely assume that the facilities are not meant to include car parking as that has already been asked about.

Where a random presentation of statements is used, care must be taken to ensure that such explanatory pairs of statements always appear together and in the same order.

Types of prompts

Prompts can be scale points, attitudinal phrases, image dimensions, brands, income ranges or anything that the questionnaire writer wants to use to guide the respondents or to obtain reaction to. They can be purely verbal or they can utilize pictures, illustrations or logos. However, it is important to be clear about the different jobs that verbal and pictorial stimuli do.

Picture prompts

Pictures can be used in a number of different ways as prompts. If they are to be used, then questionnaire writers must be careful to ensure that they know exactly what role the pictures are playing.

Brand awareness

One use of picture prompts is to show brand logos or icons (instead of a list of brand names) to measure prompted brand awareness. This is generally straightforward to do online; is offered as an option by several of the DIY survey providers; and is often included to make the interview more interesting for the respondent. However, questionnaire writers should be aware that they might be changing the question. For example, prompted awareness is a question of recognition. If a list of names is used, the respondents are being asked which of the names they recognize. If brand logos are shown, the question becomes which of the logos they recognize. The researcher infers awareness of the brand through recognition of the logo. This is likely to be higher than simple name recognition, as the logo gives more clues.

The improvement in apparent brand awareness is likely to be stronger for the smaller brands in a market. Prompted awareness of Coca-Cola does not require the use of a visual prompt to be very high among carbonated drink consumers. There is little opportunity for visual prompts to make an improvement. But for smaller brands, the opportunities for improvement offered by visual prompts are much greater. The total average number of logos recognized per respondent is usually likely to be greater than the average number of brand names from a simple list. Neither approach is necessarily incorrect, but each is likely to give a different level of response.

Likelihood to purchase

When asking about likelihood to purchase, much more information is given to respondents if a pictorial stimulus is used. Rather than show a list of brands and prices, a mocked-up shelf can be shown, as in Figure 9.3. The cues and information that are given by the pack shots mean that respondents do not have to rely on memory and recall of the brands when making their decision. Price information can easily be excluded, included, or changed as required.

Figure 9.3 A mocked-up shelf of the brands' desired positionings

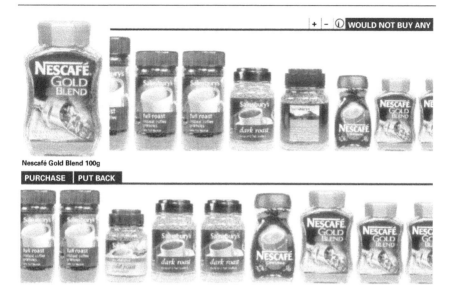

Brand image

Showing logos can also alter the responses to questions about brand image. It is normal to establish prompted brand awareness before asking about images of certain brands. If prompted brand awareness is established using a list of names, the mental picture taken into the image question is the image of the brand as it exists in isolation within the respondents' minds. The image is purely what the brand name stands for and the images that are associated with it. After prompting with a logo or pack shot, however, respondents are given clues and reminders of what the brand is trying to stand for. The logo or pack will have been designed to reflect the desired brand positioning and may well communicate something of those values to the respondents in the interview, or at least act as a reminder of them. The image question is therefore also prompted with at least a partial reminder.

Again, it is not a question of one approach being incorrect. Using a brand list may be described as giving a 'purer' measure of an image. This is an image, it can be argued, that the potential purchasers have in their minds before leaving home to go shopping, and it will act upon their intent to purchase the brand. But it can be equally argued that most brands are rarely seen without their logos, and that it is the image in the purchasers' minds at the point of purchase that is important.

The questionnaire writer should consider which is the more appropriate approach for the market in question and decide which approach to use accordingly.

Advertising recognition

Establishing recognition of advertising relies on showing picture prompts. These often consist of a series of stills taken from the advertisement in question. It also may or may not have all references to the brand removed, depending on whether being able to name the correct brand is to be asked. Online (or with CAPI) there is a choice between showing still shots and showing the actual ad as film. The two methods will generally lead to different responses, with higher awareness recorded among respondents shown the film.

Before using pictures or graphics, think carefully about:

- how it changes what you are measuring;
- what respondents will take out of the graphic;
- how consistent that take-out will be between respondents.

Generally, avoid using pictures of people – including cartoons – unless you know exactly what each picture communicates.

Influence of preceding questions

Chapter 3 covered broad guidelines for ordering questions, including:

- No prompting of any information before spontaneous questions on the same subject.
- Key questions should come as early in the questionnaire as possible.
- The interview should normally start with the more general questions relating to the topic and work through to the more specific or detailed subject matter.
- Behavioural questions should be asked before attitudinal questions on the same topic.

These issues should have been considered when the questionnaire was planned, but still need to be thought about as the detailed questionnaire is written. In particular, the question writer needs to consider what the respondent's frame of reference is likely to be by the time they come to each question. For example, in an employee study if there has been a series of questions about the team and then the focus switches to the individual then this change should be explicitly highlighted. Otherwise, some may not notice and be answering on the wrong basis. Consistent use of language and terms is important – don't vary them unnecessarily as some people will think it signals that they should be taking other things into account.

In a questionnaire exploring reaction to a website transaction the terminology kept varying:

Q1 'online facility'

Q2 'website'

Q3 'site'

Q4 'internet facilities'

Q5 'Internet site'

There would be a high likelihood of confusing some respondents as to what they should be considering at each question.

Once all the questions have been written it is sensible to review how the language flows throughout the questionnaire as a whole. Does it feel like it has been written by one person? Is the style and tone consistent throughout? This is particularly important when questions are copied from other surveys that may have been written by someone else. A questionnaire that keeps changing tone or style can irritate by making the respondent feel that insufficient effort has gone into its creation – why, therefore, should they continue to make effort themselves?

Funnelling

Funnelling sequences are used to take respondents from general questions on a topic through to questions that are more specific without allowing the earlier questions to condition or bias the responses to the later ones.

Typically in the funnelling sequence, whether respondents are asked a question depends on their response to the previous one. This means that people for whom questions are irrelevant can be routed round them. Because people continue in the question sequence without knowing what the criteria are for doing so, we can be more confident that the response we obtain to the final question is not biased. In the example in Figure 9.4, had we just asked one question, ie, 'If you have seen any advertising for Bulmer's cider on television recently, what did it say?' this question would lead to overclaiming of

Figure 9.4   Funnelling sequence

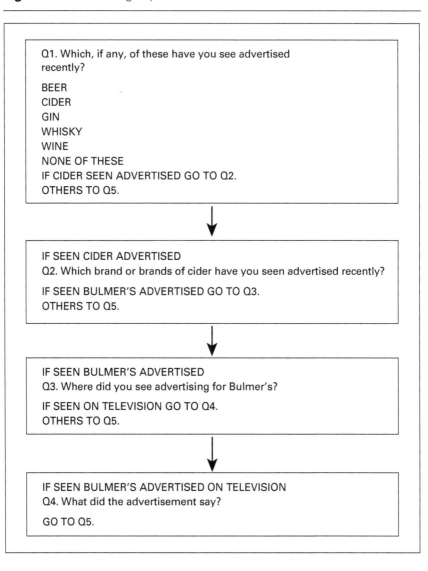

Q1. Which, if any, of these have you see advertised recently?

BEER
CIDER
GIN
WHISKY
WINE
NONE OF THESE
IF CIDER SEEN ADVERTISED GO TO Q2.
OTHERS TO Q5.

IF SEEN CIDER ADVERTISED
Q2. Which brand or brands of cider have you seen advertised recently?

IF SEEN BULMER'S ADVERTISED GO TO Q3.
OTHERS TO Q5.

IF SEEN BULMER'S ADVERTISED
Q3. Where did you see advertising for Bulmer's?

IF SEEN ON TELEVISION GO TO Q4.
OTHERS TO Q5.

IF SEEN BULMER'S ADVERTISED ON TELEVISION
Q4. What did the advertisement say?

GO TO Q5.

having seen the advertising, because there is an assumption that Bulmer's cider has been advertised on television recently. Some respondents would then claim to have seen it, even though they had not.

Funnelling sequences are straightforward with online questionnaires, although the logic routines used by some DIY survey providers are easier to follow than others. For paper self-completion questionnaires, the logic is there for all to see and so is best avoided.

Question order bias

Priming effects

Where there is a key question to be asked, such as approval of a proposal, response to a new concept or rating of an issue, the act of asking questions about the respondent's feelings about the proposal, concept or issue prior to the key questions can have an effect on the response to it.

This can be desirable, as the researcher will want respondents to give an answer that takes into account their considered view. However, the researcher can be inadvertently suggesting to respondents what they should answer. McFarland (1981) reported that asking a series of specific questions about the energy crisis led to a higher rating of the severity of the crisis than when the questions were not asked. Questionnaire writers need to be aware of the influence that prior questions can have and write the questions and interpret the responses accordingly. In particular, introducing financial considerations can affect responses. In an experiment by the Minnesota Department of Transportation, questions were asked about the acceptability of levels of service (for road maintenance, traffic signals, rest areas, etc) and how people thought the budget should be allocated (Laflin and Hanson, 2006). Asking about budget allocation before levels of service gave lower expectation scores than if these were asked first. Making people think about money and budgetary constraints appeared to make them more willing to accept lower service levels.

Consistency effect

A particular type of priming effect is the consistency effect. This can occur because respondents are led along a particular route of responses to a conclusion to which they can only answer one way if they are to appear consistent.

Consider and compare the sequence in Figure 9.5 and Figure 9.6. It should be expected that the responses to Q2 will show significant variation between Figures 9.5 and 9.6. By using statements that reflect one side of an argument – in this case for and against the building of a new airport – respondents are led to Q2 along different paths. Most people like to appear to be consistent. If they agree with the statements in Q1, it is then very difficult not to answer 'yes' at Q2 in the first example, or 'no' in the second example.

To be even-handed, the preliminary question should contain statements that relate to both or all sides of an argument. The researcher may want to put questions to respondents about the issues before asking the key question, to help them to give a considered answer to that question. However, the preliminary questions must fairly represent all the issues if they are not to bias the response to the key question.

How is the survey introduced?

The way the survey is introduced will set some expectations in respondents minds that will affect what they are thinking as they approach the questions. Details of information that respondents need to be given before agreeing to

Figure 9.5 The consistency effect (first sequence)

Q1. How strongly do you agree or disagree with these statements?

	Agree strongly	Agree	Neither agree nor disagree	Disagree	Disagree strongly
Delays at airports in this country are becoming unacceptable.	❒	❒	❒	❒	❒
There is insufficient capacity at this country's airports.	❒	❒	❒	❒	❒
Airports in this country are dangerously overcrowded.	❒	❒	❒	❒	❒
There is a shortage of jobs in this region.	❒	❒	❒	❒	❒

Q2. Do you support the government's proposal to build a new airport in this region?

YES ❒

NO ❒

DON'T KNOW ❒

Figure 9.6   The consistency effect (second sequence)

Q1. How strongly do you agree or disagree with these statements?

	Agree strongly	Agree	Neither agree nor disagree	Disagree	Disagree strongly
The countryside round here is disappearing too quickly for my liking.	❐	❐	❐	❐	❐
There is too much building on green-field sites.	❐	❐	❐	❐	❐
I would not want to see this country's plant and animal life killed off.	❐	❐	❐	❐	❐
Noise pollution is a major nuisance round here.	❐	❐	❐	❐	❐

Q2. Do you support the government's proposal to build a new airport in this region?

YES ❐

NO ❐

DON'T KNOW ❐

the interview are covered in Chapter 15. Here we will focus on how the requirement to introduce the survey topic and any screening question needed to identify the right respondents might influence them.

The subject matter should sound interesting in order to gain their cooperation, but bear in mind the data that you want to collect when deciding how much to reveal. For example, if you wish to measure the penetration of ownership of diamond jewellery, do not say that the survey is about diamond jewellery. If you do, people with no diamond jewellery and no interest in it will think that the survey is not for them and will not respond. Any measurement of penetration will then be over-estimated. In other markets light users of the product may be under-represented.

Using the company name in the introduction

If the survey is coming from an organization with which the respondent already has a relationship, then you may wish to be very specific about the content (eg a customer satisfaction survey from their mobile phone provider). The survey may well be heavily branded as being from this provider, so you have given nothing away and highlighting the relationship is likely to improve response rates.

In many instances, though, the survey will be carried out under the name of the research company and the client's name will not be revealed. This is partly for security in that the client does not want to tell the world that they are carrying out this survey, but also because to do so is likely to bias responses by highlighting the client's name. That would be sufficient to increase the mentions given to the client in awareness and image questions; would completely remove the possibility of asking about spontaneous awareness; and some respondents will think that they may not get their reward if they are critical of the client or their products.

Under some circumstances it is necessary by law to be prepared to reveal where the research company acquired the contact details of the respondent. This is returned to as an ethical issue in Chapter 15.

Screening questions

Frequently we want to include in the sample only people with certain characteristics, which can be demographic or product-focused. There may be quotas that we want to fulfil and want to screen out people who are in quota cells that are complete. The first few questions are therefore often screening questions to determine whether we want the respondent to continue with the main questionnaire as part of our sample.

These questions should be relatively few in number. An online panel member who gets screened out after five minutes and receives no payment may feel justifiably aggrieved. A two-tier payment system may be appropriate in these circumstances. Equally, someone stopped on the street or in a mall, who agrees to be interviewed but is then told after a few questions that they are not wanted may also be puzzled or perplexed.

Typically, screening questions will follow a funnel:

- Which of these do you own/do…?
- How often do you…?
- Which brand do you own/buy…?

At each stage, respondents who do not meet the criteria are politely screened out and told that they are not the person we are looking for – in a way that makes it clear that it is not their fault.

It is important that our selection criteria are disguised (see Chapter 7), so that the respondent does not know (or cannot guess) what to answer in order to qualify and use this to self-select. Experienced online panel members will often try to work out what they should answer in order to qualify and earn points/money.

If we are looking, for example, for people who visit Starbucks at last once a week we do not ask:

- Do you visit Starbucks at least once a week?
  - Yes
  - No

We ask:

- Which of these coffee shops do you ever visit?
  - Caffè Nero
  - Caffè Ritazza
  - Coffee Republic
  - Costa Coffee
  - Pret A Manger
  - Starbucks
  - None of these

If the respondent visits Starbucks, we ask:

- How often do you visit a Starbucks?
  - Every day
  - Several times a week
  - At least once week
  - At least once a month
  - At least once every three months
  - Less often

In this way, our interest is disguised and it is difficult for respondents to self-select.

Standardizing questions

Where a question has been asked in a previous study it is usually to the advantage of the researcher to ensure that, unless there is a good reason otherwise, the same question should be used and the same pre-codes. Doing this allows the researcher to build up a body of knowledge about how this question is answered, and so spot any response pattern that deviates from it. It also means that results from different studies can be compared more easily.

Many major manufacturers and some research companies have standard ways of asking particular questions that allow them to build up this body of knowledge. The value of standardized questions becomes clear when we realize that even small changes in the wording of a question can change responses (Converse and Presser, 1986). For example, changing 'forbid' to 'not allow' has been shown to significantly change response patterns. Unfortunately, because language is subtle, there are no general rules about when a wording change will change responses, so the questionnaire writer must be cautious about making changes if comparison with other surveys is a priority. If there is doubt, alternative wording should be tested before being used.

Tracking studies

Consistency of question wording is important in ongoing or tracking studies to ensure that changes in data over time are not due to wording changes.

To ensure data consistency, it is also important to maintain the order in which the questions are asked so that any order bias that exists is itself consistent. Keeping the question order means that adding new questions can cause problems, and the positioning of them must be considered very carefully. If possible, new questions should be added to the end of the questionnaire so as not to affect responses to any of the earlier questions. For the sake of the interview flow, though, this is not always possible.

For example, in an ongoing customer satisfaction survey, respondents were asked to give a rating of their overall satisfaction with the service received on their most recent visit to the client company. This had been followed with questions rating various staff and service attributes, including one on efficiency. After a while, a competitor introduced a guarantee that all transactions will be completed within 10 minutes or customers get their money back. To measure the impact of this, the client now asks that, on the next wave of the survey, a new question is inserted between the overall satisfaction question and the service attribute ratings. This question asks how quickly the customers perceive their transaction to have been handled, and how satisfied they were with that. The introduction of these questions at this point could influence the way in which respondents rate the individual service attributes – in particular the one relating to efficiency – as the speed of transaction has been raised higher in their consciousness than in previous waves of the study. Researchers must alert the client to the potential impact of such a change in the questionnaire on the comparability of data with previous waves, and endeavour to find an alternative solution – such as a less sensitive position.

If no alternative solution can be found and the question changes are to be included for the foreseeable future, then it may be worth considering having a split run for one wave. For this, the sample is split randomly into two. One half is asked the existing questionnaire, while the other half is asked the new questionnaire with the changes incorporated. An assessment of the impact of the changes can thus be made.

CASE STUDY   Whisky usage and attitude

Writing the questionnaire

In Chapter 3 we planned out the questionnaire in order to collect the data that will meet the objectives. Since then, we have looked at different types of data and different types of questions. Now comes the time to actually write the questions.

We have decided that the survey will be conducted online, so the question wording will be consistent with that (ie as short as possible).

Following the plan established in Chapter 3, and the discussion in Chapters 4 to 8, we can now begin to write the questions:

Table 9.1 (Lists of response codes have been omitted for clarity.)

Questionnaire plan	Questions required
Screening (see Chapter 7)	A Do you or any of your family work in the following industries? B Which of these have you drunk in the last three months? C How often do you drink Scotch whisky?
Spontaneous brand awareness	Q1 Which brands of Scotch whisky have you heard of?
Spontaneous advertising awareness	Q2 Which brands of Scotch whisky have you seen or heard advertising for recently?
Prompted brand awareness	Q3 Which of these brands of Scotch whisky have you heard of?

(continued)

Table 9.1 (Continued)

Questionnaire plan	Questions required
Prompted advertising awareness	Q4 Which of these brands of Scotch whisky have you seen or heard advertising for recently? Q5 [IF SEEN/HEARD ADVERTISING FOR CRIANLARICH] Where did you see or hear advertising for Crianlarich? Q6 What do you remember about the Crianlarich ad? [WRITE IN] Q7 [IF SEEN/HEARD ADVERTISING FOR GRAND PRIX] Where did you see or hear advertising for Grand Prix? Q8 What do you remember about the Grand Prix ad? [WRITE IN]
Behavioural information – consumption (see Chapter 7)	Q9 Do you drink Scotch whisky on licensed premises, or at home, or both? Q10 [IF ON LICENSE] How many glasses of Scotch whisky have you drunk in the last seven days in licensed premises? Q11 [IF DRINKS OFF LICENSE] How many glasses of whisky did you drink in the home in the last seven days?
Behavioural information – brand choice	Q12 [IF DRINKS OFF LICENSED] Do you drink Scotch whisky in your own home, in someone else's home, or both? Q13 [IF DRINKS IN OWN HOME] Do you usually buy the Scotch to drink at home or does someone else buy it? Q14 [IF SOMEONE ELSE BUYS IT] Do you have a say in which brand is bought or do they decide, or is it always the same brand? Q15 [IF ALWAYS THE SAME BRAND] Which brand do they buy? Q16 Was that originally your choice, or someone else's choice, or a joint decision? Q17 [IF NO SAY AT Q14] Which brands do they buy? Q18 [IF MORE THAN ONE BRAND] Which do they buy most often?

(continued)

Table 9.1 (Continued)

Questionnaire plan	Questions required
	Q19 [IF BOUGHT BY SELF AT Q13 OR HAVE A SAY AT Q14] Which brands do you buy or ask for? Q20 [IF ONE MOST OFTEN BRAND] Which do they buy most often?
Image factor importance in brand choice (Chapter 6)	Q21 For each pair of attributes, move the slider to show which is the more important to you when choosing a whisky.
Brand image association (Chapter 8)	Q22 Which brand or brands do you associate with each of these statements?
Recognition of unbranded ads	Q23 [SHOW UNBRANDED CRIANLARICH AD] Have you seen this ad before? Q24 [IF YES] Which brand of Scotch whisky is it for? Q25 [SHOW UNBRANDED GRAND PRIX AD] Have you seen this ad before? Q26 [IF YES] Which brand of Scotch whisky is it for?
Classification data, to confirm panel-provided details	Age Gender

This gives us our first draft questionnaire, but some of these questions will be returned to in later chapters as we consider other issues.

Key take aways: writing effective questions

- When writing each question ask yourself whether the respondent will:

  o Understand the question in the way that you meant it. Will this understanding be consistent across all respondents?

  o Be able to answer it with the level of accuracy and detail that you need?

- o Be willing to answer it – and honestly? Have you implied that some answers are more interesting or acceptable to you than others?

- Prompted questions using lists of response options are susceptible to primacy effects:

  - o Items at the start of the list often receive more attention.

  - o Randomizing the list items can balance (but not eliminate) this effect.

  - o Keeping the list shorter, with similar items next to each other, will help respondents navigate to the answer that is right for them.

- Always consider the possible influence of preceding questions.

  - o will they affect how a question is understood?

  - o will they have introduced any bias?

Creating a questionnaire for an online survey

10

Introduction

Online has become the most common mode of survey interviewing as access to questionnaire writing software has become more widespread; as commercial research panels have grown; and as online interaction becomes a default communication mode for many.

Some compromises with the quality of the sample may be needed as online typically has a more self-selecting/opt-in component that may create greater sample bias. However, it clearly offers many practical advantages. Of particular interest to the question writer are the potential advantages in information quality that stem from the respondent being more in control of the experience: being able to take the survey at a time that best suits them and in a way that is more discreet than if an interviewer were involved. Against this upside, the question writer needs to be aware of the greater responsibility placed on the questionnaire itself to hold the attention of the respondent – and to be aware that the visual layout is of particular importance.

Type of device

An important challenge is that online surveys are likely to be taken on a range of devices (Figure 10.1). Questionnaires that in the past may have been taken exclusively on a PC must now work across devices including tablets and smartphones. Indeed, with mobile phone ownership exceeding 90% in most developed economies (and the majority owning smartphones) if a survey does not work on the small screen, then it is likely to either deter the participation of a significant proportion (sample quality issues), or create a sub-optimal experience for those that do persevere (data quality issues).

Figure 10.1 The continuum of devices on which online questionnaires can be accessed (Courtesy of Kantar)

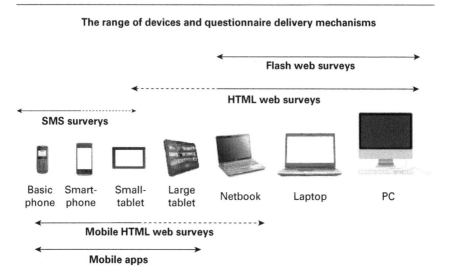

The range of devices and questionnaire delivery mechanisms

Flash web surveys

HTML web surveys

SMS surverys

Basic phone · Smart-phone · Small-tablet · Large tablet · Netbook · Laptop · PC

Mobile HTML web surveys

Mobile apps

Designing surveys for mobile phones

The good news is that most survey software almost universally automatically adapts questions so that they are seen as intended on both of the major operating systems – iOS and Android – which account for almost all smartphones. Also, studies that look at the quality of the data being returned conclude that it can be comparable with data from PC-completed respondents, with only minor differences (Antoun et al, 2017). Even with open-ended questions, long answers were frequently entered, indicating that these verbatim questions need not be a problem. However, you should always check to see how your questions appear on a mobile. Not everything might appear as you would want it to (see Figure 10.2). The best thing to do is to check how well your questionnaire works on a range of devices. You may need to adapt the questionnaire, for example, by skipping non-core questions

Figure 10.2   Some questions translate well onto mobiles

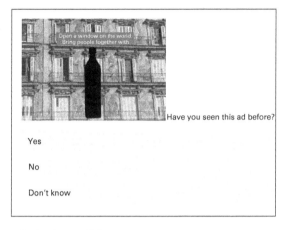

...but not everything.

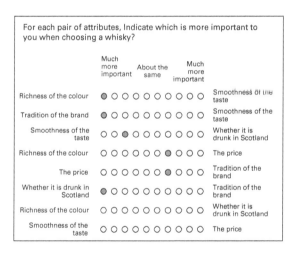

on devices where they cause problems, or excluding certain types of device where there are bigger issues.

Many research companies impose question guidelines to ensure that the mobile experience is prioritized when designing questionnaires, with the logic that if it works well on a small screen it will almost certainly work on a PC. For example, one major company's guidelines are:

- no more than 160 characters in a question;
- a maximum of 15 answer codes;
- no more than two open-ended questions;
- grids limited up to five by five cells (preferably no grids at all).

The main issue for mobile phone users is likely to be the time that are prepared to give to the survey. Macer and Wilson (2013) measure the median acceptable time for a mobile phone survey at 7 minutes, compared to 15 minutes for a PC-based survey. This comes back to the importance of keeping it short, if necessary, by chunking the survey as discussed in Chapter 3 so that the data needed is collected while keeping the experience short for each individual. If the survey is not suitable for mobile, an option is to ask respondents to return to it on a PC later, but this inevitably leads to drop-outs. (Johnson and Rolfe, 2011).

User experience

Progress indicators

Experiments have shown that telling respondents how far through the questionnaire they are affects how difficult they expect the task to be and whether or not they continue or break off (Conrad et al, 2005). If respondents believe early in the questionnaire that they are making good progress, they are more likely to persevere than if they think progress is slow. The inference from this is that progress bars may be positive with shorter questionnaires, but discourage continuation with long questionnaires, and their inclusion must be considered carefully. An alternative is to provide occasional progress information, or to provide this information only later in the questionnaire once significant progress has been made. If the questionnaire contains routing such that time taken to complete it varies greatly between respondents, then a meaningful progress bar is difficult to achieve.

Figure 10.3  Progress bar

Single or multiple pages

A key layout issue for online surveys is whether to:

- ask one question per page or screen;
- group questions into logical sets that follow on the same page, requiring respondents to scroll down; or
- have the complete questionnaire as a single scroll-down page.

This last format has the advantage that respondents can see all of their answers to previous questions by scrolling up and down and be consistent in the way they respond. This is the approach recommended by Dillman (2000). However, this approach is generally only used for short, simple questionnaires. The reasons for this are that:

- If the complete questionnaire is contained in a single scroll-down page, the data is not sent to the administrator's server until and if it has been completed.
- If it is abandoned part-way through then no data is collected from that respondent, and it may not even be known whether or not the respondent started the survey.
- This approach also rules out routing between questions on the same page and so fails to take advantage of one of the medium's key assets.
- It has been shown (Van Schaik and Ling, 2007) that respondents complete the questionnaire more quickly when there is a single question per page. They are thought to be less distracted without the text and answers to other questions on screen at the same time.

It has become general practice for most research companies to use a single page per question, although a question may include more than one part. This makes it possible to include routing between questions and helps to make the screen appear clear and uncluttered.

An exception is where there are a series of attributes to be assessed, usually using scales, when a group of attributes may be shown on the same page. There is some evidence (Couper et al, 2001) that this gives greater consistency between the items than if each one is shown on a separate page. When answer lists across two questions are the same (Figure 10.4) then displaying both questions on one screen can improve logical consistency.

Figure 10.4   Two questions on a screen

Which of these flavours of yogurt do you eat at all these days?
Which others have you ever eaten in the past?

	Eat at all these days	Have eaten in the past
Apricot	☐	☐
Black cherry	☐	☐
Blackcurrant	☐	☐
Gooseberry	☐	☐
Mandarin	☐	☐
Peach	☐	☐
Pineapple	☐	☐
Raspberry	☐	☐
Strawberry	☐	☐
None of these	O	O

Look and feel

If you are working in a research company, then there is probably a standard questionnaire design template. This maintains consistency between surveys, and where you are surveying the same respondents (as with a panel), ensures that they recognize the source of the survey. It also does not introduce different biases between surveys or between waves of the same survey.

If you are designing your own questionnaire without this sort of restriction, you should aim to keep it looking clean, easy to read, and simple. You want nothing to distract the respondent from answering the questions. Use colour sparingly. It has been shown that using excessive or coloured backgrounds can affect how people respond.

For a survey that is clearly associated with a particular company, such as a customer satisfaction survey, you may want to dress the page in the corporate identity. This identifies the survey as being from the company with which the respondent may already have a relationship, which helps response rates. Be aware, though, that the colours may affect responses, and that responses to image questions will be influenced by the corporate identity.

Utilizing the benefits of scripting software

A digitally-scripted survey offers a number of functions both to improve the quality of the data collected and the respondent's experience. These were discussed in Chapter 2, and include the ability to:

- Rotate or randomize the order in which questions are asked.
- Rotate or randomize the order of response codes between respondents.
- Sum numeric answers (eg to ensure that answers add up to 100 per cent or to check total expenditure).
- Insert responses to one question into the wording of another, known as question piping (eg 'Of the £105 that you spent on wine, how much was spent on *Australian* wines?' Here, both the total amount spent and country of origin were inserted from previous questions).
- Adapt response lists according to answers to previous questions, known as response piping (eg the brands listed as possible responses may include only those previously selected by the respondent).
- Ensure consistency between answers, and query apparent inconsistencies.
- Require that a response be given before moving on to the next question.
- Include complex routing between questions.

Minimizing effort and frustration

Minimizing the number of mouse clicks a respondent has to make and the distance the cursor has to travel is important because this reduces the effort required from respondents and improves the probability of them continuing to the end.

If respondents fail to answer a question or complete it incorrectly, they may be directed back to the page on which the error occurred and asked to answer the question again. Clear instructions about how to complete answers can help respondents get it right first time and avoid the annoyance of being returned to the page. Explicit instructions can be complemented by visual cues. In an experiment it was shown that when asking for the month and year of an event, providing a smaller box to enter the month and larger for the year (rather than both being the same size) helped significantly more respondents to enter a four-digit year as required, rather than a two-digit year (Christian et al, 2007). This reduces the frustration of being asked to correct a response.

Question types

Open-ended questions

For open-ended questions respondents are usually asked to type the answer into a box provided. The response box should not be too small, as the size of the box supplied will affect the amount of response given. Even if it enlarges as text is typed, it can be advantageous to make it large to begin with to set the expectation of a full response. It has also been shown (Couper et al, 2001) that altering the size of the box even for a numeric answer can change the distribution of responses.

In an online questionnaire, an open-ended question can be used to measure spontaneous awareness. Frequently, the researcher wishes to know which was the first brand that came to mind. The online questionnaire writer has the choice of asking this as two questions:

- Which is the first brand of shaving cream that comes to mind?

or:

- Which other brands of shaving cream can you think of?

The alternative is to ask one question: 'Which brands of shaving cream can you think of?' and to record responses in a series of boxes that can be labelled 'First brand', 'Second brand' and so on (as shown in Figure 10.5).

Figure 10.5 Open-ended response box; entry in box 1 can be taken as 'top of mind' awareness

What brands of jams and preserves can you think of?

Please type in as many brands as you can think of in the boxes below. Type in brand names only. Do not include flavours.

1		7	
2		8	
3		9	
4		10	
5		11	
6		12	

Next

This is generally preferable as the respondent has only one screen to read and complete rather than two. It also does not highlight the first brand, which may affect later responses. It has been shown that the two approaches give comparable results (Cape et al, 2007) so there is no benefit in the longer approach.

Single response questions

By convention, they are often identified by the use of radio buttons as answer codes with check boxes being used instead to denote a multiple response question.

If you have a lot of response codes but they are short, for example a list of countries, consider using a drop-down box instead.

Multiple response questions

These are straightforward and much used. Respondents may wish to tell you that none of the responses offered apply to them, so you will often need to include a 'none of these' option. This is a single code, as no other answer should be given. Not all DIY survey providers allow for automatic editing of this, though, and you may find 'none of these' checked along with other answers.

An 'other, please write in' (or 'please enter') code often needs to be offered, with a box for the respondent to enter their own response. Note how the question changes from 'which of these…' to just 'which…' and 'none of these' to just 'none' (Figure 10.6).

Where a single question per screen is used, ideally the respondent shouldn't be required to scroll down. All response codes should be included on the same screen if possible: they may not realize that further options are available and even if they do the primacy bias evident in any list may be more marked. An exception might be for a factual question where respondents have to scroll down to find the answer they need, such as their make of car or country of residence. Double- or triple-banking them might offer a solution for longer lists (Figure 10.7) but this often isn't possible on a mobile.

The need for horizontal scrolling should always be avoided. Many respondents will either not see that they should scroll across or not bother to do so. This will lead to bias against the responses that are not apparent on the initial screen.

Figure 10.6   Questions with the 'other' response

	Eat at all these days	Have eaten in the past
Which flavours of yogurt do you eat at all these days? Which others have you ever eaten in the past?		
Apricot	☐	☐
Black cherry	☐	☐
Blackcurrant	☐	☐
Gooseberry	☐	☐
Mandarin	☐	☐
Peach	☐	☐
Pineapple	☐	☐
Raspberry	☐	☐
Strawberry	☐	☐
Other (please enter)	☐	☐
None	O	O

When writing your list of response codes try to ensure that nothing draws the eye:

- Items should be roughly the same length; shorter and longer items stand out.
- Don't have a block of responses that start with the same phrases or words; randomizing the order will avoid this.
- In brand lists, don't make one brand stand out by listing individual variants just for that brand (typically the client's brand!).

Figure 10.7   Triple-banked response list

Where do you live?		
Algeria O	Iraq O	Spain O
Argentina O	Italy O	Sudan O
Bangladesh O	Japan O	Tanzania O
Brazil O	Kenya O	Thailand O
Canada O	Malaysia O	Turkey O
China O	Mexico O	Uganda O
Colombia O	Morocco O	Ukraine O
Dem Rep of Congo O	Nigeria O	United Kingdom O
Egypt O	Pakistan O	United States O
Ethiopia O	Philippines O	Uzbekistan O
France O	Poland O	Venezuela O
Germany O	Russia O	Other write in
India O	Saudi Arabia O	[_____] O
Indonesia O	South Africa O	
Iran O	South Korea O	

Scales and grids

For grids of statements and responses there are a number of options. One is to replicate the layout of paper questionnaires with statements displayed down one side (or both sides if bi-polar) with the response options given as

Figure 10.8   Scale grid using radio buttons

How much would you agree that the following brands taste good?

(Select one answer per row)

	Agree Strongly	Agree Slightly	Neither Agree Nor Disagree	Disagree Slightly	Disagree Strongly
Cadbury's Dairy Milk	O	O	O	O	O
Smarties	O	O	O	O	O
Toblerone	O	O	O	O	O

« | »

radio buttons across the page (see Figure 10.8). This is a familiar layout to most questionnaire writers.

Online, the number of attitude dimensions or brand attributes shown per screen should be limited so that the task does not appear too daunting. Puleston and Sleep (2008) found that grid questions, either as scales or brand association grids, resulted in more dropouts from the survey than any other type of question. Confronted with a screen full of text and boxes, many respondents just give up.

One way of reducing the impact is to spread the attributes over more than one screen. Many research companies adopt conventions such as having no more than five statements to a screen to avoid scrolling down with this type of question. This then presents the researcher with issues of how to group the attributes and which to show on the same screen. It is usual to group them by topic, and possibly label them as such, but this needs to be considered alongside other requirements that may demand separating similar attributes.

For scalar questions, you can also use slider scales or drop-down boxes. The use of different types of slider scales (see Figure 10.9), visual analogue scales or graphic rating scales in online questionnaires was discussed in Chapter 6.

An option available with digitally scripted questionnaires is the drop-down box (see Figure 10.10). A drop-down box following the statement can contain the full scale. Respondents only have to click on their choice of response for it to be displayed and recorded. Again, a little more effort is required than with radio buttons.

Figure 10.9   Slider scale (courtesy of Kantar)

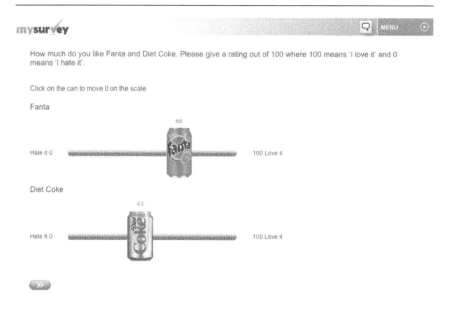

Figure 10.10   Scale using drop-down box

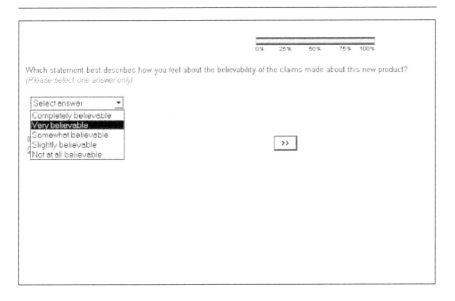

Work carried out by Hogg and Masztal (2001) compared radio buttons with write-in boxes and drop-downs. This showed that both write-in and drop-down boxes gave greater dispersion of responses across a five-point scale than did radio buttons. With radio buttons there was a greater likelihood for respondents to use one point of the scale repeatedly (a type of pattern responding known as 'flatlining'). The more deliberate process of choosing a response option with the write-in and drop-down methods could mean that more consideration is given to what that response should be.

The results for the two versions of the drop-down, one with the positive end of the scale at the top of the box, the other with the negative end at the top, were almost identical, indicating that order is not a crucial issue, at least for five-point scales. However, it may become more so for longer scales. It is important when using drop-down boxes that the default option, which shows prior to it being answered, is not one of the responses but a neutral statement such as 'select answer'.

There may be a concern that the additional time taken to complete the questionnaire could result in an increased rate of drop out. Hogg and Masztal (2001) found that although there was a small increase in the time taken, confirmed by Van Schaik and Ling (2007), there was no evidence of any increased drop out as a result.

> If you have a lot of pre-codes but they are short (eg country names or car manufacturers), consider a drop-down box to save space.

An advantage of both the drop-down and the write-in box is that more responses can be accommodated on one page. However, the questionnaire designer must take care not to make the page look overly complicated or daunting (as shown in Figure 10.11).

Dynamic grids provide a more graphic way of presenting responses, and are particularly good for scales. (Figure 10.12). This technique presents one

Figure 10.11   Drop-down boxes: the temptation to put too many on one page

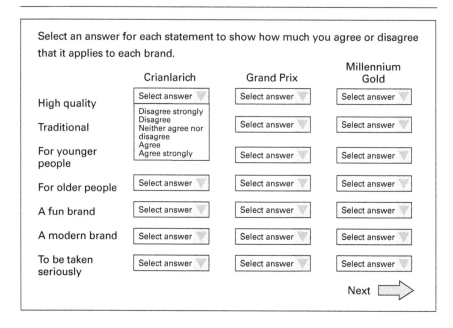

Figure 10.12   Dynamic grid (courtesy of Kantar)

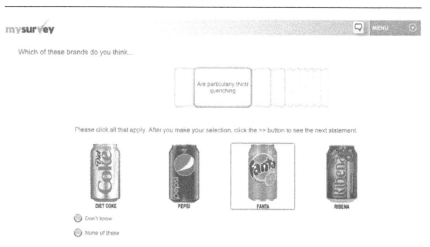

Figure 10.13   Drag-and-drop used for brand attributes (courtesy of Kantar)

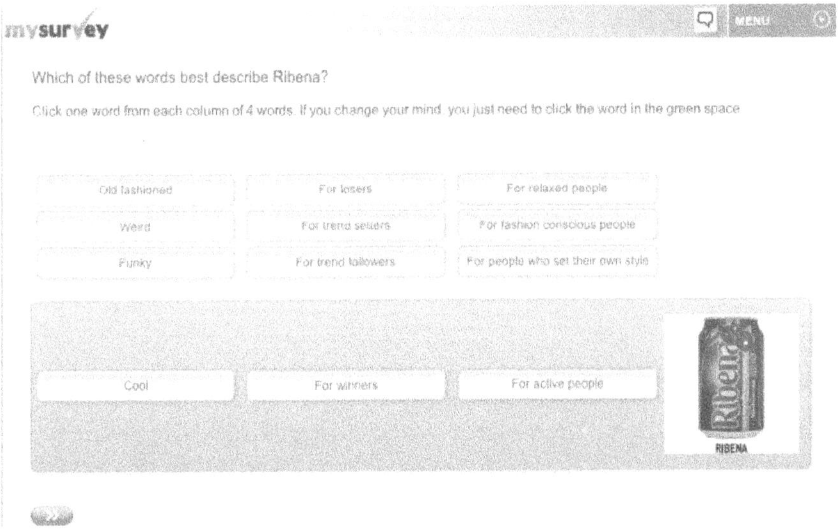

statement or attribute at a time in a horizontally scrolling format, with the response scale static. The respondent has to consider and respond to a statement which then automatically scrolls on to the next one, clearing the response to the previous statement. While this technique can be used in many ways in the online questionnaire, its main use is to present attributes for scale rating in a quick and dynamic way.

Puleston and Sleep (2008) tested slider scale, drag-and-drop (See Figure 10.13), horizontal dynamic grids and vertically scrolling versions, against the standard grid presentation for a bank of attitude statements answered with a five-point scale. They found that the drag-and-drop and dynamic grid options all reduced the amount of pattern answering, or flatlining, but slider scales showed no improvement, consistent with Van Schaik and Ling (2007) referred to previously. They also found that the horizontally scrolling dynamic grid was preferred by respondents.

Avoiding grids

Behavioural questions also frequently involve having response grids on screen. For example, frequency of use of a series of brands can be presented as a grid with brands across the top and the responses vertically to the side. However, these do not encourage respondents to give full consideration to their answers. Alternatively, a dynamic grid can be used as shown in Figure 10.14, with each brand being considered individually. This is almost certain to give better quality data, removing the temptation to flatline, even on a behavioural question.

Figure 10.14 Dynamic grid used for a behavioural question (courtesy of Kantar)

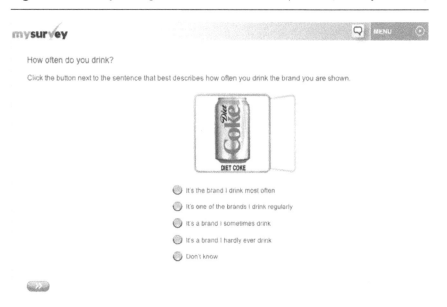

'Don't know' and 'not answered' codes

With online questionnaires the issue arises as to whether the respondent should be allowed to continue to the next question if no answer is recorded at all. Respondents may feel they have permission to simply skip questions that they do not want or feel unable to answer. For this reason, many web-based surveys do not permit the respondent to continue to the next question until an answer has been provided. The absence of a 'don't know' code and a requirement to enter a response before being able to proceed thus forces the respondent to give an answer. Several companies have carried out their own investigations that show that very few respondents terminate an interview because of the lack of a 'prefer not to answer'/'no opinion'/'don't know' codes, nor does this significantly alter the distribution of responses. Against this, it can be argued that there is an ethical issue that respondents should be allowed not to answer a question without having to terminate the interview or provide a random answer. There is also the question as to the value of an answer that a respondent has been forced to give unwillingly and that may simply be a random choice.

In a parallel test, Cape et al (2007) asked about brand ownership, using one sample with a 'don't know' code provided and one without. For the version with a 'don't know' code, 10 per cent selected that as their answer. In the version without that code, the 'other answers' response was 9 percentage points higher. Without a 'don't know' code these respondents were selecting 'other answer' as the closest they could get. But if 'other answer' had not been provided, where would they have gone? Similarly, Albaum et al (2011) found that when a 'prefer not to answer' code was offered, a significant proportion of respondents used it, so when it was not there, how would these people have answered and what would their answers have meant?

If 'don't know' and 'no opinion' codes are included, the questionnaire writer must be aware that the positioning of them on the screen can affect the responses to other codes. If they are added to the end of a list of codes with no visual break between them, this can alter the way in which the respondent regards the list. This is particularly important if the response is in the form of a scale, as it alters the perceived mid-point of the responses. In an experiment by Tourangeau et al (2004) it was shown that when 'don't know' and 'no opinion' codes were simply added to the end of a five-point scale presented vertically, a higher proportion of responses were given to the bottom two codes of the scale than when the 'don't know' and 'no opinion' responses were separated from the scale responses by a dotted line (see Figure 10.15). Without the dotted line, the two codes at the bottom of the scale were visually closer to the middle of the response options. The questionnaire writer needs to make it visually clear that the 'don't know' and 'no opinion' options are not part of the scale.

Figure 10.15 Two presentations of 'don't know' and 'no opinion' codes

Version 1	Version 2
☐ Far too much	☐ Far too much
☐ Too much	☐ Too much
☐ About the right amount	☐ About the right amount
☐ Too little	☐ Too little
☐ Far too little	☐ Far too little
☐ Don't know	☐ Don't know
☐ No opinion	☐ No opinion

Enhancing the experience

Many questionnaire's software packages offer options for enhancing the survey experience that are not available for other modes. It has been shown that online questionnaires that utilize techniques such as these lead to fewer breakings-off during the survey for reasons unrelated to speed of download, and a greater willingness to participate in future surveys (Reid et al, 2007).

> Avoid series of screens that all look the same: repetitive behavioural questions; screen after screen of radio buttons; banks of attitude statements. Introduce variety, but not so much as to confuse respondents.

Drag-and-drop

With drag-and-drop, items can be organized by the respondent into response boxes. This makes the technique suitable for a range of questions, including associating brands with image dimensions, grouping of similarly perceived attributes, and rating brands, products or statements on a scale.

Reid et al (2007) compared responses to a series of attitude statements asked as five-point scales shown as radio buttons with a drag-and-drop technique, where each statement was dragged by the respondent into one of the five response areas. For an example of drag-and-drop see Figure 10.16.

Figure 10.16   Drag-and-drop

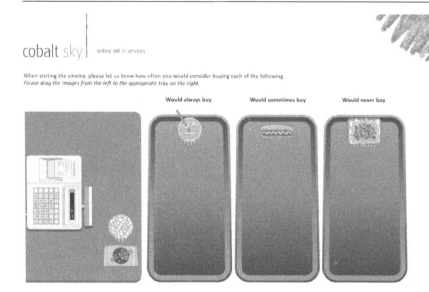

They found that the drag-and-drop technique resulted in fewer mid-point or neutral answers, mainly with an increase in negative answers, and less flatlining. Using drag-and-drop for this type of question would therefore appear to improve both the respondents' experience, so maintaining their engagement better, and the quality of the data. However, it does require more actions by the respondent, so be careful not to overuse it.

For an example of improving the respondent experience we shall look again at the question in Figure 5.4, where respondents were asked to rank order their three preferred yoghurt flavours and the three least liked from a list of 15. Translated directly on to the screen using radio buttons the question looks something like Figure 10.17.

Figure 10.17   Ranking question translated from the paper questionnaire

	Preferred	2nd preference	3rd preference	Three liked least
Below are 15 different flavours of yoghurt. Please indicate the three that you like best in order of preference and the three that you like least.				
Apricot	○	○	○	○
Banana	○	○	○	○
Black cherry	○	○	○	○
Blackcurrant	○	○	○	○
Gooseberry	○	○	○	○
Grapefruit	○	○	○	○
Mandarin	○	○	○	○
Passion fruit	○	○	○	○
Peach	○	○	○	○
Pear	○	○	○	○
Pineapple	○	○	○	○
Raspberry	○	○	○	○
Rhubarb	○	○	○	○
Strawberry	○	○	○	○
Tangerine	○	○	○	○

The screen is a mass of radio buttons and does not look at all enticing. With drag-and-drop, however, the question can be asked similarly to Figure 10.18. The screen is now more attractive and the engagement of the respondent improved by making the task simpler. Card sorting as a data collection technique has long been used in face-to-face interviews, and drag-and-drop generally makes this simple to execute.

Figure 10.18   Ranking question using drag-and-drop (courtesy of Kantar)

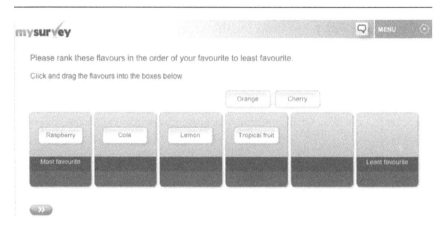

In Figure 10.19, drag-and-drop has been used to enable respondents to place brands on a scale. This enables the respondent to see the relative position of each brand in a simple way. Note that the brand image turns to a label once placed on the scale, so that they can be placed close together if required.

Figure 10.19   Combining drag-and-drop and scale question

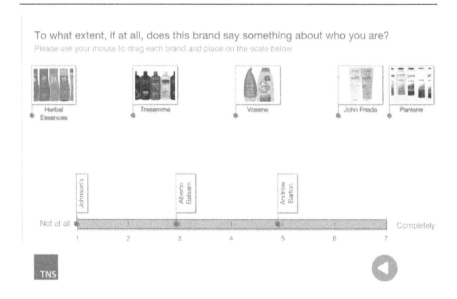

Highlighter

On-screen respondents can be asked to highlight sections of text or graphics relatively easily. The number of times a section of text or a graphic is highlighted can then be counted. (eg in response to questions such as what particularly catches the respondents' eye.)

Figure 10.20 shows a page containing a press ad where respondents are being asked to highlight parts of it depending on whether they feel positive about it, negative or neutral. In this example, clicking once turns the text green to indicate a positive response, and clicking twice turns it red to show negativity. This technique allows heat maps to be displayed, responding to the frequency with which each section has been selected for each purpose asked about.

Highlighting need not be restricted to questions about advertisements. It can also be used, for example, with maps to determine where respondents would or would not want to live, or where they went on holiday, or where they live and work. This is a technique that really is open to the creativity of the questionnaire writer.

Figure 10.20 Press ad for highlighting (courtesy of Kantar)

Here is a recent ad for Ocean Spray. We'd like to know which bits you find most interesting.

To do this, move your cursor over the picture. This will make a highlighter pen appear. By clicking you can then highlight or draw circles around the bits of the picture you find most interesting. Click on the reset button at the bottom of the picture if you want to change your answer.

THE INSIDE STORY OF
WHAT'S HELPED
KEEP OCEAN SPRAY
DRINKERS HEALTHY
ALL THESE YEARS.

Reset

Page turning

Some techniques are available to help reduce the artificiality of the interview. One such technique is the page turner, which many leading agencies include in their tool kit. This enables 'pages' to be turned forward and back by 'grabbing' one of the corners with the cursor and folding it over, simulating page turning in a magazine or newspaper. Figure 10.21, from Ipsos MORI, shows a simulated magazine that the respondent has been asked to look through. In the illustration the right-hand page is in the process of being turned as if the reader is progressing through the magazine. If the respondent wants to turn back to look again at a previous page, the technique works equally well. The purpose is to help respondents react more similarly to the way that they would if it were a real magazine.

Magnifier

When respondents look at magazines or press ads on screen the text is frequently too small to be easily readable. A common technique is to use a magnifier to help respondents; Figure 10.22 shows an example of this. Here

Figure 10.21   Page turner

Figure 10.22   Example of magnifier in use

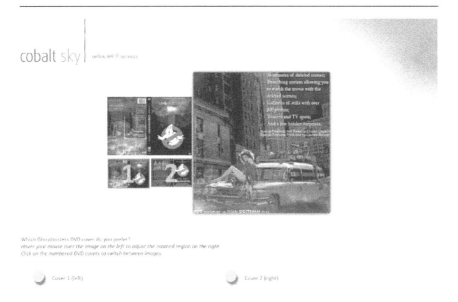

the respondent has moved the magnifying glass over the particular piece of text of interest to be able to read it better. These types of techniques have come to be expected by respondents who see them being used elsewhere.

Using graphics for answer codes

Simple questions can be made visually more interesting, breaking up the repetition of screens and adding interest for respondents. Used well, they can make the question quicker to answer by providing visual cues that can be accessed faster. Figures 10.23 and 10.24 show two simple examples.

Brand prompts

An area where care must be taken with the use of graphics and pictorial prompts is when using brand prompts. It is relatively straightforward with online questionnaires to incorporate logos or pack shots as stimuli for brand recognition or brand image questions. The use of these as prompts has already been discussed in Chapter 9.

Figure 10.23   Enhanced visual appearance

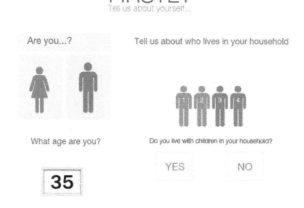

Figure 10.24   Using simple graphics

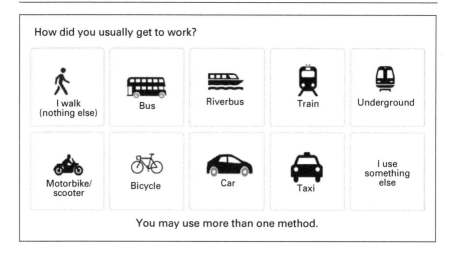

Adding brand logos or pack shots can be a good way of obtaining greater respondent involvement. However, including such visuals will often change the data that is collected. Brand awareness data may change because:

- respondents are better able to distinguish between similar brands or brand variants;
- they do not recognize the pack from the picture used;
- it reminds them of another brand with a similar looking pack.

The larger the pack shot appears on the screen, the less likelihood there is for confusion. However, the larger the pack shots, the greater likelihood there is that the respondent will have to scroll to see them all. It is better to avoid scrolling with this type of question. The aim should be to have all brands visible to the respondent at the same time to allow them to discriminate properly between them.

Care must be taken with the relative sizes of the prompts. All should be given equal prominence, or this can affect measures such as recognition.

With image questions, data will also often change between questions asked using a verbal descriptor and those asked using logos or pack shots. This should not be surprising as much effort will have gone into the logo or pack design to ensure that it conveys messages and brand cues to the viewer, and these are prompting the respondent on these attributes. It can be hypothesized that for a grocery product, the brand image collected using only verbal prompts represents the image that exists in the respondents' minds in the absence of any prompts (that is at home, before going shopping), whereas the image obtained using pack shots is that which the respondent has when seeing it on the supermarket shelf.

In an experiment conducted by the author (Ian Brace), in a brand image association question, 36 out of 85 brand-image association scores changed significantly when pack shots were used instead of brand names.

Colour cues

Another temptation is to use colour to enhance the appearance of the page and make it more attractive to respondents. Great care, though, must be taken with the use of colour. The highlighting of particular answer codes must always be avoided. Also, different colours can have different subconscious associations, which may themselves vary depending on the context. Thus, blue can suggest 'cold' and red 'warmth', but red coupled with green can mean 'stop' with green meaning 'go'.

The fact that colour can affect how people respond to a question has been demonstrated by Tourangeau et al (2007). In experiments they showed that the use of colour in scales had a noticeable impact on responses in the absence of verbal or numerical cues, and hypothesized that in this context, colour provides cues to respondents. Toepoel and Dillman (2010) found that positive responses were given more often when they were shaded green, but that this effect could be reduced by using fully labelled scales. The implication is clear: the use of colour must be treated with care.

Simulated shopping

In this technique, supermarket shelves are simulated and packs displayed. This creates opportunities to simulate a presentation, as it would appear in a store, with different numbers of facings for different products, as an attempt to better reproduce the actual in-store choice situation. Respondents can be asked to simulate their choice process. Or they can be asked to find a particular product with the time taken to find it automatically recorded. Three-dimensional pack simulations can be shown and rotated by the respondent, while questions are asked about them.

Illustrated in Figures 10.25 to 10.29 is the 4D Shopper Plus from Advanced Simulations LLC of Atlanta, Georgia. These show a series of screenshots from the system that allows respondents to simulate a shopping trip on the

Figure 10.25   Approaching the store

Figure 10.26   Inside the store

Figure 10.27   Looking at a shoppable category

Figure 10.28   A shoppable category

Figure 10.29   Looking at product, turning, magnifying, buying

computer screen. It can also do it in full virtual reality, but that is beyond our scope. The respondent can enter the store, approach the aisles, scan the shelves, pick up items, turn them to read the labels for nutritional or other information, and decide whether or not to purchase. The predominant colouring of the store, or its look and feel or layout, can be changed to simulate each respondent's regular supermarket.

Keeping respondents on-side

With any self-completion questionnaire, it's easy for a respondent to stop answering and drop out of the survey if they become bored or irritated with it.

For online surveys one such frustration is slow loading times between pages. This can occur because the questionnaire contains too many advanced features for the download speed available to the respondent's device.

Another consequence of different hardware and software configurations is that what respondents see on their screens may not match what the researcher sees when writing the questionnaire. It is frustrating for these respondents if the formatting of the questionnaire they see is wrong, with text and response boxes out of line, or screens difficult to read. Most survey software will detect what the respondent's device is using and adjust the display accordingly. The researcher must be satisfied that the questionnaire as written will appear intelligible to all respondents or it will be another cause of breaking off.

In the next chapter we consider in more detail how to manage engagement in an online survey.

CASE STUDY   Whisky usage and attitude

Online surveys

We now have a first draft of the questions that we are proposing to ask and need to consider how they are to be presented, both in terms of screen layout and how we can best make use of the opportunities offered by online questionnaires.

Screen layout

Should we have more than one question on a screen, requiring the respondent to scroll down? Our opportunities to have more than one question per screen are limited:

- Firstly, by the amount of routing that there is between questions, which requires that questions be on separate screens, and

- Secondly, by the need not to reveal following questions which might influence how the first question on the screen is answered.

The advantage of having more than one question per screen is that it reduces the number of clicks the respondent has to make, and so reduces the workload. There is an opportunity to achieve this with Q3 and Q4. Q3 (prompted brand awareness) and Q4 (prompted ad awareness) use the same list of brands as pre-codes. It is possible, therefore, to show Q3, and when the respondent has completed that, to show Q4 – with Q4 utilizing the same list of pre-codes. This does not reduce the number of clicks, because the respondent will have to click 'next' to indicate that they have completed Q3. It does, however, reduce the number of screen changes, and gives the respondent the ability to amend their answer to Q3 if Q4 brings more brands to mind.

This also allows us to lose several words from Q4:

- Which of these brands of Scotch whisky have you seen or heard advertised recently?

Becomes:

- Which of these have you seen or heard advertised recently?

Note that this is reduction in words is always an objective when writing questions.

Interactive tools

From Q17 (Which brands do they buy?) we can pipe the answers to form the pre-code list for Q18 (Which do they buy most often?) This reduces the load on the respondent by tailoring the list only to those brands already mentioned. It also prevents respondents from mistakenly clicking a brand at Q18 that they had not previously mentioned at Q17.

Rotating questions

At Q5–8 we ask spontaneous advertising recall for the Crianlarich and Grand Prix brands. As written, Crianlarich advertising is always asked first. Where a respondent answers for both brands this could lead to an order effect. It is prudent therefore to rotate the order or presentation of these question blocks between respondents, so that half see Q5 and Q6 followed by Q7 and Q8, and half see Q7 and Q8 followed by Q5 and Q6. To answer these questions, respondents have to say that they had seen advertising for the relevant brand at Q4, so not everybody will see all of these questions – or indeed any of them.

More important is to rotate the advertising recognition questions – Q23 and Q24 for Crianlarich, and Q25 and Q26 for Grand Prix – where an order effect is more likely. If a respondent mistakes the Grand Prix ad for Crianlarich, then they are less likely to say that if they have previously been presented with an ad which they know is for Crianlarich. They will have just been shown what a Crianlarich ad really looks like, and they may feel that they are not going to be

Figure 10.30   Second question appears when the first question has been completed

Which of these brands of Scotch whisky have you heard of?	
	Heard of
Bell's	☐
Chivas Regal	☐
Crianlarich	☐
Famous Grouse	☐
Glenfiddich	☐
Glenmorangie	☐
Grand Prix	☐
Johnnie Walker	☐
Teacher's	☐
Whyte & Mackay	☐
None of these	☐

Which of these brands of Scotch whisky have you heard of? Which have you seen or heard advertised recently?		
	Heard of	Seen or heard advertised
Bell's	☐	☐
Chivas Regal	☐	☐
Crianlarich	☐	☐
Famous Grouse	☐	☐
Glenfiddich	☐	☐
Glenmorangie	☐	☐
Grand Prix	☐	☐
Johnnie Walker	☐	☐
Teacher's	☐	☐
Whyte & Mackay	☐	☐
None of these	☐	☐

asked about the same brand's ad twice and will look for a different answer. We will therefore think that brand confusion between the ads is all in one direction unless we rotate the order in which they are seen.

In a number of places in the questionnaire we present a list of brands: for Q3 (prompted brand awareness), Q4 (prompted advertising awareness) and for brands purchased off licence, (Q15 and Q17–20). To avoid order bias, these lists should be randomized between respondents. It is important, though, to maintain the same order throughout for a respondent, who might otherwise be confused by an ever-changing order.

Dynamic grid or drag-and-drop?

At Q22, we ask respondents to associate a number of image dimensions with the core set of brands in which we are interested. There are several ways in which the question can be presented:

- as a grid;
- as drag-and-drop;
- as a dynamic grid.

In this questionnaire, the number of image dimensions is only eight. Nevertheless, a grid of eight dimensions listed vertically and six brands, together with 'none' and 'don't know' options present a daunting sight on screen, encouraging flatlining or pattern answering in an attempt by the respondent to get through it quickly without having to think too much.

As a drag-and-drop, each image dimension could in turn be required to be dragged into a 'bin' for each brand it is thought to apply to. This requires the respondent to consider each dimension as it appears on screen. The cognitive load is thereby increased. The workload is also increased by the task of clicking to capture the item, dragging, and then releasing them into the appropriate bin. If the dimensions are associated with an average of two brands each, then this is sixteen separate tasks, and could be more for many respondents. As this is a multiple response for each dimension, the respondent also has to indicate when they have finished allocating the dimension with a further click, adding more to the workload. Whist this technique will force greater consideration of each dimension, there is a danger that the increased workload will lead respondents to adopt strategies to minimise it, such as only choosing one brand, possibly the same brand, each time.

The dynamic grid, by presenting one image dimension at a time, also forces consideration of each dimension in turn. The workload is less than with drag-and-drop, though, as each response requires only one click per brand. It is possible for someone to speed through by choosing the same single brand each time, but we would hope to be able to spot that in the data, because we have opposite dimensions ('cheaper' and 'more expensive') which should not be applicable to the same brand. We choose to use a dynamic grid here.

The order of the brands presented on screen will be randomized between respondents, but kept constant for each respondent.

Key take aways: creating a questionnaire for an online survey

- Online questionnaire software typically provides greater options for question format and interactive techniques than interviewer-administered modes.

- However, you now have to give even more thought to the visual presentation and usability including:

  o look and feel;

  o amount on one screen and issues with scrolling;

  o clarity of instructions.

- Think how you can make the most of the routing, piping and editing capabilities of the questionnaire software to manage flow and quality through the interview.

- The appearance may be altered by the device used to take the survey:

  o PC screens offer most visual space and flexibility for the question writer, but with the growth of smartphones it is becoming best practice to work within the limits of the smaller mobile screen as the priority when designing questions.

  o Reducing word load in questions and answers is vital for optimizing the mobile experience.

Engaging respondents in online surveys

11

Introduction

We have already discussed many challenges the question writer faces that might affect the quality of the information a respondent is able to provide (eg their understanding of the question; memory limitations; their inability to identify or articulate reasons underlying their behaviour; and other potentially subconscious pressures that might influence the accuracy of their answers).

However, an overriding requirement for good quality information is that a respondent is sufficiently engaged and interested in the survey to want to make the effort to try.

With any self-completion survey the questionnaire itself must do all the work to keep the respondent motivated as there is no interviewer to help maintain their attention. Online surveys typically face even more pressure to engage than pen-and-paper self-completion, in part because respondents' expectations are influenced by their everyday online experiences (eg seeing how company websites, e-commerce platforms and social media interact with them to keep their attention). In addition, many online surveys use panels as the source of respondents; these volunteers may have many re-quests to participate in surveys and therefore they have more opportunity to assess what is and isn't enjoyable. So, the bar is raised in terms of what will encourage them to continue making an effort throughout a survey.

Length of interview

Few structured interviews can retain the interest of any respondent for a lengthy amount of time, however inherently interesting the topic might seem to the researcher. Keeping the questionnaire short is key. Cooke (2010), reporting on 'bad survey behaviour' (like speeding or pattern answering) noted a six-fold increase between a 15-minute and a 30-minute question-naire. In Chapter 3 we looked at keeping the survey to a manageable length of 10 to 15 minutes maximum, and that should be the first objective in order to maximize data quality.

Respondents who are bored or fatigued may simply log off if they are online. Figure 11.1, taken from Cape et al (2007), shows how drop-out is a function of length of questionnaire. It can be seen that in a large number of projects more than 20 per cent drop out.

Figure 11.1   Online drop-out rate by length of interview (Cape et al, 2007)

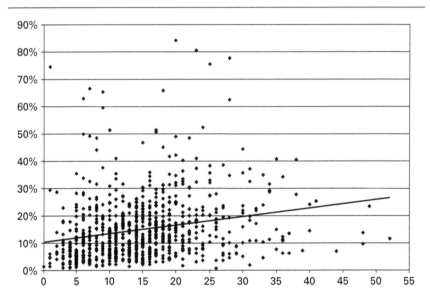

Figure 11.2 shows that ratings of how enjoyable survey participation is de-cline the longer it goes on. Using the author's (Brace) previously unpublished work based on more than 50 surveys, around half of respondents say the experience is very enjoyable for a 5-minute online survey, but this falls to around a third for a 15-minute survey, and continues to decline beyond that. If we take 'enjoyability' as a proxy for 'engagement', this demonstrates how the quality of data is likely to decline the longer the questionnaire.

Figure 11.2   Enjoyability decreases with length

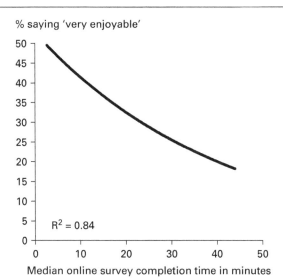

% saying 'very enjoyable'

$R^2 = 0.84$

Median online survey completion time in minutes

Respondent boredom and fatigue

The variability in the data at any one time point in Figure 11.1 demonstrates that the length of the questionnaire is not the only factor in the decision to drop out. Cape et al (2007) attribute this largely to the quality of the questionnaire design. This shows that with poor questionnaire design, fatigue is likely to set in earlier and results become unreliable sooner in the interview.

Response mistakes made by respondents because of failure to understand the question or to give sufficient thought to their response are exacerbated when they become tired of or bored by the interview. When that happens, respondents will adopt strategies to get them to the end of the interview quickly and with as little thought or effort as possible. Thus, with repeated questions, such as rating scales, they will often go into a pattern of response that bears little or no relationship to their true answers.

Sometimes any answer will be given just to be able to proceed to the next question. These may contradict or be incompatible with those given earlier, making interpretation of data harder.

Puleston and Eggers (2012) reported that 85 per cent of respondents in their experiments over 11 countries showed evidence of speeding at some stage of their online survey. They concluded that the only weapon we have to combat this is 'effective questionnaire design'.

Using questionnaire design to engage

In Chapter 10 we looked at some response techniques that can be used to break up the questionnaire, involve the respondent more and minimize some of the effort-avoidance techniques that lead to unreliable data. These included:

- drag-and-drop;
- slider scales;
- dynamic grids.

But to get the best out of an online questionnaire, and to really engage and involve respondents, it is necessary to think differently about how the questions themselves are asked. There are three ways we should be thinking differently:

1 Making the questions more accessible by keeping down the number of words, laying out the page well, avoiding repetition, etc.

2 Changing what is asked so respondents can relate more directly, and with more interest, to the questions.

3 Introducing elements that feel more like games but that collect the data in the process.

Using these techniques makes a difference. In an experiment by the author (Brace), many of the techniques covered in Chapter 10 – and several which will be discussed in this chapter – were incorporated into an online questionnaire with a median completion time of 25 minutes. The expected level of respondents saying that they found the experience enjoyable from previous experience is under 30 per cent for this length of questionnaire. With the incorporation of these techniques that figure increased to 48 per cent, demonstrating that respondents remained engaged longer than would otherwise have been the case (see Figure 11.3). Importantly we could expect the quality of the data to be correspondingly improved.

Figure 11.3   'A well-constructed questionnaire improves the experience'

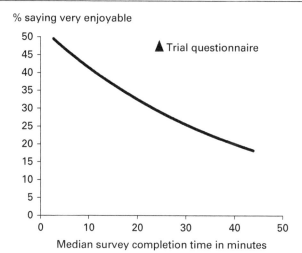

Writing to be read rather than spoken

One of the key causes of disengagement with online interviews is that the questions and the screens simply contain too many words. Large blocks of text are daunting and will not be read. There is evidence that most people have made up their minds what the question is about by the time they have read about 10 words (Tourangeau et al, 2000). They don't read beyond that and go straight into answering the question they think is being asked.

However, many people write questions as if they are to be asked by an interviewer. But when this goes on to the screen as an online question, it does not work. Often it is far too wordy, so that not only does the respondent not read all of it, but it creates a visual impression of making the questionnaire appear as an effortful chore.

To obtain a person's age it may be asked in a face-to-face interview as: 'Please would you tell me how old you are?' or, 'In which of the categories on this card does your age fall?' Online it needs to get straight to the point:

- Your age:
  - 16 to 34
  - 35 to 54
  - 55 or older

If the screen is headed 'some details about yourself' or something similar, then even the word 'your' may be omitted. This format is what respondents are used to online and is the least visually oppressive.

Using response codes to frame the question

Long explanations are rarely necessary with online interviews. Often the response list provides the entire context that is required:

- Please read the following list of statements and indicate which apply to you.

Can be replaced with:

- Which of these apply to you?

In Figure 11.4 it is clear from the scale itself that the answer is required on a scale from 0 to 10 and what the end point anchors, and does not need to be repeated in the question. The heart of the question gets relegated to the end of a long sentence. The question length is halved if written as:

- How likely would you be to recommend Joe Bloggs's Internet Banking Service based on today's experience?

Frequently in interviewer-led questionnaires we read out the response codes to define the question to the respondents. Online, the response codes can be made to do the work of the question (Figures 11.5 and 11.6).

Figure 11.4 Unnecessarily detailed question

Based on your experience today, on a scale of 0 to 10 where 0 is not at all likely and 10 is extremely likely, how likely is it that you would recommend Joe Bloggs's Internet Banking service to a friend or colleague?

   O 10 Extremely likely

   O 9

   O 8

   O 7

   O 6

   O 5

   O 4

   O 3

   O 2

   O 1

   O 0 Not at all likely

   O Don't know

Figure 11.5   Reduce the number of words

Did you know who was advertising when you first saw it, or did showing the ad remind you, or did you previously not know who the ad was for at all?

  O Knew who was advertising when first seen

  O Showing the ad reminded me

  O Previously didn't know who the ad was for

(LET THE RESPONSE PRE-CODES DO THE WORK. DON'T REPEAT THEM IN THE QUESTION.)

When you first saw the ad did you:

  O Immediately know who it was for

  O Was reminded who it was for

  O Didn't previously know who it was for

We can also remove most of the pleasantries – these are important in interviewer surveys where a relationship is being built, but on screen they add word load. Just keep a few occurrences to manage the overall tone. Figure 11.6 gives a further illustration of reducing wordage.

Keep explanations separate from the question

Separating the core question from instructions or supporting information can help to reduce the blocks of text and keep the screen uncluttered. An interviewer-administered question might be:

- 'Have you travelled from London to Birmingham in the last three months by public transport, that is by train, coach, aeroplane or taxi, but not by private car?'

For an online questionnaire this would be too much text for a single sentence. On the screen this would look less daunting as:

- Have you travelled from London to Birmingham in the last three months by public transport?

The additional information can be added a couple of lines below:

- Public transport includes train, coach, aeroplane and taxi, but not private cars.

Figure 11.6 Reducing wordage

Now please look at the names of some companies that provide telephone services into the home. For each company, please click on one statement that best describes how you feel about it for telephone services. Just click on the one that best applies in each case.

Company A

O The only company I would ever use

O One of a number of companies I would prefer to use

O From what I've heard I might try that company in the future

O I'd use this company in certain circumstances

O I've heard of this company but didn't know they provided this service

O I've never heard of it

O I would never use this company

Only a third of the words are required in the question if it is online:

Here are some providers of home telephone services. How do you feel about each of them?

Company B

O The only company I would ever use

O One of a number I would prefer to use

O From what I've heard I might try them in the future

O I'd use them in certain circumstances

O I've heard of them but didn't know they provided this service

O I've never heard of them

O I would never use them

If we do not need to emphasize the service provision context, then even more words could be saved online:

How do you feel about each of these providers of home telephone services?

Put additional information in a separate box away from the question. It helps ensure that the question is read.

Personalizing the questions

Too often questionnaires are designed simply to extract information without sufficient thought given to how well it works as a conversation. This can make the questions very formal and sometimes difficult for respondents as it requires them to work harder to understand the task they are being set. For example, a frequently asked question is:

- Please select the three items from the list below that are the most important to you.

This has been written from the researcher's point of view, who has formulated the question in terms of importance, the language of the research brief. This question could be written as:

- If you could only have three of these items, which would they be?

This changes the question from an abstract notion of importance, which may be something that respondents have never considered before and so requires some cognitive processing, to a more personal and easier to answer construct that relates to their behaviour. If the data changes as a result, then it may well better reflect the respondents' real notions of importance.

Starting at the beginning

Engaging the respondent begins with the first screen they see. From the start the survey should be seen as something interesting to do (see Figures 11.7 and 11.8). We want respondents to want to continue and complete the survey, not just because they are going to be rewarded with points from their panel but because they are motivated to give good quality answers. 'Another tedious survey' is not a mindset that will deliver high quality. Some of the ways of achieving this are:

- Including some questions they find enjoyable – even fun – to complete. These may not be directly relevant to the subject of the main survey, although equally they should not be completely dissonant. They must not influence or bias responses to later questions, so need to be carefully constructed.

- Starting with a question framed as a short quiz with feedback on the respondent's performance can be engaging, as well as getting the respondent to thinking about the topic – which may not be one that they think about every day. This approach will be returned to later.

- Constructing the questionnaire as an interactive website rather than a typical survey. With customer satisfaction surveys, for example, where the client is apparent to the respondent, it can be constructed as the client's feedback site, with appropriate characters and animation.

Figure 11.7 Introducing the survey in a more interesting way

We're a market research agency and we're going to ask you how you feel about some everyday products you may buy and use at home.

We'll tell you more about our client and why we're doing this research at the end of the survey.

Figure 11.8 Using graphics to add interest

FIRSTLY
tell us about yourself...

Who does the grocery shopping in your household?

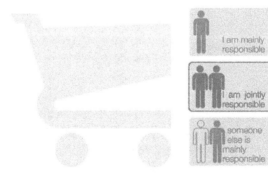

Including animation, particularly at the beginning of the questionnaire, has been shown to increase the involvement of respondents and cause them to spend more time on the following questions (Puleston and Sleep, 2008).

Adding interest

In Chapter 10 we saw how slider scales and other techniques can be used to vary the task and make it easier. To make it more entertaining and involving, this can be taken further by, for example, making the slider scales look like a mixing desk, or turning the radio button on a scale into a series of facial expressions. By doing this, Malinoff and Puleston (2011) found that respondents enjoyed the experience more and the quality of the data improved in that flatlining was reduced or eliminated. However, they also found that the distribution of responses was different, and that it could be varied in particular by changing the face used to depict the facial expressions. Thus, introducing pictorial images has an effect and they must be used with caution.

In Figure 11.9, the size and number of hearts increases the higher the score that is given to the brand using the slider scale.

In Figure 11.10 the depiction of how you feel changes for different points on the scale. Clearly great care has to be taken with this so as not to bias responses.

Figure 11.9   Graphics make it more fun

Move the slider to indicate how you feel about yourself and each of these brands

Figure 11.10   Different depictions appear for different points on the scale

Which of these emotional states most closely reflects how you feel when you buy shampoo!

They never quite sell the type of product I am looking for | I find it really difficult deciding what to buy | I take a while thinking about it | It's simple I always buy the same product

Learning from gamification

Some of the engagement techniques already described are steps towards the full gamification of questionnaires (ie making it an entertaining, interactive experience).

The balance of evidence is that gamification can make questionnaire completion more interesting and enjoyable; and promotes greater satisfaction with the experience. (Keusch and Chang 2014, Harms et al 2014) There is growing evidence that it can increase the level of completions, by reducing the number who terminate the survey early; that the effect is consistent across all demographic groups; and the quality of the data is maintained and often improved (Bailey, Pritchard and Kernohan 2015, Cechanowicz et al 2013). The techniques do, however, have to be applied appropriately and sensibly, or they can introduce biases to the data which may be difficult to detect, and if too complex can cause increased drop out (Baker and Downes-Le Guin, 2011).

There are many types of gamification techniques to enhance questions. Findlay and Alberts (2011) list 47 different game mechanisms from games company SCVNGR, many of which could be used to create engaging ways of asking questions.

Here we will be looking at five of the more commonly used ones:

- personal scenario;
- projective scenario;
- presenting a challenge;
- providing rewards;
- arbitrary rules.

Many of the gamification suggestions were originally pioneered in questionnaires by Jon Puleston and Deborah Sleep (2011).

Personal scenario

With this approach we put the respondent into a scenario in which they could imagine themselves having to make a decision. We have already seen the simple version of this with the question, 'If you could only have three of these items which would they be?' This idea can be extended to create an imaginary situation. Instead of asking:

- What are your three favourite yoghurt flavours?

We ask:

- In a promotion at your supermarket, you are offered three free yoghurts. Which three flavours would you go for?

Or we change:

- What flavour of pasta sauce do you prefer?

To:

- Imagine you've run out of pasta sauce and only have enough money to buy one jar. You're the only one who'll be eating it...so what flavour will it be?

These types of questions draw respondents in and help them to focus on what is important to them as an individual. In another example, Bailey, Pritchard and Kernohan (2015) changed:

- Please tell us what your family's favourite foods are.

To:

- You have an opportunity to go to the supermarket with an unlimited budget and buy all your family's favourite foods. What would you buy?

This increased the average number of responses from six to 14. A clear example of getting greater engagement.

Another example of this type of question is given in Figure 11.11 which also combines drag-and-drop and some simple graphics.

This is a scenario to which the respondent can personally relate, and does not require them to make too big a leap of imagination.

Projective scenario

With a projective scenario, the respondent is put into a situation which they would not normally expect to come across, or where they are asked to project themselves into someone else's shoes. So they might be asked to imagine that they are the shop manager and have to suggest what would sell best in their store. Or, they might be told they are the captain of a sinking ship with the opportunity to rescue only one product from the cargo they are carrying.

Figure 11.11   Combining a scenario, with drag-and-drop and simple graphics

DISASTER! All your apps have been deleted!

But you can retrieve three of them if you are quick.
Drag the three you most want from the bin to the screen to keep them.

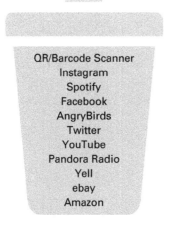

QR/Barcode Scanner
Instagram
Spotify
Facebook
AngryBirds
Twitter
YouTube
Pandora Radio
Yell
ebay
Amazon

The aim is to engage the imagination of the respondent and so involve them more in playing the game.

If we are looking for new product ideas, instead of asking:

- What new pizza toppings would you like to see?

We can change this to:

- Imagine you're the manager of a pizza restaurant. Head office have asked for suggestions for new toppings, and they'll give a bonus to the manager who comes up with the biggest sellers. What are your three suggestions?

Now we are asking respondents to think on behalf of someone else, freeing them from their own constrictions, helping them to be more creative. The original question would probably have been given little thought and generated some unusable answers. By asking respondents to think about what other people might want, we are more likely to get some suggestions with potential.

Puleston and Sleep (2011) tested various variations of both personal and projective scenarios or frameworks, some of which are given in Table 11.1.

In each case, the respondents spent longer on the questions posed in the imaginary framework than the standard question. For the question describing the advertising, the average number of words in the answers rose from 14 in the standard question to 53 for the imaginary framework question.

This demonstrates that the respondents were more engaged, and importantly gives the researcher a far more detailed evaluation of their response to the ad. For the last question, the average number of foods given per respondent increased from 6 to 35. This may be more than the researcher needs, but to increase discrimination the analysis can look only at the first 10 or 15 given – and that is still a big improvement. Note that this question also introduced an arbitrary rule by limiting the answer to two minutes.

All of these questions appear to violate the rule of keeping the number of words to a minimum. What they are doing, though, is intriguing the respondent within the first few words, which maintains the attention and ensures that they read them through fully.

Presenting a challenge

Presenting the question as a challenge has been found to increase respondent involvement and to increase the number of responses significantly. Puleston and Sleep (2011) found that asking for advertising recall in this way increased

Table 11.1   Tapping into the respondent's imagination

Standard wording	Question using imaginary framework
What is your favourite meal?	Imagine you are on death row and had to choose your last meal. What would it be?
How much do you like each of the following recording artists?	Imagine you were in charge of your own private radio station. From the following list of artists we want you to build up a play-list by deciding how much each artist should be played.
What did you think of the advertising?	Imagine you work for an advertising agency. One of your key client's rival brands has just released a new ad, and you are about to see a sneak preview before anyone else. You have to report back to the agency what you thought of it.
Please name your favourite foods.	You have an opportunity to go to a supermarket with unlimited budget and buy all your favourite foods. The catch is you only have 2 minutes.

Adapted from Puleston and Sleep (2011)

the number of brands mentioned threefold. They also found that adding the words 'can you guess' to a question increased the time spent on considering the response from around 10 seconds to up to 2 minutes. Clearly these fairly small changes had increased the engagement of respondents. For example, asking:

- We challenge you to name as many brands of (product) as you can that you have seen advertised recently.

Instead of:

- Which brands of (product) have you seen advertised recently?

The former is more likely to give a longer list of responses, which may be important where the brand of interest is not the most salient in the category.

Of course, they may not always be appropriate. If it is a quick, front-of-mind response that you are seeking, then you may not want respondents to give it too much consideration. Then, you might change the question to:

- As quickly as you can, name one/two/three brands that...

In Figure 11.12, the respondent is challenged to match the brands with the ads. The serious purpose is to obtain brand association with the ads but presented in this way respondents find it much more fun.

Figure 11.12 Challenge the respondents – they find it fun

Here are five pictures from adverts for different brands, but 8 brands. Your goal is to find the brand that goes with each picture by dragging the brand's logo into the picture. See how many you can get right; and see if you can find the odd ones out.

Providing rewards

Helping the respondent to measure their achievements helps to maintain engagement.

Providing scores for some of the games has already been discussed, either providing a score based on speed of response or telling how many brands they recognised correctly (Figure 11.13).

Figure 11.13 Comparing scores turns it into a game

There is a danger that telling respondents which brands they got right and which they got wrong can influence their later responses and so bias the data.

Cechanowicz et al (2013) showed that if the respondent learnt which answers they got wrong, then this did alter their later responses. However, if they were told only those for which they were correct, it did not. There is a logic to this, as knowing that you got something wrong would be likely to make you re-evaluate your thinking at later questions. Reaffirming where you were correct, however, can enhance the feeling of involvement.

Another form of reward is to provide badges as marks of achievement as the respondent progresses through the questionnaire. Harms et al (2015) created a survey in which ten badges could be won for various achievements during the course of the survey. These were shown, greyed out, at the top of the screen, and changed as they were completed. The badges, though, were awarded at random, not necessarily linked to specific achievements. The survey was about sport and aimed at 14 to 26 year olds, and was run in parallel with the same survey without the badges. While they found that the quality of the data between the two forms of the survey was identical, the respondents competing the badged survey showed a much higher level of positive feedback about the survey. This suggests that this is thus a relatively low-cost way for creating happier respondents who are more likely to participate again – which is one of our objectives.

Arbitrary rules

Adding arbitrary rules to a question can turn it from a task into a game. Many sports would be no more than a task if there were no rules, and teaching children is often made easier and more engaging by turning it into a game.

One type of rule is a time limit, as used in the previous example. A question about naming brands could be turned into:

- You have 10 seconds to name as many brands as you can that ...

The question in Figure 11.10 could be enhanced by asking the respondent to complete it in an arbitrary time – say 15 seconds. A counter in the top right corner would show how many seconds they have left, so the respondent is competing against the clock. This encourages respondents to be spontaneous in their answers, more closely matching the associations they would normally make without the benefit of unlimited time to consider it. A score on the following screen could then be arrived at by summing the seconds left when the response is completed, and a comparison against the average. This turns it into a game, where respondents can assess their performance against that of others.

A variation on this is to identify a slowly revealed ad (Cechanowicz et al, 2013). The ad is revealed one block at a time over a 15 second period, and the respondent is challenged to name the brand as soon as possible. This was shown to increase engagement.

Bailey, Pritchard and Kernohan (2015) changed the question:

- Please tell us what your favourite brands of crisps are?

To,

- You have one minute to tell us as many of your family's favourite brands of crisps as you can.

The result was that the average number of responses given increased from two to six.

Another type of rule is to ask respondents to use an exact number of words to describe something. Puleston and Sleep (2011) tested the two questions: 'How would you describe yourself?' and 'In exactly seven words how would your friends describe you?' With the standard question, 18 per cent failed to respond and those that did gave an average of 2.4 descriptors. With the rule added, only 2 per cent failed to respond and the average number of descriptors given rose to 4.5.

Just for fun

Sometimes it is difficult to avoid having a tedious section in the questionnaire and there is a need to re-engage respondents. Then you might consider including a question that has no purpose other than to re-engage. It ought to have some relevance to the survey, but it should surprise the respondent by being not what they might expect. In a travel survey, for example, you might ask:

- On a long-haul flight, which of these people would you most like to find yourself sitting next to?

Named photographs of a dozen celebrities, politicians and other well-known people selected to have some relevance to the target group would follow from which they have to choose one. You could also or alternatively ask who they would most not want to sit next to! The aim is not to collect data of any immediate value to the research objectives, but to protect the integrity of the data that you are yet to ask for by bringing the respondent back to being engaged with the survey.

CASE STUDY   Whisky usage and attitude

Engaging the respondents

At the end of Chapter 9 we had a first draft of the questions, and in Chapter 10 we looked at some of the tools that we could use to ask them. Now we are going to return to the questions themselves and look at ways of making them more likely to be understood and to make them more engaging.

Question wording

It is essential to keep the number of words to a minimum at the same time as ensuring that we get the information we are looking for.

Q12–14 are relatively lengthy questions, with up to 21 words. These can be reduced by using the response codes as part of the question. So Q12 changes:

Table 11.2

Do you drink Scotch whisky in your own home, in someone else's home, or both?	Do you drink Scotch whisky:
In my own home O	In your own home O
In someone else's home O	In someone else's home O
Both mine and others' homes O	Both mine and others' homes O

Active engagement

We now want to see if we can improve engagement and the quality of our data by utilizing gamification techniques.

The first question in the main questionnaire presents us with an opportunity to involve respondents by challenging them. The first draft is:

- Which brands of Scotch whisky have you heard of?

This question at best makes the respondent sit back and think, and at worst it makes them think that as long they name a couple of brands we'll be happy with the response and they can move on. We can actively involve them better by challenging them:

- Can you name eight brands of Scotch whisky?

The number of brands we ask for is based on prior knowledge of the market – there are a lot of brands and our desire is to get past the dominant three or four. Our brand, Crianlarich, is not one of the best-known brands, so if we only get two or three responses from each respondent, it is less likely to be mentioned. By seeking up to eight brand names, the 'second tier' of brands will get more mentions and we learn more about how well-known Crianlarich really is. For the responses we provide eight boxes for the names to be entered into. Employing this technique enhances the quality of the data that we collect.

We do not repeat this approach for spontaneous advertising awareness, because that would be likely to encourage respondents to drag up from their memory old campaigns that they recall just in order to meet the challenge, where our interest is in recent advertising. By having been forced to think about the brand names at the previous question, that will help to remind them of recent advertising that they are aware of.

Q25 and Q20 are currently two questions as follows:

- Have you seen this ad before? [SHOW UNBRANDED CRIANLARICH AD]
- Which brand of Scotch whisky is it for?

These could be replaced by a single question, by slowly revealing the ad and asking the respondent to name the brand as quickly as possible. This would then be repeated for the Grand Prix ad. However, this changes what we are asking. Our objectives for these questions are to determine:

- whether the brand has been seen (ie its reach);
- how well the branding on the ad is working.

With the changed question, this could leave us with some interpretation issues. For example, if they correctly name the brand they may simply be responding to the style of ad which they identify with the brand. Also, if they incorrectly name the brand, we cannot know whether that is because they have not seen it and are guessing a brand, or that they have seen the ad and failed to recall the brand. The latter is important for us to know in assessing how well the ad is working. The technique should increase engagement, but as these are the final questions in the survey, that is of less importance to us. Therefore, we decide to keep with the original questions.

We must always examine whether an engagement technique delivers the information that we seek, and not just use it because we can.

Key take aways: engaging respondents in online surveys

- The length has a direct impact on response rates and drop-out rates, so keeping the questionnaire below 15 minutes (and ideally nearer to 5 minutes) is a key aim.

- However, with online questionnaires – whatever the length – you need to actively consider the respondent experience of completing the survey to manage their motivation to give considered answers.

- Keep the words to a minimum to encourage respondents to read them. Edit out superfluous language that is a carry-over from the wordier style needed in interviewer-led surveys.

- Drop the key parts of the question into the response lists. The respondent's eye often spends more time here.

- Explore question approaches that will draw the respondents in by:

  o creating scenarios that they can relate to;

  o introducing an element of competition.

- The challenge is to adopt more engaging approaches, but also ones that you can still interpret reliably. Occasionally a question whose sole purpose is to re-engage the respondent might earn a place in the questionnaire.

Choosing online survey software 12

Introduction

The way in which a questionnaire is written for an online survey is at least, in part, dependent on the options offered by the software being used.

Some of the approaches described in the preceding chapters may only be available to the questionnaire writer who is using one of the survey software programs used by the major research agencies, such as Confirmit, IBM Dimensions or Merlinco. These are professional software packages, utilized by professional script writers, which occasional users of surveys would usually be prohibited from using by their cost and complexity.

However, there are a large number of people, companies, individuals and students, who carry out surveys themselves, without using a research company as intermediary. They are using survey and questionnaire packages or apps that are available off the web, and for which relatively little training is required. Whether a one-time or ongoing user, these can be very cost effective for the researcher who does not want the functionality, or cost, of one of the major software solutions.

Which platforms are available to choose from?

As with any technology-driven market, the providers and capabilities are rapidly multiplying. Many of the packages are more suitable for those wishing to conduct quick polls among friends and colleagues, predominantly for social or team interaction reasons rather than as objective information gathering to aid organizational decision making.

With the dynamic nature of the market, any listing or review of specific suppliers will become outdated too quickly. To help you choose at the point in time when you are trying to make that decision, this chapter provides a list of considerations against which to evaluate the offers.

First, there are different business models for survey software including:

- **Free access**: the number of surveys you can run on a free basis may be limited. Similarly, there may be limitations on the number of questions, types of questions and number of responses/completes. There are then options for various monthly fee structures which give you more question features and/or more surveys/completes per survey. If they offer access to a panel of respondents there will be a fee for that or sometimes for hosting the questionnaire.

- **Free set-up of a questionnaire**: with a charge per completed questionnaire collected, dependent on length of questionnaire.

- **Free set-up of a basic survey**: with charges for additional features that can be added as you write the questionnaire and for hosting the survey.

- **Monthly charge with no fee option**: There may be different levels of charge. For an increased fee some will give you more question types. Others give all question types for the lowest fee, but limit the number and size of surveys, a limit which is then removed for the higher fee. Monthly charges vary considerably depending on the market that is being targeted and the sophistication of the software.

In addition to evaluating the fit to your needs of the questionnaire design capabilities, you may also need to consider:

- Whether the provider offers access to a panel of respondents, or whether it can host the questionnaire for your own mailing list.

- The analysis capabilities linked to the questionnaire software. Some have much more flexibility and allow more complex analyses than others – with varying degrees of user-friendliness.

- The security protocols in place to protect data and respondents' personal information.

This chapter, however, will focus on aspects related directly to questionnaire design.

How to evaluate which platform is right for you

The criteria for assessing the functionality of the questionnaire offered fall into three areas:

1 The range of question types.

2 The range of functions.

3 The look and feel.

Range of question types

Simple response questions

- **Multiple response options, single choice:** The basic one-answer question, usually with radio buttons or a drop-down box. Can an edit be scripted to ensure only one answer is given?

- **Multiple response options, multiple choice:** Can you ensure that a 'none of these' response cannot be used if other responses are made? (ie is 'none of these' a single response option?) Can you set a maximum number of answers to be given? This can be useful for 'pick up to three' type questions.

- **Number and layout of response codes:** Is there a limit and is that adequate for your purpose? Do you have the choice of responses being vertically or horizontally displayed?

Scales

- **Semantic scales:** Can you choose the number of scale points or are they fixed? Is there a range to select from? Are they all odd numbered or can you use even numbered scales if you want to? Can the scale be shown as radio buttons, stars, hearts, boxes or a slider scale? Are there bi-polar semantic differential scales? Sometimes these are hidden within matrix/ grid questions.

- **Carousel scales:** Do you have grid questions? Carousel scales will allow you to use dynamic grid approaches.

- **NPS:** Are there templates for this? This could save you design time.

- **Rating scales:** Can these be slider scales, stars, radio buttons? What choice is there? Whichever you choose, you should be consistent for similar questions.

- **Slider scales:** Can you define where the default opening position is for the cursor? This can introduce significant bias if it is not in a neutral position.

- **Drag-and-drop:** This is often offered as a means of ranking, but can be used in many other ways where items have to be sorted into categories. Does the platform allow you to do that?

Open-ended questions

- **Open-ended or free text questions with single text box:** Check to see if they are limited to the number of characters allowed, or if limited to a single line of text.

- **Multiple text boxes:** Do you want to be able to record the order of responses eg to identify brands most front-of-mind at spontaneous awareness questions? Having a different box for each one means that you don't have to do quite so much disentangling at the analysis stage.

Specialist questions

Is the survey software able to cope with how you want to ask more complex or specialist questions?

- **Matrix/grid questions:** These come in a variety of formats: single answer per row, multiple answers per row, single answer per column, multiple answers per column. You will need to determine exactly how you want to ask this type of question beforehand.

- **Numeric response questions:** When asking 'how many…' in behavioural questions, you may need the granularity that a restricted number of response bands in a single choice question cannot give. This can also be used for some rating questions.

- **Ranking questions:** These can be numeric or drag-and-drop.

- **Conjoint questions:** Some platforms build in a discrete choice conjoint capability. This can be used to assess the importance of different attributes in a product or service when they come bundled together, such as a phone provider (number of free minutes, data allowance, subscriptions to services, monthly cost) or train services (frequency, journey time, reliability, cost). Specialist analysis skills are required.

- **Max Diff:** This is offered by some platforms. The technique enables sets of attributes to be assessed for preference or importance in a user-friendly way. It is a form of conjoint and requires specialist analytic skills.

- **Heat maps and hot spots:** These are some very specific functions but may be what you need.

- **Time taken:** Can they record the time between opening the screen and clicking the response? This can be valuable when measuring stand out of items in a list or in a picture.

- **Text highlighter:** Useful for assessing advertising or other communication material.

- **Video/audio sentiment:** Some platforms have a template for continuously measuring how respondents feel as they watch or listen to a video or audio. This can be used for evaluating the impact of visuals or messages in advertising.

- **Card sort:** Useful if a large number of items (features, brands etc) need to be sorted into groups typically to reduce the consideration set before some other more involved activity (eg important/not important, aware/not aware). You will probably need a paid-for version to do this.

Range of Functions

- **Limits on questions:** Is there a limit to the number of questions? This is more common with free services, but also with some paid ones. Make sure you can complete your questionnaire within that limit.

    Are questions limited to a number of characters? A limit can be good because it makes sure that you keep it short, but it also needs to be adequate for your requirements.

- **Limits on characters:** Does the number of characters vary by the language the questionnaire is written in? Some languages take longer than others to ask the same thing.

- **Limits on response codes:** Are response codes limited to a number of characters? Again, this can be a good discipline to avoid you cluttering the screen with unnecessarily long responses that won't get read. But if the limit is too short, you might not be able to describe a brand name, flavour or variant accurately. Are open-ended questions limited to one line?

- **Routing**: Can you route people to subsequent questions based on their answers – and how complex can this routing be? Can it come from more than one question? Can it cope with syntax? (eg if 'A' and not 'B'?) Can it cope with multiple routings from the same question? (eg to question loops of follow-up questions for each brand used.)

- **Masking and Piping**: This functionality helps to get closer to the feeling that the survey is an intelligent conversation. It can have a marked effect on engagement when implemented well (eg piping through answers from one question so that the wording of another is seamlessly tailored). Is it intelligent enough to cope with any necessary changes in grammar or upper/lower case? Masking can reap benefits in reducing the word load by only showing answers that can be deduced to be relevant based on earlier responses.

- **Rotating and randomizing**: Can you randomize the order of responses and keep 'other answers' and/or 'none of these' at the bottom? If you can't, this can limit your ability to randomize response lists, because you do not want 'none of these' appearing in the middle of the list. Can you randomize the order of questions? Sometimes it is not just individual questions that you need to randomize, but question blocks, so if you need to do that, is that possible? With drop-down response options, can the response categories be rotated or randomized within the drop-down boxes? If you have a series of drop-down boxes with the same response codes, will the order of presentation be consistent for a respondent?

- **Information boxes**: Is there a notes box separate from the question where you can add explanatory material without obscuring the question? Some offer this automatically, some can be found with a bit of work, and some don't offer this at all. The font size may be automatically lower than that of the question which differentiates it from the question. Such boxes can be very useful to provide additional information or explanation of terminology in the question. Can additional information be provided by a box that appears when the item is rolled over or tapped?

- **Media**: Can you add pictures, video or audio to questions? This is important if you want to get reaction to a product or an advertisement. You need to be able to insert this at the relevant question, which may not be the question that the platform provides for this type of material. Can you add pictures/pack shots/logos to response codes? Using logos or pack shots helps to ensure that respondents are thinking about the brand you want them to. Be careful about using them for questions on brand image or communication as they will suggest attributes that they want to be known for. Are there limitations to the size or length of audio or video material? This can be an advantage to stop the screen slowing up but must be adequate for your needs. Can you show pictures or graphics side by side? You may need to do this to ask preference questions.

- **Image clicking**: When you present a set of images, can respondents click on the images to select them, or does it require separate radio buttons to be selected? Clicking on the image reduces the load on the respondent. Does the image change to show that it has been selected, or is there a radio button that automatically fills in image selection? The latter can sometimes be difficult to see, and the respondent is not certain that the image has been selected.

- **File upload**: You might want to ask respondents to upload a file such as a photograph. If you want to do this, is it possible?

- **In-survey calculations**: Is it able to run algorithms in real time within the survey as the basis for routing to subsequent questions? (eg Identifying respondent fit with predetermined segments/typologies from their answers across a range of questions/attitudes and tailoring the presentation of subsequent questions on this basis.)

- **Process**: Can you preview what each question will look like on screen as you write it, or do you need to preview the whole questionnaire each time? For longer questionnaires that can significantly add to the writing time. Can you easily change the order of the questions? It is common to want to move questions after they have been written. You will want to be able to do this easily without having to delete and rewrite. Is it easy to group questions on to the same page or create new pages as required? Filtering or skipping will only work between pages, so if you are filtering respondents between questions you need to think about whether you can group them on to the same page. Is there support for languages that do not read left-to-right? If you are using Arabic languages this will be an issue. Can you import questions and response codes from other questions that you have already written? Having to keep entering the same set of response codes is time-consuming. Does the platform have a bank of predetermined questions that you can take advantage of? It can be time-saving to have someone else already write the question, but make sure that it is exactly what you require. Is there a test function, which estimates the length of time the survey will take, and highlights questions that might be difficult?

- **Engaging with respondents:** Is there a progress bar? Letting respondents know how far they have got is important in keeping them motivated. Can you show results or give feedback to participants? Showing them how they compare with other people can keep them involved. It also gives you the opportunity to create some basic quizzes and games in order to help maintain engagement. Some offer a specific quiz function. Are there standard graphics such as smiley faces, thumbs up/down icons that you can use? What types of questions can you use these on? Does the questionnaire offer click-on maps of countries/continents? A more engaging way of collecting geographic data.

- **Structure:** Can you randomly allocate respondents to different questions or block of questions? This can be used to minimize the length of the survey to individual respondents. Some platforms allow you to set the percentage of respondents that see each block. Others allow more complex allocation (eg switching off blocks when statistical significance of results is achieved).

- **Mobile friendly:** Does it automatically configure for mobile users? If it says it does, check just how good that is. If it is not satisfactory you will lose people taking it on their mobile. Can respondents scan bar codes and/or QR codes? This can be very useful if they are recording what they have bought. Can you ask respondents to time themselves doing a task in their mobile? This could be selecting a product or time taken to find a product on a shelf.

Look and Feel

- **Professional fit:** What impression does it give? Is this acceptable for your purposes? How prominent is the software provider's name or logo on the page? This can sometimes be an issue for users of free software. What flexibility is there within the standard packages? Are a variety of themes offered to enable you to choose the best match for your purposes?

- **Flexibility to customize:** Can you create your own theme? Can you add your logo? Together with creating your own theme, you may want to make sure that the questionnaire meets your corporate design style. This might be especially important if you are sourcing respondents from a high-value or limited customer list and need to carefully consider the impact of the survey interaction on the relationship.

- **Layout**: How flexible is the layout? (eg If you do not want the question or the response codes to appear on screen in the supplier's default position, can you change the page heading between pages – which is useful to indicate the subject matter?) Can radio buttons be customized by size and colour? Can you change font size and/or colour between questions, response codes and other material that appears on screen? If there is a lot of information on the screen this can be a way of differentiating it. Can radio buttons be customized by size and colour?

- **Scrolling**: Do you have to scroll down more than necessary? (eg does inflexibility in line-spacing mean that longer lists require more scrolling effort).

Making the choice

There are more than 50 questions here that you could ask of the questionnaire design software before you make your choice.

How rigorously you evaluate the alternatives will clearly depend on your situation, including the volume and importance of surveys that you need to undertake.

If it is for a one-off survey, first write out and plan your questionnaire so that you can see all of the different types of questions that you will need, the complexity of any routing, and the need to use any media such as images or video.

If it is for a greater volume try and create a list of primary considerations given the subject matter and respondent challenges you are most likely to face.

If you have a preferred or recommended supplier, look at their offer and see if it meets your needs. If there is a free version, or if the supplier allows you to create a questionnaire without payment, you can construct the questionnaire at no cost to see if it works.

CASE STUDY   Whisky usage and attitude

Selecting a survey supplier

We know what questions we want to ask, and now want to see which of the leading suppliers is the best to use in order to give us the questionnaire that we want.

First, we categorize the questions by type to see what range of question type we are going to need:

Table 12.1

Single code	QC, Q9, Q12, Q13, Q14, Q15, Q16, Q18, Q19, Q20, Q25, Q26, Q27, Q28
Multiple responses	QA, QB, Q3, Q4, Q5, Q7, Q17, Q21, Q22
Open-ended with multiple boxes	Q1, Q2
Open-ended	Q6, Q8
Numeric	Q10, Q11
Bi-polar scale	Q23
Grid, multiple responses in rows and columns	Q24

Then we assess other considerations:

Table 12.2

Show image	Q25, Q27 We require to upload passive images to these questions.
Rotate response codes	All multiple response questions response codes should be in randomized order, but with 'other' and 'none of these' anchored at the end where applicable.
Number of response codes	The maximum number of response codes at any one question is 17. A limit of less than that will not be acceptable.

(continued)

Table 12.2 (Continued)

Routing	We require complex routing/filtering between questions.
Look and feel	We want to be able to customize the look and feel to our corporate design guidelines.
Add our logo	As part of the customization we want to show our logo.
Piping	We shall want to only show brands that are heard of at Q3 at later questions.
Preview	Can we preview individual questions or have to work through the whole questionnaire every time?
Progress bar	We want our respondents to know how far through the survey they have got.
Can I move questions easily?	As we write the questionnaire we want the flexibility to easily change the order of the questions.

The next step is for us to assess our preferred suppliers to find out if we are going to be able to write the questionnaire satisfactorily. We choose to look at the three largest suppliers as most of our needs are met by all three. It is clear that we are going to be unable to use a free version because of the limit on the number of questions on all of them.

Table 12.3

Question types	Supplier 1	Supplier 2	Supplier 3
Single code	Yes	Yes	Yes
Multiple responses	Yes	Yes – vertical or horizontal	Yes – vertical or horizontal
Open-ended with multiple boxes	Yes	Yes	Multiple lines are provided, but not multiple boxes.
Open-ended	Yes	Yes	Yes

(continued)

Table 12.3   (Continued)

Question types	Supplier 1	Supplier 2	Supplier 3
Numeric	No, but a numeric scale can be used.	No, but a numeric scale can be used.	No, but a numeric scale can be used.
Bi-polar scale	Yes, but only one line per question.	Yes, with multiple lines on page.	Yes, with multiple lines on page.
Grid, multiple responses in rows and columns	Yes	Yes	Yes
Other Functions			
Show image	Yes	In paid version	Yes
Rotate and randomize response codes	Yes, while keeping last answer in place.	Yes, while keeping selected answers in place. Advanced randomization options available in paid-for.	Yes, with ability to hold selected answers in place and to randomly choose a subset.
Number of available response codes	Unlimited	Unlimited	Unlimited
Routing	Skipping and advanced branching in paid version.	Skipping and complex logic in paid for version.	Skip logic included in free version
Look and feel	Some standard themes in free version. Custom themes and logo in paid for version.	Colouring of standard themes and logo in free version. Custom themes in paid for version.	Limited number of themes in free option. Custom themes in paid for version.

(*continued*)

Table 12.3   (Continued)

Question types	Supplier 1	Supplier 2	Supplier 3
Add our logo	Paid version	Yes	Paid version
Progress bar	Yes	Yes	Yes
Moving the questions	Yes	Yes	Yes
Piping	Paid version	Yes	Yes
Preview	Complete questionnaire	Per question	Per question

Figure 12.1   Different forms of open-ended response entry

Q1 Name up to eight brands of Scotch whisky.

Given our need to show an advertisement as a picture for recognition and brand identification, Supplier 2 would seem to be ruled out. Our choice then is between Supplier 1 and 3.

As we are going to be using a paid version, the differences between them are not significant. Supplier 1 allows individual entry boxes for Q1: 'Name up to eight brands of Scotch whisky.' With Supplier 3, all responses will be collected in one box. The advantages of multiple boxes are:

● They encourage respondents to provide more answers because there is a challenge to complete all the boxes.

- In analysis, we have eight sets of text with each entry differentiated. In the single box the text is one entry, which will need to be disentangled.

Supplier 3 gives a better option for Q23: 'Relatively how important are these to each other when you are choosing a whisky?' With Supplier 1, only one pair of features can be shown on a screen at a time. As this is a repetitive question it requires the respondent to forward to the next screen unnecessarily often. Supplier 3 offers us the possibility of having the whole question on one page, which also allows respondents to see what they have answered for preceding lines, to give more consistency in the answers.

Other factors will undoubtedly come into the decision, such as cost and previous experience, but as questionnaire writers, we must make our choice based on these criteria.

Key take aways: choosing online survey software

- The options you have available as a question writer will vary depending on the survey software you are using.
- The dynamic nature of the market – with new suppliers and new functionality – means possibilities will continue to evolve.
- Evaluate who is the best fit with your needs by creating a checklist that considers:
  o the range of question types that are offered;
  o the functions and controls;
  o the look and feel.
- Balance this scorecard against cost constraints and other associated factors such as analysis capabilities and whether the platform also provides direct access to respondent panels.

Considerations for interviewer-administered and paper self-completion surveys

13

Introduction

Most principles of questionnaire design apply to all modes, however there are some considerations that are mode-specific – particularly regarding layout and instructions. Chapters 10 and 11 dealt with creating online questionnaires. Here we highlight issues that arise with alternative data collection approaches: interviewer administered (face to face or telephone) and those that are self-completed on pen and paper.

Challenges with interviewer-administered surveys

From a questionnaire design perspective, the benefits of interviewer involvement typically arise from the rapport that can be built with the respondent. This rapport helps if the interview involves complex questions, (eg to establish correct understanding), or where open-ended verbatim questions are key (eg to encourage maximum detail and depth). Interviewers can also hold respondents' attention for longer if the survey is face-to-face and conducted in an appropriate environment, ie not on the street nor on the telephone.

However, there are a number of challenges and sources of possible error when an interviewer is involved.

An unusual conversation

Questionnaires are often described as conversations by proxy between the researcher and the respondent. However, it is not the sort of conversation that two people who know each other would have.

With interviewer-administered surveys it is not unusual for respondents to try to enter into conversation with the interviewer, to give their views and elaborate on their responses. Only when the interviewer insists on reducing this answer to one of the pre-codes on the questionnaire does the respondent appreciate that this is not really a conversation but an interaction in which they have a specific and limited role to play (Suchman and Jordan, 1990).

The lack of conversation can mask incorrect answers. Through elaboration of answers such as 'yes, but...' or 'I agree, except that...' it can become clear that the true answer is 'no' or 'I disagree'. If respondents are not allowed to elaborate in this way, their true answer may not become apparent, and an incorrect answer may be recorded. With self-completion surveys we rely on respondents to think it through, to in effect elaborate to themselves, and not necessarily give their first reaction. Thus, while we conceptualize the questionnaire as the medium of conversation, we must recognize that it is not a true conversation. This may mean that we do not acquire all of the information that respondents could give us; and that it can, on occasion, lead to incorrect answers being recorded.

To write better questions for interviewer administered surveys it is important to more fully understand the problems that we touched on in Chapter 2 relating to the interviewer's role.

Questions asked inaccurately by the interviewer

It is not uncommon to hear an interviewer paraphrase a question. This may be done because:

- The interviewer finds the wording stilted. However natural it appears on the page, when spoken aloud it can sound awkward. Interviewers will paraphrase to make it flow better.
- The interviewer may think that the question is too long. One of their aims is to maintain the attention of the respondent and a long, detailed question with several sub-clauses detracts from that.

- The interviewer may think it is repetitive, either through repetition within the question; or repeating instructions or descriptions given in a preceding question; or they may think that the question has already been asked. To keep the respondent engaged they may omit the elements they see as repetitive.

- They may not understand the question or feel that the respondent is unlikely to. With business-to-business interviews, there may be terminology that is completely new to the interviewer who then mispronounces key words or possibly substitutes them for other, more familiar, words. A thorough briefing of the interviewers in the technical terms used and the provision of a glossary of terms that are likely to be used by respondents is worthwhile here. This glossary may also be of value to coders and analysts in later stages of the survey process. With consumer interviews, overuse of marketing jargon can have the same result.

However it is paraphrased, it is likely that some aspects of the question change, and the response will be different to the one that would have been obtained from the original question. Good interviewer training will instil into the interviewer that the wording on the questionnaire is to be kept to. If the interviewer still feels the need to alter the wording, then it is a sign of a poorly written question.

Failure of the interviewer to record the reply accurately or completely

Interviewers record responses inaccurately in many ways. They may simply mishear the response. This is particularly likely where there are complex routing instructions on surveys that use a paper, rather than scripted CAPI or CATI, questionnaire. The interviewer's attention may be divided between listening to the respondent's answer and determining which question should be asked next.

With open-ended (verbatim) questions, interviewers may not record everything that is said. There is a temptation to précis the response, to keep the interview flowing and to not make the respondent wait while the full response is recorded.

If a list of pre-codes has been provided for the interviewer as possible answers to open questions (eg spontaneous awareness or spontaneous reasons for purchase), interviewers must scan the list and code the answer that most closely matches the response given. This is open to error. None of the answers may match exactly what the respondent has said. The interviewer then has the choice of taking the one that is closest to the given response or writing it in verbatim if space for 'other' has been allowed. However, there is a strong temptation to make the given response match one of the pre-coded answers, thus inaccurately recording the true response.

Mistakes made by the interviewer because of boredom and fatigue

An interview that is tedious for the respondent is also tedious for the interviewer. This can be made worse for the interviewer by the embarrassment felt in boring the respondent. The interviewer responds by reading the questions more quickly, leading to an increase in the number of errors of misunderstanding as well as recording errors on the part of the interviewer.

Interviewer-administered CAPI or CATI questionnaires

If the survey is using scripting software (ie Computer Aided Personal Interviewing (CAPI) or Computer Aided Telephone interviewing (CATI)) then many of the considerations for managing order and flow through the interview are similar to online. For example, question order can be rotated or randomized, as can response codes; answers from one question can be piped into the questionnaire or response codes of a later one; calculations and checks can be carried out in real time; and complex routing can be included. However, there are some additional considerations when a scripted survey involves an interviewer.

Look and feel

The first difference between online and interviewer administered electronic questionnaires is that online the priority is for it to be visually attractive, easy to read and clear of clutter. However, the emphasis for an interviewer-administered questionnaire is to be efficient and functional for the interviewer. The interviewer will have been trained to expect certain formats and to use certain conventions, and the screen layout needs first and foremost to follow these.

Pleasantries

The main wording differences between online and interviewer-administered questionnaires stem from the fact that the questions are spoken aloud rather than simply read. Here it is important that the interviewer builds up a rapport with the respondent, to relax them, to get the maximum cooperation from them, and, if necessary, keep them going to the end. The pleasantries and courtesies of conversation play a big part in question wording. We want to include phrases such as 'please can you tell me…' which online would be considered screen clutter.

Pleasantries can also help in getting the respondent attuned to the interviewer's voice before the key words of the question arrive. A baldly stated question such as 'what brands can you name?' not only sounds abrupt and likely to alienate the respondent, but the suddenness of the question means that it may not be heard properly.

Pre-coded responses

The respondent does not see the questionnaire, so the questionnaire writer has the option to pre-code likely responses for open questions avoiding the need for coding later. As the interviewer's task is to match the verbatim response given to one of the pre-codes supplied there is a reliance on them to interpret that correctly. The questionnaire writer must help them navigate this task by providing comprehensive pre-codes with the desired level of discrimination between them – listed in a helpful order. If two pre-codes are quite similar, they should be next to each other so the interviewer is encouraged to discriminate. If they had been randomized then error could creep in as interviewers are likely to scan the list and stop at the first one of the pair on the basis that it is 'near enough'.

Usually, lists of brand names or simple categories would be given in alphabetical order. However, sometimes it is preferable to group them by categories or sub-categories if that makes it quicker for the interviewer to find them.

Note in Figure 13.1 the inclusion of an 'other answer' code, together with an instruction that the interviewer should type in what that 'other' is. It is rare that the questionnaire writer can assume that all possible responses have been thought of and included in the pre-coded list. It is therefore generally prudent to allow for other answers to be given and recorded.

Figure 13.1   Inclusion of an 'other answer' code

Q12. What was the main method of transport you used to get here today?

BICYCLE	1
BUS	2
CAR	3
MOTORCYCLE	4
TRAIN	5
WALKED	6
OTHER ANSWER (WRITE IN)	7

Additional instructions

The respondent does not see the screen from which the interviewer is reading, so the screen can contain additional information to help the interview or to clarify responses. For example, if the question 'why did you choose that store?' receives the answer 'because it is convenient', the interviewer can be instructed to probe as to exactly what the respondent means by 'convenient'.

Prompt material

With face-to-face interviews, the question writer has the options of showing it physically (eg prompt codes on a card, printed text or pictorial material such as ads) or of showing it on screen to the respondent. The latter is often the simpler, but care must be taken that there is nothing else on the screen that might bias their response, such as interviewer instruction or a list of pre-codes.

With telephone interviews this is more problematic: response codes must be read out, and other material can only be shown by sending it in advance or asking the respondent to log on to a website where it is displayed. The questionnaire writer therefore needs to think carefully about whether and how any material is to be displayed. This can be a particular issue with business-to-business research where telephone interviewing is the most feasible medium. Here, though, you often have a better chance of the respondent being in front of a computer so they can log on to your website. It may be possible to get the respondent to then complete the questionnaire online.

Self-completion sections

For attitude questions, or for sensitive questions, the computer can be handed over to the respondent to self-complete the section. This can be especially useful where there is an expectation of socially desirable responding (see Chapter 16) or where there is a concern that the respondent may not be honest if other people, such as family members, can hear their responses.

> With CAPI questionnaires, the layout is designed for the interviewer's needs, not those of the respondent.

Interviewer-administered paper questionnaires

If a paper questionnaire is being used, there is a lot more for the questionnaire to take into account than with CAPI or CATI questionnaires. There is now a concern with the layout, which must allow the interviewer to follow the questionnaire sequence easily, and accurately record the answers. This is the case for both face-to-face and telephone interviews. If the layout causes the interviewer difficulty, the flow of the interview can be lost, together with the interest and attention of the respondent.

Most research companies adopt a set of conventions and standardized templates for questionnaire layout that are designed to help the interviewer.

Font size and formats

It may be tempting to use a small font size to fit more questions on to each page, particularly with interviews that are relatively long, but a crowded layout may just lead to interviewer error.

Bold and italic formats can be used to draw attention to instructions and key points, or to emphasize particular words in a question.

It is important that formatting is used consistently so that interviewers can distinguish clearly between instructions and what is to be read out. Most companies adopt the convention of upper case for instructions and lower case for items in the questionnaire that should be read out.

This upper- and lower-case convention is often extended to the responses to pre-coded questions, which are given in upper case if they are not to be read out and lower case if they are meant to be. Other agencies use lower case for all pre-coded responses. The former approach may distinguish better between what is and is not meant to be read out – thus helping to avoid unintended prompting. The latter may be easier and therefore faster for the interviewer to read and to code – thus helping to maintain the flow of the interview.

A question should never be allowed to go over two pages. This is likely to lead to errors as the interviewers turn the pages backwards and forwards trying to match the respondents' answers to the given pre-codes.

Single and multiple responses

Frequently, it is clear from the question whether the anticipated response is a single answer or whether each respondent could give more than one. In the question about how the respondent travelled (Figure 13.1), the use of the term 'main method of transport' indicated to both respondent and interviewer that only one answer was expected.

Had the question been asked as in Figure 13.2, more than one answer would have been possible. Wherever there is any possibility of ambiguity as to whether only one response or more than one is permissible, an instruction to the interviewer should be used to make it clear what is expected.

Figure 13.2   Possibility of multiple responses

Q12. Which method or methods of transport did you use to get here today? RECORD ALL THAT APPLY.

BICYCLE	1
BUS	2
CAR	3
MOTORCYCLE	4
TRAIN	5
TRAM	6
WALKED	7
OTHER ANSWER (WRITE IN)	8

Common pre-code lists

Successive questions frequently use the same list of pre-codes. When that occurs a single set of responses can be used with the codes for each question next to each other, as in Figure 13.3. This arrangement saves space on the questionnaire, but also allows the interviewer to see what was coded for the first question and to ensure that the same answer is not coded for the second one. If the survey had been scripted this could have been programmed as an edit. Note the inclusion of a 'no others' response category for the second question.

Figure 13.3   Common pre-code list

	Q12 MAIN METHOD	Q13 OTHER METHODS
Q12. What was the main method of transport you used to get here today? SINGLE CODE ONLY.		
Q13. And what other methods of transport did you use, if any? MULTIPLE CODES ALLOWED.		
BICYCLE	1	1
BUS	2	2
CAR	3	3
MOTORCYCLE	4	4
TRAIN	5	5
TRAM	6	6
WALKED	7	7
OTHER ANSWER (WRITE IN)	8	8
NO OTHERS	–	9

Open-ended questions

Open-ended questions should be laid out with sufficient space for full responses to be written in. Interviewers will often stop probing once they have filled the space available to record the answer. More space can mean fuller responses.

'Don't know' responses

The example of the method of transport used does not include a 'don't know' category in the list of possible responses. In this instance that is justified because respondents are being interviewed shortly after arriving at the place of interview and it is reasonable to assume that they will remember how they travelled there.

However, had the question been about which brands of grocery products they had bought most recently, a 'don't know/can't remember' category should have been included. It is not reasonable to assume that everybody will remember an event that may have taken place some time ago, particularly if it is an event that they see as being of little importance. (There is a fuller discussion of this in Chapter 4.)

'Not answered' codes

Some researchers argue that every question should include a 'not answered' pre-code, so that, should it not be answered for any reason, there is a record that it has been asked. The argument against this is that having such a code could encourage interviewers to accept a refusal to reply too easily.

Occasionally respondents will refuse to answer or are unable to answer a question. If this occurs, it is most likely to be because the question is sensitive in some way or because the response options are inadequate for the answer they wish to give. An example of the latter might be that the question asks for a single response but the answer given is a genuine multiple response. If the question asks which brand was most recently bought, but two different brands were bought at the same time, the interviewer or respondent may consider a multiple response as being contrary to instructions, leaving the question unanswered or coded 'don't know'.

Where questions go unanswered, it is generally a shortcoming on the part of the questionnaire writer. Sensitive questions should be recognized as such and a 'refused' category included on the list of pre-codes.

Show cards

Show cards are commonly used to prompt respondents with lists of possible responses. These can be lists of brands, time periods, behaviours, activities or attitude scales. It is important in face-to-face interviews that interviewers show the correct card at the correct time – so clear instructions and labelling of cards are needed.

Sometimes the questionnaire writer wants to ensure that the card is removed from the respondent's sight before subsequent questions are asked. This may occur when the card contains the description of a new product concept or an advertising idea, and the researcher wants to establish which parts of it have stuck in the respondent's mind.

Read-outs

Where an interviewer is to read out a number of response options, this should be clearly indicated as an instruction at the appropriate place.

Reading out is frequently used where respondents are asked to react to a list of attributes by associating them with brands, or to a list of attitude dimensions to which they indicate strength of agreement. The questionnaire writer should instruct interviewers as to whether or not the question should be repeated between each attribute or statement being read out. The initial question might be: 'Which of these brands do you think is...? [READ OUT]' If the questionnaire writer intends that it should be read out before each phrase, then this should be made clear.

Battery rotations

It is unlikely to be possible to print different versions covering every unique rotation so an alternative, which is usually acceptable, is to have a limited number of start points, and to print a reduced number of versions corresponding to these. Thus, if there are 30 statements, six different start points can be used, spread throughout the battery. The statements are still reasonably well rotated, with only six versions of the page to be printed.

A less robust option is to ask each interviewer to tick at random a start point in the list for each respondent. They would typically be instructed to mark-up the questionnaires before they set out interviewing. It is important that every interviewer understands the process of rotating start points. In particular, interviewers must understand that every statement must be read out. It has been known for interviewers to read out only the statements from the designated start point to the end of the battery, and not to return to the beginning of the battery for the remaining statements. This is more likely to occur where the battery is on more than one page and the start point is not on the first page.

Grids

A commonly used format is to have a number of brands across the top of the grid, which appear on a card shown to the respondent, and a list of attributes down the side of the grid that the interviewers read out. It can be difficult for interviewers to read across a large grid, and they may miscode an answer on to the wrong line, particularly when standing on a doorstep or in a shopping centre. Sight lines going across the page and shading of alternate lines are simple but effective ways of helping interviewers to avoid this type of error.

Routing

Clarity of routing is one of the key challenges for an interviewer-administered paper questionnaire. If interviewers get lost in deciding which questions they should or should not be asking, the credibility of the survey is damaged in the eyes of the respondent and it is almost certain that questions will not be asked that should have been, so data will be lost.

Where routing is dependent on the responses given to a question, the number of the subsequent question to be asked should be indicated alongside. In Figure 13.4, respondents who answered 'car' at Q12 are routed to Q13, whereas all others are routed to Q14. The heading at Q13 confirms to interviewers that this is the correct question to be asked of people who travelled mainly by car, and the heading at Q14 confirms that everybody should be asked this question.

Figure 13.4   Routing in a questionnaire

Q12. What was the main method of transport you used to get here today?

BICYCLE	1	
BUS	2	Q14
CAR	3	Q13
MOTORCYCLE	4	
TRAIN	5	
WALKED	6	
OTHER ANSWER (WRITE IN)	7	
_____		Q14

Q13. ALL WHO TRAVELLED MAINLY BY CAR.
    Were you the driver of the car or a passenger?

DRIVER	1	
PASSENGER	2	Q14

Q14. ASK ALL.
    Will you mainly use the same method of transport for your return journey?

YES – USE SAME METHOD	1	
NO – WILL USE DIFFERENT METHOD	2	
DON'T KNOW/NOT DECIDED	3	Q15

Occasionally routing can become very complex with respondents coming to a question from a variety of routes or with routes that depend upon the responses to more than one question. In these circumstances the questionnaire writer should consider including the same question more than once in the questionnaire if doing so makes it less likely that routing errors will be made.

Thanking and classification questions

Interviewers rarely need reminding to thank respondents for their time and cooperation, especially if they have built up a rapport with them. However, it is good practice to include a line on the questionnaire thanking respondents for their time.

Some research companies record all classification details on the front page of the questionnaire even though they may not be established until the end of the interview. This is to facilitate the checking of quota controls and demographic details when the questionnaire is returned to the office. If this is the case, it is prudent to include a reminder at the end of the questionnaire for the interviewer to return to the front page and complete the classification questions.

Administrative information

Each questionnaire will require a unique identifier or serial number so as to be able to distinguish between respondents. Interviewer-administered questionnaires should also include an interviewer identification code. Interviews can then be analyzed by interviewer to determine any between-interviewer effects, or to identify interviewers who may have made errors in their interviews. If there is more than one version of the questionnaire, the different versions will also usually need to be identified for analysis purposes.

Data entry

The format and layout for data entry will depend on the way in which the data is to be entered and the program that will be used to analyze them.

If data is to be scanned in, using optical mark reading, there will be specific instructions on the layout, depending on the type of scanning equipment used. This usually involves having fixed points on each page from which the position of the marks made by the interviewer or respondent is measured. In Figures 13.5 and 13.6 the fixed marks are the diamonds in the four corners of the page. Note that the job identification and page numbers must also be included on each page to identify the scanned data correctly.

Figure 13.5   Questionnaire for scanning (1)

J.012345

Q11. You said that you had switched energy company recently. Which energy supply did you switch to Powerplus?

Both gas and ☐   Gas only   ☐   Electricity only   ☐
electricity

Q12. Why have you decided to switch to Powerplus?

Tick one main reason in the first column and any other reasons in the second.

	Main	Other
To have both gas and electricity supplied by one company	☐	☐
They said they could offer lower prices	☐	☐
No standing charge	☐	☐
Moved house	☐	☐
They offered me internet account management	☐	☐
I was unhappy with the customer service at the previous company	☐	☐
I did not receive bills in a timely manner before	☐	☐
I was unhappy with the accuracy of my bills	☐	☐
Bills were not easy to understand before	☐	☐
Too many estimated meter readings	☐	☐
Inaccurate estimated meter readings	☐	☐
They offered me green energy	☐	☐
Other (tick box and write in space below)	☐	☐

Q13. If Powerplus said they could offer lower prices, what were the approximate savings per year you expected?

Up to £20 per year   ☐

£21 to £40 per year   ☐

£41 to £60 per year   ☐

£61 to £80 per year   ☐

£81 to £100 per year   ☐

More than £100 per year ☐

Not sure   ☐

Q14. Which supplier were you with before?

Powergen   ☐

British Gas   ☐

EDF Energy   ☐

Npower   ☐

TXU Energi   ☐

Scottish Power   ☐

Other   ☐

03

Figure 13.6   Questionnaire for scanning (2)

J.012345

(OFFICE USE ONLY)   SERIAL NO

Dear Research Club Member

Thank you for taking the time to complete this questionnaire. Please answer all the questions by putting a cross ☒ in the appropriate box or by writing in the boxes provided.

Q1.   Are you male or female?

PLEASE GIVE ONE ANSWER ONLY

Male . . . . ☐

Female . . . . ☐

Q2.   Into which of the following groups does your age fall?

PLEASE GIVE ONE ANSWER ONLY

18–25 . . . . ☐

26–29 . . . . ☐

30–34 . . . . ☐

35–39 . . . . ☐

40–44 . . . . ☐

45–49 . . . . ☐

50–54 . . . . ☐

55–59 . . . . ☐

60–65 . . . . ☐

Over 65 . . . . ☐

Q3.   How many times a week do you brush your teeth, if at all?

PLEASE WRITE IN BOXES – USE LEADING ZERO IF NECESSARY

Q4.   What is your regular brand of toothpaste, the one you use more than any other brand nowadays?

PLEASE WRITE IN BOXES – USE 3-DIGIT CODE FROM OVERLEAF

Q5.   Would you be willing to take part in surveys where we send you a tube of toothpaste to try?

PLEASE GIVE ONE ANSWER ONLY

Yes . . . . ☐

No . . . . ☐

Q6.   If you are not the Research Club member to whom this questionnaire was addressed, please write in your name here. Otherwise leave this blank.

| First Name | | | | | | | | | | | | | | | | | |
| Surname | | | | | | | | | | | | | | | | | |

THANK YOU FOR COMPLETING THIS QUESTIONNAIRE.

PLEASE NOW RETURN IT TO US USING THE REPLY-PAID ENVELOPE PROVIDED

01

Telephone interviews

An additional challenge for interviewer-administered surveys conducted on the phone is posed by the lack of eye contact and the respondents' inability to see what the interviewer is doing. If the interviewer falls silent, the respondent is not to know this is because the interviewer is trying to make sense of complex instructions or trying to navigate poorly organized lists of pre-codes. This puts extra pressure on the questionnaire writer to ensure that the survey is as user friendly for the interviewer as possible otherwise rapport will soon be lost. Since all questions need to be read out, this typically means that the interviewer talks for 70–80% of the time. Anything that can be done to create a more even balance is helpful (eg making sure that there are some open verbatim questions where the emphasis is on the respondent talking).

The respondent's short-term memory also has limits. Keep any itemized scales short – or use a numeric scale instead where only the end points are labelled. If they need to remember a specific set of brands for a brand association question, ask them to write them down – and get them to read them back to you before asking the question so you can be sure they haven't missed out any.

Self-completion paper questionnaire

Much of the success of a paper-based self-completion survey depends on the appearance of the questionnaire and the ease with which respondents can use it. An unattractive questionnaire that is difficult to follow will reduce the response rate, and suggests to the respondents that you don't really care about the project, so why should they?

Making it attractive

There are many ideas about how to make a questionnaire attractive to potential respondents. However, it is almost certainly true that time, effort and money spent on improving the appearance are rarely wasted.

The paper should always be of sufficient quality that the printing on one side cannot be seen from the other side. Using different colours in the printing can increase the attractiveness if used sparingly. Colour can be used to distinguish instructions from questions, or to provide borders to questions. Coloured paper, though, should be used with care. Avoid darker colours and gloss-finish paper, either of which makes the print difficult to read or write on.

If the budget allows, the questionnaire may be presented in the form of a booklet. This looks more professional and is easier for respondents to follow. With a questionnaire printed on both sides of the paper and stapled in one corner it is easy for respondents to miss the reverse pages, and it is possible that some later pages will become detached or inadvertently torn off.

To help make the respondents feel that the survey is worthwhile, the study should have a title, clearly displayed on the front page of the questionnaire, together with the name of the organization conducting it and the return address. Even if a return envelope is provided, it may get mislaid by respondents.

Use of space

Little is more daunting for potential respondents than to be confronted with pages crammed full of print that they must struggle to find their way through, in the same way that a cluttered screen is daunting in an online interview. Lay the questions out sparingly.

Dividing the questions into sections with a clear heading to each section helps respondents understand the flow of the questionnaire and focuses their attention on the topic of each section. It also helps give them a small sense of achievement when a section is completed, particularly if the questionnaire is long. Vertical listing of responses should be used in preference to horizontal listing, as this is often easier to follow and creates a more open appearance. However, it does require more space.

Figures 13.7 and 13.8 show the same questions with responses listed horizontally and vertically, respectively.

Figure 13.7   Horizontal listing

Q8. Do you think the property will require any of the following repairs or improvements in the next five years?

Please tick all that apply.

Additional ☐   Improved ☐   Rewiring ☐   Damp- ☐   Roof ☐   Window ☐
security   heating   proofing   repairs   repairs

Q9. Do you intend to carry out any of the following repairs or improvements in the next five years?

Additional ☐   Improved ☐   Rewiring ☐   Damp- ☐   Roof ☐   Window ☐
security   heating   proofing   repairs   repairs

Figure 13.8   Vertical listing

Q8. Do you think the property will require any of the following repairs or improvements in the next five years?

Please tick below all that apply.

Q9. Do you intend to carry out any of the following repairs or improvements in the next five years?

	Q8	Q9
Additional security	☐	☐
Improved heating	☐	☐
Rewiring	☐	☐
Damp-proofing	☐	☐
Roof repairs	☐	☐
Window repairs	☐	☐

Never allow questions to go over two pages, or over two columns if the page is laid out in columns. If a response list continues on another page, it may not be seen. Avoid, if possible, a short question being placed at the bottom of a page, preceded by a question with a large response grid. The short question is likely to be overlooked.

In Figure 13.8 the response codes are evenly spaced vertically. If, however, one of the response codes had been so long that it had had to go on two lines, this would have resulted in uneven spaces between the boxes as shown in Figure 13.9.

It has been shown by Christian and Dillman (2004) that uneven spacing of the category responses can significantly bias the response to the category that is visually isolated. This effect is likely to be greater for attitudinal questions than for behavioural questions, or where there is an ordinal scale. However, for all questions it is good practice to avoid the possibility of this bias by ensuring that the response boxes are equally spaced, as in Figure 13.10.

Open-ended questions

Open-ended questions can be a deterrent to respondents as they require more effort. If the level of interest is low, then open-ended questions tend to be at best poorly completed and at worst can damage the response rate. Avoid starting the interview with an open-ended question. If possible, keep open-ended questions until the latter part of the interview. The questionnaire can be read through before being completed, so the respondents must be

Figure 13.9 Question with uneven spacing between response boxes

Q8. Do you think that the property will require any of the following repairs or improvements in the next five years?

Replacement of central
heating including boiler ☐

Electrical rewiring ☐

Brickwork repointing ☐

Renewal of roof ☐

New window frames ☐

Additional security ☐

None of these ☐

Figure 13.10 Question with response boxes evenly spaced

Q8. Do you think that the property will require any of the following repairs or improvements in the next five years?

Replacement of central
heating including boiler ☐

Electrical rewiring ☐

Brickwork repointing ☐

Renewal of roof ☐

New window frames ☐

Additional security ☐

None of these ☐

assumed to be prompted by any information that is on the questionnaire. There is thus no issue of having to ask an open-ended question before one that shows pre-codes that might prompt the open responses, as long as this likelihood is remembered when interpreting the data.

As with interviewer-administered questionnaires, the more space that can be left for respondents to write in, the fuller the response they are likely to give.

> Spend time on making the questionnaire look attractive. It will be repaid in improved response rates.

Routing instructions

Routing should be kept to a minimum. Where they are necessary, routing instructions must be clear and unambiguous. If the questions can be ordered so that any routing only takes respondents either to the following question or to the next section – both of which are easy to find – errors of omission are more likely to be avoided.

The routing instruction (which tells them where they should skip to) should be placed after the response codes of the branching question. This makes it less likely that respondents will read the routing instruction before answering. It has been shown by Christian and Dillman (2004) that placing the routing instruction before the response codes (as in Version 1 in Figure 13.11) can

Figure 13.11   Location of routing instruction

Version 1	Version 2
Q1. Have you visited the cinema at all in the last seven days?	Q1. Have you visited the cinema at all in the last seven days?
If you have not visited the cinema, skip to Q5.	Yes ☐
	No ☐
Yes ☐	
No ☐	If you have not visited the cinema, skip to Q5.

(Adapted from Christian and Dillman, 2004)

increase the number of non-responses to the question, probably because respondents believe that if they meet the branching criterion, they should skip directly to the later question without having to answer this one. When the instruction follows the response codes (Version 2), nearly all respondents complete the question before moving on to the next one.

Covering letter

When the questionnaire is to be completed unsupervised or if it is a postal or mail survey, a covering letter and instructions will be required. The covering letter may be printed on the front page of the questionnaire if the layout allows sufficient space. There is then no danger of it becoming separated from the questionnaire. This also simplifies the production process if you wish to print a respondent identifier (eg customer type) on the questionnaire, as this can be printed on to the latter page, avoiding the need to match the letter to the questionnaire when mailing out.

Data entry

With a paper questionnaire, data entry will be required. Data entry instructions and codes should be kept as unobtrusive as possible. Where numeric codes are used to identify the responses, there is a danger of suggesting to respondents that there is a hierarchy of responses, which have been numbered from one onwards. For this reason, circling of codes – in the way that is often used with interviewer-administered questionnaires – should be avoided. Ticking or checking boxes should always be preferred to avoid any such bias, and response codes should be kept as small as is possible while still compatible with accurate data entry.

Where data is read by optical scanning, data entry codes can often be completely removed or confined to the margins of the questionnaire. This has the benefit of removing some of the visual clutter from the page, making it more attractive to the respondent. It also removes any concerns that the responses may be biased by the data entry number codes.

CASE STUDY   Whisky usage and attitude

Interviewer-administered questionnaires

Our whisky usage and attitude survey is going to be conducted online, so here we shall look at how it would have been different had we decided instead to use an interviewer-administered face-to-face survey using CAPI. (We can rule out using a telephone survey because of the need to show advertisements as prompts.)

Tone

The main difference will be one of tone. What we want to know from each respondent remains the same, but the way in which we ask it will change in many instances. The tone will change from the efficient tone of the online questionnaire, where we seek to minimize the number of words in a question and the amount of clutter on screen, to one that helps the interviewer to build a relationship or rapport with the respondent. Pleasantries and explanations now play a big part in achieving that.

Table 13.1 shows some of the changes that would be made to make it suitable for a face-to-face interview.

Notice that all of these questions are longer. This is partly because of the increase in the instructions that the interviewer has to provide, given that the respondent can see nothing except the occasional card with a list of brands on. This also helps the interviewer to build up a rapport with the respondent.

Table 13.1

Question	Face-to-face question
Q1 Can you name eight brands of Scotch whisky?	Which brands of Scotch whisky have you heard of?
Q3 Which of these brands of Scotch whisky have you heard of?	Which of the brands of Scotch whisky on this card have you heard of? Please include any you have already mentioned.
Q4 Which of these brands of Scotch whisky have you seen or heard advertising for recently?	Which of the brands of Scotch whisky on this card have you seen or heard any advertising for recently? Please include any you have already mentioned.

(continued)

Table 13.1 (Continued)

Question	Face-to-face question
Q6 What do you remember about the Crianlarich ad? [WRITE IN]	Please describe to me everything that you can remember about the advertising for Crianlarich. [PROBE] What was it about? What did it say or show? [PROBE] What else?
Q9 Do you drink Scotch whisky on licensed premises, or at home, or both?	Do you drink whisky only on licensed premises such as a restaurant, pub or bar; or only at home or at someone else's home; or do you drink it both on licensed premises and at home?
Q23 For each pair of attributes, move the slider to show which is the more important to you when choosing a whisky.	I am now going to read out a number of pairs of phrases that describe some of the things that you might take into account when choosing a brand of Scotch whisky. For each pair, I would like you to please tell me which is the more important by allocating eleven points between them. If one was a lot more important than other you might give it all eleven points. If they are about equal you would give them nearly equal numbers of points.
Q24 Which brand or brands do you associate with each of these statements?	I am now going to read out a number of words and phrases that have been used to describe brands of Scotch whisky. For each one I would like you to tell me to which of the brands on this card you think it applies to. There are no right or wrong answers and each phrase could apply to all of them, none of them or any number of them.
Q25 [SHOW UNBRANDED CRIANLARICH AD] Have you seen this ad before?	Here is an advertisement for Scotch whisky. Have you seen this before?

Q23 and Q24 could be done as self-completion, with the interviewer handing the CAPI machine over to the respondent. This would more closely correspond to the online questionnaire but would still require some explanation from the interviewer.

Note how Q25 describes what is being shown as an advertisement to allow the respondent to understand what it is before being asked the question. Online, that is taken to be apparent.

Key take aways: considerations for interviewer-administered and paper self-completion surveys

- Having an interviewer involved can create greater rapport and engagement, so help the interviewer to focus on achieving this rather than on navigating your questionnaire.
- Interviewers make mistakes too – and speed up if the survey is long and dull. Ensure:
  - Clear routing (vital if the survey is on paper and not scripted).
  - Well-organized lists that are easy to navigate, especially at spontaneous questions using pre-codes that only the interviewer can see (a particularly common format in a telephone interview).
  - Questions that sound natural and polite when read out.
  - More pleasantries and slightly wordier questions than online self-completion.
- Paper self-completion surveys must look good: professional, uncluttered and with simple navigation.

Piloting your questionnaire

14

Introduction

In creating the questionnaire, the researcher has been considering what could go wrong and taking steps to try to ensure that each question – and the questionnaire overall – will deliver useful and good quality information. In the process of doing this they will have become very familiar with the questionnaire. While an experienced questionnaire writer should still be able to review the questionnaire objectively, they will be too close to it to fully appreciate its impact on a respondent who will be experiencing it for the first time.

Unfortunately, it is very common for insufficient piloting time to be built into the project schedule. This stage in the process is often seen as expendable in the light of the pressure for information to be delivered as fast as possible, but some kind of pilot testing is always advisable.

Why pilot questionnaires?

The aim of a pilot is, at minimum, to catch accidental errors including any arising during the production of the actual document or script (eg routing errors, missing instructions or technological issues).

A pilot also aims to investigate whether our questionnaire is delivering information that is both valid and reliable. Validity refers primarily to our confidence that we really are measuring what we want to measure. This includes confidence that our questionnaire will provide the type of information needed to answer our objectives. It also refers to our confidence in the likely accuracy of the data. Will all respondents understand the questions in the same way? Are they able to answer with the level of detail we want? Are they willing and able to answer our questions truthfully?

Reliability refers to confidence that, if we asked the same questions of those respondents again (assuming we could wipe their memory of their previous answers) they would give the same answer. Direct testing for reliability is clearly very difficult. If we attempted to administer the same questionnaire to the same sample of respondents again to test for consistency, it is likely that their answers will be affected by their memory of the first time. The length of time required for them to forget the first experience would likely be quite long, and much else may have changed in the intervening period that could lead to true differences in their answers. In practical terms, therefore, investigations of reliability centre on establishing that the respondent is able to answer accurately in the first place – in effect overlapping with our investigation of validity.

Investigating influences on reliability and validity

A pilot could investigate a range of aspects to build confidence in a questionnaire's validity and reliability and highlight where changes are needed:

- Do the respondents read and understand the questions? How successful have we been in designing a question short enough to be read yet precise enough to be interpreted unambiguously?

- Is the language as natural and simple as possible? Do any words or terms confuse?

- Can respondents answer the questions? In that level of detail? Over that time period? Are any generalizations we are asking them to make manageable? Or is the answer too often 'it depends'?

- Does the interview flow well? Does it help the respondent to think? (eg unfolding in a way that makes sense to them, following their natural thought processes?)

- How is the question order influencing respondents' thinking? Inevitably, every question risks changing the way they think, and compromises in ideal order will be necessary. Can the impact be reduced, for example, by randomizing questions or sections?

- How well does it control the respondent's frame of reference in moving from one question to another? Is it clear when the context has changed? (eg when questions switch from asking about 'buying' to 'eating'?)

- Are any important response options missing in answer lists? Are answers being forced to fit into the codes provided? Is 'other' frequently used? A respondent to the question in Figure 14.1 may have travelled by tram. Omitting this from the response options may have been an oversight if the researcher was unaware that the tram was an option, or maybe they assumed respondents would include trams with buses. Reviewing these 'others' will highlight important amendments to the response list.

- Do the response codes provide sufficient discrimination? If most respondents give the same answer, then the pre-codes may need to be reviewed to see how discrimination can be improved, and if that cannot be achieved, is there still value in including the question?

- Does the questionnaire retain the attention and interest of respondents throughout? Can we identify points at which motivation dips? Maybe an intervention such as a change in question format might help?

- Does all of this vary by the type of device being used by respondents? If there is any evidence that those using a mobile phone give different responses from someone using a desktop, this may highlight the need for layout or question format changes to ensure presentation of the question and answers is comparable.

- Can the respondents (or interviewers) understand any routing instructions in the questionnaire? This is particularly important if the survey is on paper or if the digital scripting software does not have the capability for automatic routing.

- Do the questions sound right if read out by an interviewer? It is surprising how often a question looks acceptable when written on paper but sounds over formal or simply odd when read out. It can be a salutary experience for questionnaire writers to conduct interviews themselves and realize how often they want to paraphrase a question to make it sound more natural.

- Do the interviewers understand the question? If they cannot understand it there is little chance that respondents will.

Spotting errors and practical implementation issues

- Have mistakes been made? It is often the small errors that go unnoticed, but that can have a dramatic effect: visual inconsistencies that draw the eye, some list items in bold or much longer than others, key brands mistakenly left off a list or misspelled etc.

Figure 14.1 Spotting a missing code

What was the main method of transport you used to get here today?

Bicycle O
Bus O
Car O
Motorcycle O
Train O
Walked O
Other answer (enter)

[   ] O

- Does the routing work? Although this should have been comprehensively checked, illogical routing sequences sometimes only become apparent with live interviews.

- Does the technology work? Perhaps a new interactive element is being used. It may work perfectly well in the office, but does it work across the variety of devices, browsers and operating systems that the respondents have?

- How long does it take to complete the interview? The respondents will have been told an amount of time in the introduction; if it exceeds this the goodwill of the respondents may be lost at a risk to quality. If it is significantly shorter, you may have lost respondents at the introduction who would otherwise have taken part.

- How long will fieldwork take? Most face-to-face or telephone surveys will have budgeted for the interview to take a certain length of time. The number of interviewers allocated to the project will be calculated partly on the length of the interview, and they may be paid accordingly. Interviews shorter than allowed for does not usually present such problems, but the opposite may lead to a waste of resources.

Even if the routing has already been tested, run through the questionnaire yourself with different responses to check that you get asked the questions you expect to.

Types of pilot surveys

The type and scale of the pilot will vary according to the perceived need for piloting, time available and budget. They include:

- informal pilots carried out with a small number of colleagues;
- cognitive interviewing in which the questionnaire is tested among respondents;
- accompanied interviewing, which may be used principally to test for interviewer and routing errors;
- soft launches, where responses are reviewed for time taken, routing errors and unusual patterns of response;
- large-scale pilot studies where a larger number of interviews can be used to test for completeness of brand lists or incidence of sub-groups;
- dynamic pilots, where question wording is changed between interviews to test alternatives based on responses received.

Informal pilot

An informal pilot, among colleagues or friends, represents the minimum that any questionnaire should undergo. Although they may not be able to fully mirror typical respondents, they will be seeing the questionnaire through fresh eyes and be able to give feedback on this basis. They will also give an indication of the length of time it takes, although they may answer more quickly if they are familiar with the questionnaire conventions or indeed may answer more slowly if they do not know the subject matter as well as the intended respondent.

Ideally, your pilot testers should meet the eligibility criteria for the study, so that they can answer as target respondents. In that capacity they would be better able to highlight where question terminology or answer categories are unclear or incomplete. Even if they have to pretend to fit the eligibility criteria they can give feedback on usability, instructions and visual layout or distractions.

If a questionnaire has routing that results in some respondents having a longer interview than others, it is useful to ensure that colleagues are briefed to be able to test this. For example, asking one colleague to pretend to be a user of many brands to see how the questionnaire works when it is at its longest.

If the questionnaire is written to be interviewer-administered, then the question writer could take this role. However, their familiarity with it will mean that interviewer usability issues will not be fully tested.

Although colleagues may not be thought to be the ideal sample for testing questionnaires, it has been shown that people with a knowledge of questionnaire design are more likely to pick up avoidable errors in questions than are people who are not, so they are a good place to start (Diamantopolous et al, 1994).

Cognitive testing

Testing a questionnaire among colleagues may identify some issues with it but cannot properly replicate what will happen with real respondents, their understanding of the questions or their thought processes when answering. To test these requires interviews to be carried out with a number of respondents who fall into the survey population, usually in one-to-one interviews. These interviews can be carried out by the researchers themselves, who have a good knowledge of the subject and the questionnaire; cognitive psychologists, who have a good understanding of the processes of cognition; or specially trained senior interviewers who have expertise in this area. For online questionnaires they sit with respondents and watch them complete the survey. Although the pilot respondent could be asked about their reaction to the questionnaire throughout the completion process, this can get in the way of them experiencing it as a typical respondent. Instead, the respondent may be asked to 'think out loud' as they answer the questions, and so give a running commentary on their thought processes. Based on models put forward by Tourangeau (1984) and Eisenhower et al (1991), this type of piloting is aiming to determine whether respondents:

- have a memory of what is being asked about and hence the ability to answer the question (encoding in memory);
- understand the question (comprehension);
- can access the relevant information in their memory (retrieval);
- can assess the relevance to the question of what they retrieve (judgement);
- can provide answers that meet the categories provided, and decide whether they want to provide an answer, or whether they want to provide a socially acceptable answer (communication/response).

A question always worth asking is whether the respondents felt that the questionnaire allowed them to say all that they wanted to say on the subject. Occasionally an issue consistently comes through that is important to respondents.

Without being able to express this the respondents feel that the survey originator will not have the whole picture. If this is not central to the study objectives it may not be necessary to add detailed questions to address this, but certainly suggests that there would be benefit in saying at the start of the interview that there will be an opportunity – either then or at the end – for the respondent to express issues of particular importance to them in their own words (ie verbatim format).

> When in a cognitive test, do not correct the respondent or give new information until the end, otherwise you may not uncover later problems.

Cognitive testing of this nature can reveal a range of difficulties with the questionnaire. For example, McKay and de la Puente (1996) reported identifying problems with:

- sensitive questions that respondents were uncomfortable answering;
- abstract questions that respondents found difficult to understand and to answer;
- vocabulary problems where the questionnaire writers had used terms unfamiliar to some of the respondents;
- order effects in which responses changed depending on the order in which questions were asked.

Respondents should be chosen to represent a broad range of the types of people to be included in the main study. Any particular sub-groups whose members might experience some difficulties with the questionnaire should be represented.

Accompanied interviewing

A further stage of piloting face-to-face or telephone interviews is for the researcher to accompany or listen in to interviews carried out by regular members of the interviewing force. The questionnaire writer should be listening for:

- mistakes by the interviewer in reading the questions;
- mistakes by the interviewer in following routing instructions;
- errors in the routing instructions that take the respondent to the wrong question.

If it has not been possible to carry out a proper cognitive test, this approach can be combined with interviewing the respondents to test the question. However, this can sometimes cause conflict in the approach of the researcher due to the multiple objectives of testing both the way in which the interviewer handles the questionnaire, and the way in which the respondents understand and answer the questions.

Soft launch

It is common to conduct a soft launch of an online survey to test out as much as possible of the questionnaire before it goes to all respondents. The survey will go live for a limited period, say one or two days, or until a desired number of completions have been received. This could be as many as 100 for a large survey. The data is quickly analyzed at a top-line level and responses are assessed for issues such as:

- Routing failures, where an unexpectedly low (or high) number of respondents have answered a question, indicating an error in the questionnaire scripting.
- Unexpected response patterns that might suggest a failure to understand the question, or an inadequacy or lack of discrimination in the list of pre-coded responses presented.
- Length of time taken.
- High levels of flatlining where respondents have not engaged with the question.

If any of these, or other issues, are identified, then full launch of the survey is delayed until they have been rectified. If no such issues are identified, then the survey launch can continue. Whether the responses from the soft launch can be included in the final data set will depend on the type and severity of an issue uncovered.

Large-scale pilot survey

For interviewer-administered surveys after completion of the small-scale pilot survey, it may be desirable to move on to a larger scale. The objective here is to extend the pilot exercise to a broader range of respondents, and for there to be a sufficient number of respondents for some analysis to be carried out to confirm that the questions asked are delivering the data required to answer the project objectives. This is similar to the soft launch of an online survey in some ways, but structured as a separate exercise from the main fieldwork.

Some commentators suggest that for interviewer-administered surveys, the interviewers used in the pilot survey should be the most experienced interviewers available, who are capable of determining ambiguities and other errors in the questions. Others suggest that a mix of interviewer ability is more appropriate, as it reflects the ability range likely to be used on the main study. The principal purpose of the pilot study should be determined, and the type of interviewers chosen accordingly. Thus, if the focus of the pilot is more on the wording of the questions, more experienced interviewers may be appropriate. If the focus is equally on how well the interviewers can cope with a complex questionnaire, then a range of abilities would answer the needs better.

This type of large-scale pilot is only likely to be carried out with large-scale studies, where the cost of failure is high if the study is unable to meet its objectives. Upwards of 50 interviews may be carried out in this pilot, which should be designed to cover different sections of the market and possibly different geographical regions. It is at this stage that small regional brands may be discovered that should be added to brand lists, or unanticipated minority behaviour that had not been catered for. It is also at this stage that unusually high numbers of 'don't know' or 'not answered' responses may indicate an issue with a question.

The questionnaire writer is unlikely to be able to be present at all of the interviews. Interviewers should therefore be provided with note sheets on which to record comments – their own and the respondents' – as they go through the interview, which can be referred to later.

A debriefing of the interviewers should be held to discuss their experiences with the questionnaire. The questionnaire writer should have seen all the completed questionnaires before the debrief so as to have determined where there might still be issues with some questions, including issues that the interviewers themselves might not be aware of. If, for example, they all consistently misinterpret a question, they are unlikely to identify that as a problem. It will require the questionnaire writer to do so. Should significant changes be made to the questionnaire as a result of the pilot testing, then another round of pilot testing should be carried out.

Although not part of the questionnaire development process, a further use to which the large-scale pilot survey can be put is to give an indication of the incidence of minority groups within the research universe. If it is intended that the study should be capable of analyzing specific sub-groups, the incidence of which is unknown, the pilot sample can give a first indication of this and so suggest whether the intended sample size of the main study is sufficient for this analysis. This may lead to revision of the sample size or sample structure for the main survey.

Dynamic pilot

The dynamic pilot can be very useful where a questionnaire is experimental. It is similar in scale to the small pilot survey. However, instead of the questionnaire writer listening in to a number of interviews and then deciding what is and is not working, the questionnaire is reviewed after each interview and rewritten to try to improve it. The client and researcher will often do this together. The improved questionnaire is then used for the next interview, after which it is reviewed again.

This is a time-consuming and possibly costly process, particularly if a central location must be hired to accommodate it. However, where there is real concern about the sequence of questions or the precise wording of questions, it can be the quickest way to achieve a questionnaire that works, particularly if the client is part of the dynamic decision-making process. Online, a series of different options can be tested among small samples in parallel, making this a relatively fast and simple process.

An example of where this might be appropriate is if we wish to test the reaction to a complex government policy proposal. In this situation, it may be important to ensure that respondents understand some of the detail of the policy. A key component of the questionnaire design would be how to explain a number of different elements of the policy and gain reactions to each one. So, we may need to test the wording of the descriptions of the different elements to judge how clearly and correctly it conveys the policy; and to assess any order effects dependent on the sequence in which the components are revealed. By observing the reaction of the pilot respondents and where necessary asking them questions on what they understand from the descriptions, the questionnaire writer can adjust the wording and the order of the questions between interviews until a satisfactory conclusion is reached.

It is rare for all of these techniques to be used in a project. However, it is important that at least one type of questionnaire testing is always carried out.

CASE STUDY   Whisky usage and attitude

Piloting

With our Scotch whisky survey, we will undertake two stages of piloting:

- an informal pilot;
- a soft launch.

Informal pilot

Following scripting of the questionnaire, the researcher will check it through for any obvious errors, and to ensure that the routing works correctly. The scripters will have checked this, but the researcher will want to double check. Particular attention will be paid to Q9-22, where there is complex routing about who is the purchaser, who is the decision maker and brand repertoire for in-home drinking. Here the flow diagram is important, as the researcher will follow through each path in the flow diagram to ensure that the questions are presented as intended.

Once the researcher is happy, the link will be sent to two or three colleagues, preferably who are regular drinkers of Scotch whisky, but if not, they are asked to complete it as if they were. They are asked to make notes where they are unsure of the meaning of the question or where they feel that the response codes are inadequate for their circumstance. From these notes the questionnaire writer will revisit those questions to improve them.

Soft launch

We have carried out similar surveys in this market before and believe we are sufficiently experienced not to need in-depth cognitive testing. As a quick check, however, the questionnaire writer could sit with some colleagues at the informal pilot stage and ask them to talk through their understanding of the questions and their thought processes as they complete the questionnaire.

Once any changes from the informal pilot are made, we can move on to the soft launch.

The sample size for the survey is 1,000 Scotch whisky drinkers, so we aim to complete the soft launch among the first 100 and then pause the survey. What we will be looking for from this data is:

- Time taken to complete. Does this match the length of time we are proposing to tell respondents?

- Level of dropping out and at what point in the questionnaire – this might point to a question that requires amending.
- Whether there is a high level of 'other answers' written in where there are questions with brand lists. This could suggest we have missed out some significant Scotch whisky brands.
- Whether there are unexpected response patterns or data distributions which might suggest a failure to understand the question.
- The level of flatlining at Q24, where a high level may mean we are failing to engage respondents.

Any issues that arise can be addressed before the survey is relaunched.

Key take aways: piloting your questionnaire

- During the questionnaire writing process you will be taking steps to eliminate errors, overcome potential issues and reduce the effect of respondent limitations.
- Inevitably you will have become very close to the questionnaire and the benefit of fresh eyes on it cannot be underestimated.
- Some kind of piloting is always advisable. The scale depends on the risks associated with the project, for example:
  - extent of prior knowledge. (Is this the first study on this topic? In this country?);
  - the complexity of the questionnaire and subject;
  - the size of the project. (Is it being replicated in many countries? Is it designed to run for many waves or years?);
  - the importance of the decisions that will be based on the outcome of the research.
- The range of piloting options includes:
  - Informal testing by colleagues.
  - Talking with test respondents to understand the interview experience and the cognitive processes they use to answer the questions.
  - Feedback from interviewers on usability plus their perspective on respondent issues.

- o Check of initial data after partial launch (ie before full sample roll-out).
- o Large-scale piloting (sometimes including testing of data analysis processes).
- If significant changes are made, then a further round of piloting may be needed!

Ethical issues in questionnaire design   15

Introduction

The ability of the market research industry to continue to use sample surveys depends upon the willingness of the public to give their time and cooperation to answer our questions. We often introduce a survey saying that participation can help to improve products and services on the market but there is frequently little, if any, direct reward for them. Respondents on panels are usually incentivized with points that amass – but even here the financial rewards are not great, and most do not do it for the money. (Bruggen et al, 2011). There are three main bodies that produce codes of conduct for research. These codes are designed, in part, to help ensure that researchers maintain the goodwill of respondents:

- Market Research Society (MRS) in the UK
- The Insights Association (formerly CASRO and MRA) in the United States
- The European Society for Opinion and Marketing Research (ESOMAR)

Membership of any of these bodies requires adherence to their code which provides an overall set of principles to be followed. They also provide more detailed guidelines on specific aspects of research. As an adjunct to its code, the MRS has produced 'questionnaire design guidelines', which are regularly updated and can be found at www.mrs.org.uk/standards/guidelines. Questionnaire writers should make themselves familiar with these guidelines which not only will help with ethical issues but with legal responsibilities regarding data protection.

Legal requirements

Many countries now have legal requirements, usually in the form of data protection laws, which define certain points of information that questionnaire writers are required to give to respondents. These laws take precedence over codes of conduct should there be any conflict. In the UK, the relevant law is the General Data Protection Regulation that came into force in 2018. The regulation requires researchers to become more accountable for the data privacy of respondents than previously. Within the EU, laws are derived from the European Data Protection Directive, and so are similar but not necessarily always exactly the same. European law is different to US law, and to transfer personal data from Europe to the United States requires the recipient to have signed up to the Privacy Shield agreement. This includes cloud-based services, such as DIY survey providers, who may hold data outside of Europe of which you are not aware. It is the responsibility of questionnaire writers to ensure that they comply with the laws of the country in which they work, as well as with the laws of the country or countries in which they are carrying out the survey.

> Know and understand the laws that you operate under. This can help you to say 'no' straight away if you are asked to do something that breaks them.

General data protection regulation (GDPR)

The GDPR covers personal data, ie information relating to an identified or identifiable natural person; who can be identified directly or indirectly by that data on its own or together with other data. Note that sound and video recordings and still images should always be considered as personal data.

There are six general principles of GDPR:

- **Lawfulness, fairness and transparency**: Personal data is processed lawfully, fairly and in a transparent manner.
- **Purpose limitation**: Personal data is obtained for specified, explicit and legitimate purposes and not further processed in a manner that is incompatible with those purposes. Further processing is allowed for archiving, scientific, statistical and historical research purposes.

- **Data minimization:** Personal data processed is adequate, relevant and limited to what is necessary.
- **Accuracy:** Personal data is accurate and, where necessary, kept up to date.
- **Storage limitation:** Personal data is not kept longer than is necessary (but data processed for archiving, scientific, statistical and historical research purposes can be kept longer, subject to safeguards).
- **Integrity and confidentiality:** Appropriate technical and organizational measures are put in place to guard against unauthorized or unlawful processing, loss, damage or destruction.

Not all of these affect the questionnaire writer but refer to how the personal data is managed further in the research process. Note that personal data collected should be relevant and limited to what is necessary.

The other main issue for questionnaire writers is the requirement to be transparent. This means that, for most research purposes, informed consent must be obtained.

Obtaining consent

Where consent is obtained this must be:

- freely given;
- specific (it can cover multiple processing purposes including the research purpose, but must be highlighted from any other terms);
- informed;
- an unambiguous indication with clear affirmative action or statement.

The 'data controller' (the body you have identified as being responsible for the security of any personal data) needs to be able to demonstrate that consent was obtained. This means that you need to obtain agreement to a clear positive statement or action. Silence, pre-ticked boxes or inactivity cannot be used to give or imply consent. The consent must be specific to the purpose highlighted to individuals. If you do not already have this consent it will need to be built into the questionnaire.

Respondents have the right to know:

- the identity of the data controller;
- contact details of the data protection officer responsible;
- legal basis for processing;
- purposes of processing;

- details of any international data transfer;
- retention period for data or criteria for retention;
- existence of any automated decision making and logic, significance and consequences;
- details of all other rights including right to object, right to data portability, right to withdraw consent, and right to lodge complaints with supervisory authorities.

This does not mean that you need to take the respondent through all of this at the start of the interview. Clearly, you must say who the research organization is (or the data controller if different) and the purpose of the survey. Online, other information can be offered using techniques such as headings or boxes which reveal the detail when rolled over, or through links to the full detail held elsewhere. In very complex situations, an explanatory video might be used.

In telephone research respondents can be directed to a website or to a nominated individual for queries. To avoid lengthy explanations at the beginning of the interview and risk its early closure, essential information can be given at the start of the phone call and the rest at the end.

Where research is being used for scientific purposes; social research which is intended to be published; or public health purposes it may not be possible to predict all the purposes for which the data may be used, and a broader consent may be obtained.

Sensitive data

There is a category of sensitive 'special' data. This covers religious or philosophical beliefs, health, racial or ethnic origin, trade union membership, political beliefs, sex life or sexual orientation, genetic data and biometric data of individuals.

Further information

Laws will continue to be amended, updated, and potentially interpreted differently so it is therefore suggested that questionnaire writers consult research societies and regulatory authorities for clarification, in particular the Market Research Society, ESOMAR and Efamro. Much of the above is based on the General Data Protection Regulation (GDPR) Guidance Note for the Research Sector of June 2017, issued by the MRS in conjunction with ESOMAR and Efamro. In the UK, the Information Commissioner's Office has guidance on their website and a telephone helpline for small businesses. (See Appendix 2 for website addresses.)

Declining goodwill and response rates

The level of goodwill and cooperation has declined in most countries over the past 30 years. Possible reasons include:

- Potential respondents do not distinguish between market research and activities such as database marketing. Indeed, in one study three-quarters of respondents said that they could not distinguish between them (Brace et al, 1999).

- Direct marketing, database marketing etc have increased. Since potential respondents may find it hard to distinguish between them, they may fear they will be sold something when approached about research.

- Being too busy or not having enough time have increased as reasons for refusal to participate in a survey (Vercruyssen, Van de Putte, and Stoop, 2011). Many feel that they have less time for non-rewarding activities such as market research, although whether this is actually the case has been more recently challenged (Sullivan and Gershuny, 2017).

- There are more market research studies than there used to be, and many people are asked to participate in research surveys more often. Some markets are very over-researched, particularly business-to-business and medical markets.

- Our demands on respondents have increased as demands for information from client management have increased. Many potential respondents have been bored by a market research interview once before, or know someone who has been, and are not prepared to go through the same tedium again. Online, where there is no interviewer to act as intermediary, this can be particularly acute.

There is little that the questionnaire writer can do to free up more time in people's lives or to prevent markets becoming over-researched. However, by treating respondents honestly, openly and respectfully when writing the questionnaire, the questionnaire writer can help to distinguish genuine market research from direct marketing. By creating involving and interesting short interviews, he or she can improve the standing of market research interviews. Potential respondents may then be more willing to participate in surveys in the future.

Responsibilities to respondents

The introduction

What is said in the introduction to an interview is crucial in securing the cooperation of respondents. From an ethical standpoint the introduction should include:

- the name of the organization conducting the study;*
- the broad subject area;
- whether the subject area is particularly sensitive;*
- whether the data collected will be held confidentially or used at a personally identifiable level for other purposes, such as database building or direct marketing, and if so by whom and for what purposes;*
- the likely length of the interview;
- any cost to the respondent;
- whether the interview is to be recorded – either using audio or video – other than for the purposes of quality control.*

*See GDPR

This gives respondents or potential respondents the information they require to be able to make an informed decision about whether or not they are prepared to cooperate in the study. Sometimes it is not easy to comply with these requirements, but the questionnaire writer should make every effort to do so.

Name of the research organization

The main organization name to be conveyed is the body that is responsible for the security of any personal data. In GDPR terms this is the 'data controller', who could be:

- an online panel company, who retain respondents' personal information which is not passed on to any other organization;
- a research company that recruits respondents to the survey and retains respondents' personal information which is not passed on to any other organization;
- a client company, where the survey is run by a research organization, but the respondents' personal data is to be passed back to the client;

- a client company which runs the survey itself;
- any organization or person who organizes the survey and will retain respondents' personal data.

It is possible for a survey to be conducted by a research company, and permission sought at the end of the survey to pass personal details on to another organization, such as the client. This permission must be explicitly given only after it is explained for what purposes the personal data will be used by this other organization, and it can then be used for no other purpose. You may wish to do this where revealing the identity of the client or other organization at the beginning of the survey will bias the responses given.

Subject matter

The broad subject area should be given so that the respondent has a reasonable idea of the area of questioning that is to follow. Frequently we do not wish to reveal the precise subject matter too early as this will bias responses, particularly during the screening questions. However, every effort should be made to give a general indication. For example, a survey about holidays could be described as being about leisure activities, although such a description may be inadequate for a survey about drinking habits. 'Leisure activities' would certainly be an inadequate description for a survey about sexual activity, which is regarded as a sensitive subject.

Sensitive questions

In the UK sensitive subjects are defined as including:

- sexual life;
- racial or ethnic origin;
- political opinions;
- religious or similar beliefs;
- physical or mental health;
- implication in criminal activity or alleged criminal activity;
- trade union membership.

This list, though, is not exhaustive in terms of what respondents may find sensitive, and the questionnaire writer should examine the study for any possible sensitive content. Anyone working in areas dealing with drugs and medication, or illness, or conducting studies on financial topics should be particularly alert to this issue.

There are certain demographic questions that need to be asked with care (eg ethnicity, gender or sexual orientation). Keep up to date with changing guidelines on best practice. In the UK, the Office for National Statistics and the MRS are good sources for this.

Confidentiality

One of the key distinctions between market research surveys and surveys carried out for direct marketing or database building is that the data is held confidentially and for analysis purposes only. No direct sales or marketing activity will take place as a result of the respondent having taken part in the study. This should be stated in the introduction to the questionnaire or in the covering letter in the case of a postal survey. It is then the responsibility of the research organization to ensure that the data is treated solely in this way.

Sometimes this may not be the case. An example might be where the survey is a customer satisfaction survey intended to utilize individual-level data to enhance the client company's customer database. Nor is it likely to be the case if it is to be used to identify respondents who show an interest in a new product or service that the client can follow up with marketing activity. (This may occur in small business-to-business markets.) Such studies are not confidential research, and the questionnaire must not represent them as such. Respondents must be told which organizations are going to see their data and how they are going to use it and given the opportunity to opt out. In most European countries this is a legal requirement under data protection legislation.

Apart from it being against the law in these countries to represent such studies as confidential research, it is morally wrong to mislead respondents. It is also bad for the image of market research if respondents are wrongly led into thinking that nothing will occur to them as result of participating in the study. It can only damage response rates for future surveys if respondents become disillusioned about the reassurances they are given.

Interview length

One of the most common causes of complaints received by the Market Research Society from members of the public is that the interview in which they participated took significantly longer than they were initially told. Sometimes they were not told how long the interview would take, and wrongly assumed that it would be only a few minutes. On other occasions, though, they were told the likely duration of the interview, which was then significantly exceeded.

With online surveys this is crucial, because response rates will be dependent on the time expected to be taken.

Sometimes it is straightforward to estimate the length of the interview. When the study has a questionnaire with a simple flow path and little routing, the pilot survey will have demonstrated how long it will take, and that is likely to be about the same for all respondents. However, the time required to complete the interview can vary considerably between respondents as the questionnaire becomes more complex. It can depend on the speed with which respondents answer the questions and the amount of consideration they give to each. It can also vary significantly depending on the answers that they give. The questionnaire may contain sections that are asked only if the respondent displays a particular behaviour, knowledge or attitude at an earlier question. The eligibility of any individual respondent for these sections cannot be predicted at the outset of the interview, with the consequence that the interview length could vary between, say, 15 minutes and 45 minutes for different respondents. If the survey could be this long for any respondent, then you should look at options of chunking it (see Chapter 3), or simply reducing the number of questions.

If there is likely to be a significant variation in interview length between respondents, the questionnaire writer should try to reflect this in the introduction.

> Do not be tempted to under-state the likely length. You will end up with a high drop-out rate or speeding.

Source of name

Respondents have a right to know how they were sampled or where the research organization obtained their name and contact details. With online panels this is not an issue. Respondents will have signed up with the panel operator to receive surveys.

Where the names have been supplied from a database, this can sometimes present more of a problem. With customer satisfaction surveys, we often want to say in the introduction that respondents have been contacted because they are customers of the organization. Frequently, clients will see the customer satisfaction survey as a way of demonstrating to their customers that the organization cares about the relationship between them. It is not uncommon for the introduction to state this and for online or postal satisfaction questionnaires to include client identification and logos. It is significant enough that the UK Information Commissioners Office regard customer satisfaction surveys as part of the marketing process.

Cost to respondent

If taking part in the interview is going to cost the respondents anything other than their time, this must be pointed out. In practice it is usually only online interviews that are likely to incur cost for the respondent (Nancarrow et al, 2001) and then only occasionally eg if they are paying for data download on a mobile phone. Occasionally though, respondents will be asked to incur travel costs to reach a central interviewing venue such as a new product clinic. These costs would normally be reimbursed.

The questionnaire introduction for a telephone survey should always establish not only whether it is safe for respondents to talk on their mobile phones, but also whether doing so is likely to incur any costs for them.

Children

In the UK children under the age of 16 years should not be interviewed without the explicit consent of a parent, guardian or other responsible adult acting in loco parentis. Once this permission has been obtained, the child's wish whether or not to take part must then also be respected. The age for consent may differ by country so check the relevant sources.

This does not necessarily affect the writing of the questionnaire, as the permission may be obtained prior to the questionnaire being opened or the interview started. It is good practice, though, that it should be recorded on the questionnaire that permission has been obtained and who from (parent, teacher, etc), so that this confirmation is kept in the same dataset as the individual child's responses in case of later query.

During the interview

Right not to answer

Researchers must always remember that respondents have agreed to take part in the study voluntarily. Should they wish not to answer any of the questions put to them, or to withdraw completely from the interview, they cannot be compelled to do otherwise. With face-to-face or telephone interviews, part of the role of the interviewer is to minimize such occurrences by striking up a relationship so that respondents continue for the sake of the interviewer even when they would rather not. However, if a respondent refuses to answer or continue, this must be respected.

In Chapter 5 we examined the pros and cons of including 'not answered/refused' codes at every question and concluded that they should not necessarily be included as a matter of course. However, it should be possible to identify the questions that are most likely to be refused and to include a code for refusals as appropriate. Such questions are likely to be the sensitive questions listed above, and personal questions about income and family relationships.

With paper questionnaires the interview can progress even if a question is not answered, unless an answer is required for routing purposes. In Chapter 10 the issue of whether or not the researcher should build in an ability to move on to the next question following a refusal to answer in online questionnaires was discussed. The alternative to allowing this can be that the respondent terminates the interview rather than answer the question. Different research organizations take different views on whether to accept termination of the interview or to provide another mechanism that allows respondents not to answer.

Maintaining interest

Creating a boring interview is not just bad questionnaire design which leads to unreliable data, it also fails to treat the respondents with respect, and damages the reputation of market research. Long and repetitive interviews should be avoided. This sometimes means that the questionnaire writer must find a creative way of asking what would otherwise be repetitive questions. Chapter 11 looks at this for online surveys, but it can be a major issue for face-to-face and telephone surveys as well.

Responsibilities to clients

Ethical behaviour does not just extend to the relationship between questionnaire writer and respondent, however. The questionnaire writer also has a responsibility to behave ethically towards the client.

The questionnaire must be fit for the purpose of the study. Deliberately introducing bias to support a particular point of view is unethical and is rarely of value to the client's organization.

The client should always be given the opportunity to comment on the questionnaire. Most quality control procedures require that the client signs off the questionnaire as having been agreed. It is the questionnaire writer's responsibility to ensure that the client has sufficient time to consider the questionnaire and any implications for the data to be collected before being asked to agree it.

By implication, questions to which the client has not agreed should not be included. It can be tempting to add questions on a different topic, possibly for a different client, where the sample definition for the two subject areas is the same. It is unethical to do this without the agreement of both clients.

Also, where one client has paid for the development of a questionnaire, it is ethically unacceptable to use it for another client's survey. It is, of course, to be expected that the questionnaire writer will draw upon their experience when writing the second questionnaire, but usually the questionnaire is considered to be the property of the client who paid for its development unless specified otherwise in the contract. Questionnaires that the research company has developed itself, without being paid by a client to do so, are the property of the research company and can be used for multiple clients.

CASE STUDY   Whisky usage and attitude

Ethical considerations

The main ethical issue is to ensure that we do not interview anyone below the legal age for drinking alcohol. In the UK that is 18 years of age.

Because we are using an online panel for the survey, the panel provider will target the invitations only to panel members aged 18 or over. However, we cannot guarantee that the person completing the survey is the same person for whom the panel owner holds information. We should start the questionnaire with a screening question to determine the age of the person completing it.

- Are you:
  - 12 or under
  - 13 to 17
  - 18 to 24
  - 25 to 34
  - 35 to 54
  - 55 or over

Note, we do not simply ask if they are under 18, as this highlights what our interest is and where the cut-off is, making it easier for those who want to deceive. There is still no guarantee that the person completing the survey tells the truth about their age, but we can immediately close the survey to anyone who admits to being under 18.

The survey has been introduced as being about alcoholic drinks because anything vaguer than that could be thought of as misleading. We do not say it is about whisky because we do not want people to self-select into the sample depending on whether or not they want to answer questions about whisky, nor to pose as whisky drinkers when they are not.

There is a second issue which is common to the alcoholic drinks industry, which is that we must not ask any questions that could be seen as encouraging people to drink more. As objective researchers, questions intended to alter behaviour should never be in a questionnaire, but it is particularly important for this market.

Key take aways: ethical issues in questionnaire design

- Check relevant up to date sources to ensure that you are complying with data protection legislation (eg GDPR).
- For questionnaire design specifically this will primarily influence how you introduce the survey to obtain informed consent.

- The research industry is reliant on the goodwill of respondents as participation is voluntary. A respondent whose goodwill is lost during an interview may not want to take part in any survey again.

- Look for information provided by research bodies like the UK Market Research Society, ESOMAR and the Insight Association:

  o They have codes of conduct that help to maintain this goodwill.

  o They also produce additional guidelines (eg advice on tackling sensitive issues).

Understanding social desirability bias

16

Introduction

Respondents give inaccurate answers for a number of reasons – some conscious, some unconscious. In previous chapters some of these response biases were examined, including the problems of memory, inattention by the respondent and deliberate lying. This chapter examines the social desirability bias and considers steps that the question writer can take to reduce this category of response bias.

Social desirability bias

Social desirability bias (SDB) arises because respondents like to appear to be other than they are, and is at risk of occurring wherever there is a potentially 'right' or 'more acceptable' answer. SDB can manifest itself both in stated behaviour and in the attitudes that they express.

Sudman and Bradburn (1982) identified the following topics as being desirable and therefore areas in which behaviour is likely to be over-reported:

- Being a good citizen, including:
  - registering to vote and voting;
  - interacting with government officials;
  - taking a role in community activities;
  - knowing the issues.

- Being a well-informed and cultured person, including:
  - reading newspapers, magazines and books, and using libraries;
  - going to cultural events such as concerts, plays and exhibitions;
  - participating in educational activities.

- Fulfilling moral and social responsibilities, including:
  - giving to charity and helping friends in need;
  - actively participating in family affairs and child rearing;
  - being employed.

They also quote examples of conditions or behaviour that may be under-reported in an interview:

- Illness and disabilities, such as:
  - cancer;
  - sexually transmitted disease;
  - mental illness.

- Illegal or contra-normative behaviour, such as:
  - committing a crime, including traffic violations;
  - tax evasion;
  - drug use;
  - consumption of alcoholic products;
  - sexual practices.

- Financial status, including:
  - income;
  - savings and other assets.

When this list was created, SDB was seen as an issue mainly affecting social research. For market researchers, it has, in the past, been an issue limited to a small number of specific categories in which there is a perceived element of social responsibility or perceived social irresponsibility. In certain markets, such as tobacco, alcohol and gambling, both attitudes and behaviour are likely to be misrepresented. Researchers working in these fields have learnt that they cannot ignore SDB as an influence on the data they collect.

More recently, though, most major businesses now have a function dedicated to managing their corporate social responsibility. This need has occurred because of the increasing association between many types of businesses and the impact they have on both the physical and social environments:

- For consumer goods manufacturers and retailers, there are consumer concerns about the impact on the environment of excessive packaging and the overuse of plastic bags.

- Food and confectionery manufacturers have to be conscious of their responsibility regarding the contribution of the ingredients in their products to the health of their customers.

- For manufacturers of consumer durables, the environmental impact of the disposal of their products can be a social concern.

- In the automotive industry, the issue of car emissions and the environment has high consumer awareness.

- In individual markets, ethical sourcing is a major issue, both to provide a living wage to suppliers and to minimize environmental damage.

- Many companies engage in cause-related marketing, often related to areas of ethical concern for their business.

Therefore, SDB is no longer only an issue for social researchers. In many areas of commercial market research, the researcher may come to false conclusions from the research data if they fail to recognize that SDB may be influencing responses.

Types of SDB

Impression management

Possibly the most common cause of SDB is the need for approval, known as 'impression management'. The questions or topics on which people feel the need for approval may vary between respondents. For some people it will be a wish to appear more environmentally friendly, and they will under-state their use of plastic carrier bags, while for others it will be healthy eating, with them overstating their consumption of unprocessed foods. However, within any one study it is most likely that if impression management occurs, it will do so on a small and consistent set of questions.

Ego defence and self-deception

Here respondents' intentions are not to manage the impression that they give to someone else, such as the interviewer or the researcher, but to convince themselves that they think and behave in socially responsible ways. This is less likely to be a conscious activity than is the need for approval but can result in the same exaggeration of claimed socially responsible behaviour and attitudes. People will tell you that they eat more healthily than they do, because they (or rather, their ego or self-concept) can't accept that they don't. This type of behaviour may also affect future projections of likely behaviour, where the respondents convince themselves that they will behave in a responsible fashion in the future even if they do not do so currently. When this is carried out consciously it is known as 'ego defence'; when it is carried out subconsciously it is known as 'self-deception'.

Instrumentation

A further type of bias – and one that is totally conscious – is instrumentation (Nancarrow et al, 2000). This means that respondents give answers designed, in their view, to bring about a socially desirable outcome. Many respondents are relatively sophisticated with regard to marketing and to market research, and know that they have an opportunity to influence decision making through their responses to the survey. For example, a survey of attitudes to how lottery money should be divided between good causes and lottery administrators may suffer from this effect. Respondents may deliberately give low estimates of the proportion that should be allocated for administration because they believe that if it is seen that the public wants a higher proportion to go to charities, this could have an impact on the decisions of the regulatory body. This may be in addition to or in place of impression management, in which the respondent wishes to be seen by the interviewer to be generous to charities.

Dealing with SDB

If the questions ask about attitudes or behaviour on any subject that has a social responsibility component, then consideration should be given on how best to minimize any possible bias. Simply asking respondents to be honest has very little effect (Brown et al, 1973; Phillips and Clancy, 1972).

Research carried out under the MRS, ESOMAR or Insights Association code of conduct (see Chapter 15) should tell respondents that their responses will be treated confidentially. This could be reinforced with a restatement of confidentiality as part of the introduction to the sensitive questions. However, the effect of this appears to be slight (Dillman et al, 1996; Singer et al, 1995) or even to reduce the level of cooperation (Singer et al, 1992). This reduction in cooperation could be because the additional emphasis on confidentiality highlights to respondents that the questions are particularly sensitive, and so increases their nervousness about answering them. With postal self-completion surveys there is evidence that omission of a respondent identifier on the questionnaire reduces SDB (Yang and Yu, 2011). This suggests that assurances of confidentiality that are seen to have substance should have some effect. However, for surveys other than postal, there is still the interviewer (who will be aware of the responses), or for online surveys whoever is thought to be receiving the data. Appealing for honesty and assurances of confidentiality are insufficient. Measures that are more positive are therefore required.

Removing the interviewer

The most obvious person for whom a respondent will want to create a good impression is the interviewer. Online surveys therefore suffer less from impression management. Poynter and Comley (2003), Duffy et al (2005) and Bronner and Kuijlen (2007) have all demonstrated that the admission of socially undesirable behaviour or the admission of not carrying out socially desirable behaviour is greater with online surveys than with interviewer-administered surveys, thus demonstrating the greater honesty that is achieved with this medium (Holbrook and Krosnick 2010). In addition, Kellner (2004) demonstrated that there was less pressure on respondents to appear knowledgeable. However, impression management is not entirely eliminated, and there is no reason to believe that ego defence or instrumentation is any less significant.

Self-completion questionnaires are also good to use where the subject is potentially embarrassing for the respondent, and they eliminate much of the bias that would otherwise occur. Both online and mail surveys benefit in this respect, with internet-based surveys possibly being seen by respondents as the most anonymous form of interview.

> With face-to-face interviewing also consider who might overhear the responses. The respondent may be tempted to give socially desirable answers for that person's benefit.

Face-saving questions

Face-saving questions give respondents an acceptable way of admitting to socially undesirable behaviour, by including in the question a reason why they might behave in that way. For example, if the questionnaire writer wishes to measure how many people have read the new edition of the Highway Code, instead of asking, 'Have you read the latest edition of the Highway Code?' the writer could ask, 'Have you had time yet to read the latest edition of the Highway Code?'

The first question can sound confrontational, with an implication that respondents ought to have read the latest edition and be aware of current driving rules. This can force respondents to be defensive, or to feel guilty about not having read it, and hence to lie and say that they have read it. The second question carries an assumption that respondents know that they ought to read it and will when they have the time. This is less confrontational, eases any guilt about not having read it and makes it easier for respondents to admit they have not.

Work carried out in the United States (Holtgraves et al, 1997) has consistently demonstrated over a series of studies that questions of this type can significantly reduce overclaiming in socially desirable knowledge topics (eg global warming, health care legislation, trade agreements and current affairs), and reduce under-claiming of socially undesirable behaviour (eg cheating, shoplifting, vandalism, littering). However, the work is inconclusive regarding the impact of such questions when applied to socially desirable behaviour (eg recycling, studying, volunteering).

Rather than ask, 'How many kilometres are there in a mile?' or, 'Do you know how many kilometres there are in a mile?' the question could be made less challenging by adding the phrase, '*Do you happen to know* how many kilometres there are in a mile?' This phrase has been shown to lead to an increase in the level of 'don't know' responses, suggesting that respondents find it easier to admit their ignorance with this wording rather than guess.

The use of opt-out responses in the question like 'if any' or 'if at all' can also be useful in balancing questions where the absence of a behaviour might be a less acceptable response. For example, 'How many portions of fruit and vegetables, if any, did you manage to eat yesterday?' or, 'How often, if at all, do you go to the gym?' Even if the option 'none' is included in the list of answer responses, the question phrasing is made less leading by also explicitly offering the opt-out response in the question itself.

Indirect questioning

A technique sometimes used in qualitative research is not to ask respondents what they think about a subject, but to ask them what they believe other people think. This allows them to put forward views that they would not admit to holding themselves, which can then be discussed. It can sometimes be possible to use a similar technique in a quantitative research questionnaire. However, in qualitative research the group moderator or interviewer can discuss these views and use his or her own judgement as to whether or not respondents hold these views themselves or simply believe that other people hold them.

In quantitative research both the structured nature of the interview and the separation of respondents and researcher make this far more difficult to achieve. The researcher is therefore left with uncertainty as to the proportion of respondents who projected their own feelings and the proportion who honestly reported their judgement of others.

Question enhancements

The questionnaire writer can take a number of other simple steps in order to help minimize SDB.

Reassure that a behaviour is not unusual

Where there is a concern that people may misreport their behaviour, statements that certain types of behaviour are not unusual can be built into the question. This can reassure respondents that whatever option they choose, their behaviour will be considered by the interviewer or by the researcher to be normal. For example, 'Some people read a newspaper every day of the week, others read a newspaper some days a week, while others never read a newspaper at all. To which of these categories do you belong?'

Extended responses on prompts

In a similar way, extended responses on prompt material can suggest that extreme behaviour is not unusual and encourage honest responses (Brace and Nancarrow, 2008). For example, when asking about the amount of alcohol that people drink, the researcher can use prompts with categories that go well beyond normal behaviour, so that categories of mildly heavy drinkers appear mid-way on the list. This helps heavier drinkers to feel that their consumption might be of a more normal level than it actually is, and they may be more likely to be honest and not under-report. Care needs to be taken not to make light drinkers feel inadequate and so feel forced to over-report their weight of drinking. Having relatively small gradations at the lighter end of the scale – thus helping the lighter drinkers to see that they have more options – can help this. (See Figure 16.1.)

Figure 16.1   Two approaches to category banding

Using one of the phrases on this list, please tell me how many units of alcohol you drink in an average week.

Approach A	Approach B
None	None
1 to 2 units	1 to 14 units
3 to 5 units	15 to 39 units
6 to 8 units	40 units or more
9 to 12 units	
13 to 17 units	
18 to 24 units	
25 to 34 units	
35 to 54 units	
55 to 74 units	
75 to 94 units	
95 to 134 units	
135 to 184 units	
185 units or more	

The opposite approach can also help, ie to have very broad categories, probably no more than three in total, so that respondents can give a vaguer answer. This approach is likely to be preferred by respondents either because they do not want to admit an exact value, or because they find it difficult to calculate. However, for most research purposes the broad categories supply insufficient data to the researcher for the required analyses. A further alternative is to use this as a first part of a two-part question. The first question is used to identify which of the three broad categories the respondent falls into, and a second question is used to identify the amount more precisely within the category.

Identifying responses by codes

With interviewer-administered face-to-face interviews, code letters can be used against each of the prompted response categories and the respondent asked to read out the appropriate code letter. Respondents therefore do not have to read aloud the answer, which helps them to feel that a degree of confidentiality is being maintained. The interviewer of course knows to which response category each code applies, but respondent and interviewer do not have to share the information overtly (see Figure 16.2).

Figure 16.2   Use of code letters

ASK ALL IN PAID EMPLOYMENT.

SHOW CARD.

What is your personal annual income before tax or other deductions? Please read out the letter on this card next to the band in which your income falls.

J	UP TO £8,000
N	£8,001 TO £12,000
D	£12,001 TO £16,000
P	£16,001 TO £20,000
W	£20,001 TO £24,000
K	£24,001 TO £35,000
G	£35,001 OR ABOVE

Implicit Association Test

In Chapter 8 we introduced the Implicit Association Test as a method of getting to how people feel about brands and a range of brand-related attributes. Its strength is that it infers attitudes without asking direct questions, which it does by measuring response times in allocating combinations of primary factors (such as brands) and attitude-related dimensions to a predetermined axis (such as good-bad). This approach also makes it a good tool for getting past desirability bias because the respondent is unable to consciously or subconsciously influence their reaction times.

The drawback is that it can only discriminate between two primary factors and on one attitudinal dimension. However, that may well be perfectly adequate to get an understanding about how an individual really feels about, say, recycling or global warming. It could be used to measure anything that suffers from social desirability bias or political correctness (Brunel, Tietje and Greenwald, 2004). That information then has the capability of being used to calibrate responses given elsewhere to direct questions.

Random response technique

The randomized response technique was first developed by Warner (1965). It provides a mechanism for respondents to be truthful about embarrassing or even illegal acts without anyone being able to identify that they have admitted to such an act. This is achieved because the respondent is presented with two alternative questions, one of which is sensitive and the other not. No one other than the respondent knows which question has been answered. It allows the researcher to measure the incidence of such behaviour, but little else.

To achieve this, two questions with the same set of response codes are presented for self-completion. One of these is the sensitive or threatening question, and the other is the non-threatening and innocuous one. Respondents are allocated to answer one of these questions in a random way, the outcome of which is clearly not recordable in the survey, and, if an interviewer is involved, unknown to them. This can be by assigning the respondent to a set of questions according to whether their mobile phone number or their date of birth ends with particular digits. This information must not be known to the researcher, or the respondent will not believe in the anonymity of the process.

An example of how this might work is presented in Figure 16.3. We know from other sources that 17 per cent of the population has their birthday in November or December and, given a sufficiently large sample, we can reasonably apply this proportion. So, of a sample of 1,000, it can be assumed that 830 will have answered the threatening question and 170 the

Figure 16.3 Random response question example

Below, there are two questions with only one place to record the answers. Please answer question A if you were born in November or December, and question B if you were born in any other month of the year. No one will know which question you have answered. Please be honest about which question you answer and how you answer it.

A. TO BE ANSWERED IF YOUR BIRTHDAY IS IN NOVEMBER OR DECEMBER
Does your home telephone number end with an odd-numbered digit, 1, 3, 5, 7, 9? Answer YES if it does, NO if it does not.

B. TO BE ANSWERED IF YOUR BIRTHDAY IS NOT IN NOVEMBER OR DECEMBER
Have you used marijuana at all in the last 12 months?

YES ☐

NO ☐

non-threatening question. Of the 170, half (85) will have answered 'yes' to the question about their telephone number.

If X out of the total sample have answered 'yes' at all, we can deduce that, of the people who answered the threatening question, X – 85 answered 'yes' to the threatening question. We can therefore arrive at an estimate of the proportion of the population who have used marijuana in the last 12 months, which is (X – 85)/830.

It has been shown that the technique works effectively for subjects that are relatively unthreatening (eg having been involved in a case in a bankruptcy court), but that with more threatening subjects (eg drunken driving), it still significantly underestimates levels of behaviour (Sudman and Bradburn, 1982).

This approach is limited to providing an estimate of the proportions answering 'yes' and 'no' to the threatening question among the total sample, or among sub-groups that are of sufficiently large sample size for the assumptions regarding the proportions answering the non-threatening question still to hold. As it is not possible to distinguish individual respondents who answered the threatening question, we cannot cross-analyze them against any other variables from the survey to establish, say, the profile of those who admit to the behaviour and that of those who do not.

What the technique achieves is providing an opportunity for the respondent to answer honestly. This means that, while it addresses impression management, it can do nothing about self-deception.

Determining whether SDB has influenced responses

It can be difficult to determine whether or not the responses to a question have been influenced by SDB.

Matching known facts

Where it is possible to cross-check responses against known data from other sources, this can highlight differences that may be due to SDB. The cross-checkable facts will tend to be factual or behavioural data, such as volume of product sold. Attitudinal questions cannot be checked in this way. Even with factual data it is frequently difficult to match external data sources with survey data because of differences in definitions, time periods and so on. Survey data can sometimes provide its own internal cross-checking.

Pantry checks, to see what is actually in a respondent's store cupboard, can be used as a check against what the respondent has previously claimed to be there.

A good rule with SDB is just to be sceptical. Ask yourself if this can possibly be true and don't take it at face value.

Checking against measures with known SDB

For attitudinal questions it is possible to design a battery of scales that measure a sample's tendency towards SDB. Such a battery would include behaviours that are common (majority of the population) and socially undesirable; and behaviours that are not common (minority of the population) but are socially desirable.

Consistently low scores on the first group (indicating low levels of undesirable behaviour) and a high score on the second (indicating high levels of desirable behaviour) would suggest that the respondent either falls into a small and angelic minority of the population or that SDB exists in the responses. Individual respondents with these response patterns can be identified, and if on another topic the sample has a higher-than-expected level of claimed desirable behaviour or a lower level of claimed undesirable behaviour, the researcher knows that there is an SDB problem with the sample as a whole.

There are several published batteries of scales to help the questionnaire writer, including Edwards (1957), Crowne and Marlowe (1960) and Paulhus and Reid (1991). In addition, shortened versions of the Crowne–Marlowe scale have been tested by Strahan and Gerbasi (1972) and by Greenwald and Satow (1970) that may be more suited to market research interviews.

Rating the question for social desirability

Questions can be included that directly ask the respondents to assess the attitude or behaviour for social desirability (Phillips and Clancy, 1972). This can indicate the relative problem between different scales or questions. However, there must be doubt about whether such questions do not suffer from SDB themselves.

Noting physiological manifestations of unease

It is likely that there will be physiological signs that a respondent is trying to mislead an interviewer, such as facial muscle movement, galvanic skin response and pupil dilation. However, interpreting these even in laboratory conditions is problematic and outside laboratory conditions is likely to be impossible and beyond the skill set of most market research interviewers.

CASE STUDY   Whisky usage and attitude

Socially desirable responding

There is a clear possibility of socially desirable responding when collecting data about whisky consumption. This occurs in two places in the questionnaire:

- in the screening questions (QC);
- when asking detailed consumption (Q10 and Q11).

Screening Question QC

- How often do you drink Scotch whisky? [QC]
  - Most days
  - At least once a week
  - At least once a month
  - At least once every three months
  - At least every six months
  - Less often

Here our interest is in determining whether the respondent drinks Scotch whisky more or less often than once every three months. The question could ask that directly. However, we don't use a direct question: partly to disguise the precise point of our interest to stop people trying to opt in or out of the survey. Here, though, the subject matter could lead to some social desirability bias. If we simply asked whether they drink Scotch whisky 'more or less often than every three months', some people who would qualify may feel that they would be seen as a heavy drinker and rule themselves out by saying 'less often than every three months'. By allowing a distinction between heavier drinkers (most days/at least once a week) and lighter drinkers (at least once a month/at least once every three months), this allows these people to answer more honestly. We therefore get more people giving one of the first four response codes.

Consumption Questions

At Q10 and Q11 we could ask how many glasses of Scotch whisky they have drunk in the last seven days, firstly in licensed premises and then at home.

How many glasses of Scotch whisky have you drunk in the last seven days in pubs, bars, clubs and restaurants? A glass is equivalent to a single measure.

0	0

TYPE IN NUMBER.

There is a risk here of social desirability bias, with some respondents deliberately under-reporting their consumption rather than be thought to drink 'too much'.

However, to address the issue of SDB, we could prompt the respondent with a list of ranges, say '0, 1–3, 4–8, 9–15, 16 or more' This would have required less of a feat of memory from respondents and, if the ranges went sufficiently high – say to 50-plus glasses – could have encouraged heavier drinkers to be more truthful. Precise numbers as requested are not necessary for the researcher's purposes here. Responses separated into ranges would have given sufficient information to categorize the sample into heavy and light drinkers.

Another way of expressing this is as a scale, numbered to 50+, with a slider for the respondent to provide their answer. This both addresses the issue of SDB by suggesting that an answer of 50 is acceptable and provides the respondent with some variety in answer format. For these reasons we choose to use this.

Key take aways: understanding social desirability bias

- SDB is at risk of occurring wherever there is a potentially 'right' or 'more acceptable' answer. It leads to overclaiming of socially acceptable behaviours or attitudes and under-claiming of socially unacceptable ones.

  o It can be conscious, ie the respondent trying to manage the impression they give.

- o Or unconscious, ie being self-deceptive into believing that they are better than they are.

- SDB is more likely to be more marked in interviewer-administered surveys due to the more personal nature of the interaction, however it occurs in all data collection modes including online (despite the greater anonymity).

- The question writer needs to identify question areas that are possible sources of SDB and take steps to reduce its impact. This can sometimes be achieved with careful wording or alternative questioning approaches.

- However, it is difficult to completely remove this type of bias – or to know the extent to which the question writer has been successful. The possible impact of SDB on the answers needs to be acknowledged when interpreting the data.

Designing questionnaires for multi-country surveys

17

Introduction

Multi-country surveys encounter a number of unique problems. Clearly there will be challenges with wording if translations are needed. The question may be affected by the conventions, nuances and subtleties of language so direct translations may not be appropriate. In addition, other differences between countries will affect whether a common questionnaire can be created or whether a separate questionnaire needs to be designed for some or all countries.

Differences between countries

Structural differences

Worcester and Downham (1978) list the following aspects that the questionnaire writer needs to consider:

- **Language:** There may be different languages not only between countries but also within countries. Is it necessary to include all minority languages in all countries? Common languages may also have different usages (eg English in the UK vs in the United States).

- **Ethnic differences:** Even if different ethnic groups speak the same language, they may have different habits and attitudes.

- **Religion:** This may have implications for attitudes, lifestyle and consumption of products such as alcohol and meat, for which different questions will be required both to make sense and not to offend.

- **Culture and tradition:** Behling and Law (2000) draw particular attention to the difficulties that different cultures bring to the willingness to share personal information; what behaviours, attitudes and aspirations are thought acceptable to discuss with a stranger; expressing abstract ideas and concepts in universally understood ways; and finding the correct terms in which to express intentions and aspirations. Other examples of cultural differences that might need to be reflected in the question wording are the different levels of importance given to gifting and the issue of 'saving face'.

- **Literacy:** Literacy levels vary between countries, and even official statistics can overstate it. Low literacy levels mean that aids such as verbal prompt material cannot be used, nor self-completion questionnaires.

- **Geography and climate:** Differences in climate can mean that product usage patterns are different, particularly regarding food products that are suited to either a warmer or cooler climate, such as dairy products.

- **Institutional factors:** Different market backgrounds often require different questions to be asked. Baths are more common than showers in some countries but rarely installed in others; approaches to clothes washing, savings and credit cards all vary between countries.

- **Distribution:** Supermarkets, hypermarkets and shopping malls which dominate the distribution of many goods in some countries are unknown in others, therefore different questions may be needed.

- **Media and advertising:** Access to media and the types of media available can vary between countries.

- **Infrastructure:** Different infrastructures may have an impact on usage and attitudes. Different transport systems, different stages of development in telecommunications, and different approaches to healthcare may all affect the way in which the questionnaire is written for different countries.

Marketing differences

In addition to these structural factors, Goodyear (1996) identified a continuum of marketing literacy divided into five stages:

1 Seller's Market

2 Marketing

3 Classic Brand Marketing

4 Customer-driven Marketing

5 Post Modern Marketing

Knowing at which stage on this continuum each of the markets to be surveyed is can affect how each is approached and hence what questions should be asked and how.

> Get to understand the differences between countries by talking to local offices and absorbing local reports before you start to write the questionnaire.

Different market segments

Market segments that exist in one country may not exist in another. Low and mid-priced Scotch whisky segments, which can account for the majority of the market in Western countries, may not exist in some Asian countries where only luxury brands are available. The usage questions and image dimensions that are appropriate for a market segment with a strong mid priced segment of many brands may not be of any use in countries where the competitive set is not just Scotch but other high-priced luxury drinks.

Brands in different segments

Brands may be in different segments in different countries. This can happen in any market and is quite likely to happen in countries where distributors are independent of the manufacturer, and who have historically been given the authority to position the brand as they wish. Brands that in one country would be considered mid-priced may elsewhere be luxury brands. Good market data and local knowledge should identify this type of difference.

Market knowledge

With a multinational study, it is possible that the commissioning organization or client has a presence in most if not all of the countries that are to be covered. However, the extent and expertise of that presence may differ between countries.

With a strong presence in each country, it is likely that much is already known about the market, and certain assumptions can be made when writing the questionnaire. If little is known, the questionnaire may need to be more open in the way it addresses topics, because of the danger of making wrong assumptions. The amount that is known about each market will have an impact on the way in which the same approach can be adopted across countries.

The client may want to adopt a common marketing strategy, but the researcher would not be doing his or her job if the client was led to believe that the markets possessed only a number of common characteristics and was left unaware of the differences because they were not asked about. The biggest danger is the assumption that because a questionnaire has been used successfully in one country, it can be used in any country.

Mode of data collection

Online is an efficient way to reach samples throughout most countries. There may be issues regarding how representative of a population this may be, but in most developed markets in which commercial research is primarily interested, online access is very high. In less developed markets, online access may still be skewed towards higher economic groups, but these are typically the segments in which commercial researchers are usually most interested.

In some instances, it may be necessary to mix the modes of data collection to optimize the sample profile (eg there may be pockets of a population that are difficult to reach online but which are key to the survey objectives). The challenge for the questionnaire writer is to ensure that the different biases inherent in the different modes (see Chapter 2) are minimized using question techniques that suffer least from modal bias.

What is likely to be more of an issue for the questionnaire writer is the different ways in which online questionnaires are accessed in different regions. In many countries not only is internet penetration relatively low, but the majority of participants may be accessing the questionnaire by mobile phone rather than by PC. If the survey is to cover these countries, the questionnaire writer must therefore write the questionnaire principally for the mobile phone, with implications for length of survey and complexity of questions.

However, designing for mobile as the priority is increasingly important everywhere. Even in developed countries with high levels of home computers, mobile is growing as the main route for accessing the internet.

Comparability

There are many reasons to try to make the questionnaires, and hence the data output, as comparable as possible. Worcester and Downham (1978) suggest that:

- Time and money are saved by using a standardized approach.
- Life is simplified for the researcher.
- End-users often have greater confidence in a standardized approach, rather than one that has many variations.
- Absolute uniformity is essential in some cases, particularly in the data required for the technical development of products.

Having a common questionnaire is also likely to lead to fewer errors in survey administration than if there are a number of different ones. Given these reasons, most organizations would agree that a standardized questionnaire is always preferable and should be used unless there are good reasons why it would not be suitable for a particular country or group of countries.

One approach to writing questionnaires for a multi-country study is to start by writing the questionnaire with one country in mind. Once that has been refined, it should be tested for its appropriateness in every country in which it is to be used, even those sharing a common language. Amendments should then be made to accommodate differences between markets. This may require changes only in the brand lists, but it may also require changes in image dimensions, advertising media and prompts used, methods of distribution in the market, absolute prices, relative prices, the competitive product set, frequency of use bands, or completely different behavioural questions. The researcher can reach a point where the changes are so significant that it becomes a different questionnaire.

Coordinating common elements

Even if it is possible to conduct a study using a standard questionnaire across a number of different countries, there will nearly always be minor variations to be accommodated.

Brand lists

Almost invariably, the brand list will change in most consumer markets. There may be local brands that are available only in that country or region, and the multinational companies may sell different brands in different countries.

Some brands of Scotch whisky, for example, are sold only in the Asia-Pacific region. Others only have a significant level of distribution in a small number of European countries.

Brand image

Brand image questions are frequently asked of a small number of brands deemed to be important either in the market or in the direct competitive set to the client's brand. Even if the long list of brands available is similar in two countries, the short list of brands that are the most relevant to be asked about in image and brand-positioning questions may vary between countries.

Frequently the client will be able to advise on the appropriate brands for each country both for the long and short lists. This may come from the company's marketing plans for each country and from the company's office, representatives or distributors. It is always worthwhile to check the list with local representatives, who may be aware of new local brands that have not yet made it into the company's global marketing strategy. It is also worthwhile for the research agency to ask its own representatives in each country for their views on the brand lists, for the same reason.

Image dimensions

Often the objective is to produce a single, global, brand image map on which variations between countries can be plotted. If insufficient care is taken in choosing the image dimensions relevant to each country, this can result in a misleading picture being produced for some countries.

To achieve the ideal set of image dimensions the researcher should determine all the relevant image dimensions for each country, bearing in mind that the positioning and the competitors could be different. This may involve preliminary qualitative research or review of secondary sources such as previous research.

However it is arrived at, a distillation of all relevant image attributes across the countries in the study can be compiled to form a master set of image dimensions. If the intention is to use a technique such as correspondence analysis to produce a global map, all image dimensions may have to be used in all countries regardless of their relevance. There is a danger that the list, in trying to accommodate the key points for each country without becoming overly long, will contain too many compromises. While it will provide a global overview, it will not be sufficiently detailed to provide an accurate positioning in any one country. Supplementary questions specific to each country may be required for that to be achieved.

Attitudinal questions

Attitudinal questions can sometimes be difficult in maintaining comparability between countries. Not only may consumers have different attitudes to a market or product area in different countries, but what is important to them in arriving at those attitudes may also be completely different.

Frequently the attitude dimensions to be measured should be the same in each country, although with the expectation that response patterns will be very different between countries. If a battery of attitudinal rating scales is to be used, the wording of each dimension must be appropriate for each country, and care must be taken to avoid offence in relation to both cultural and religious attitudes.

Translating the questionnaire

Accurate translations are, of course, essential. But an accurate translation is not simply one that is literally accurate. Translations must be carried out sensitively so that meanings, shades of meaning and nuances are accurately retained.

For example, Forsyth et al (2007) advocate a five-step process which they used when translating questionnaires – in their case the translation was from English into a range of Asian languages:

1 Translation – using professional translators.

2 Review.

3 Initial adjudication – to propose revision using bilingual adjudicators.

4 Cognitive interview pre-test.

5 Final review and adjudication.

Such a translate-test-review process represents the ideal for all multilingual projects, to tease out the nuances and shades of meaning that can ruin comparability between languages.

Possibly the most difficult to translate are brand image and positioning statements, and attitude dimensions. There may be subtle but clear distinctions in one language that cannot be translated into another. In English there is a clear difference of understanding between 'old-fashioned' and 'traditional'. In some languages this distinction cannot be made. The word 'warm' is frequently used as a brand image descriptor in English, to describe the warmth and affection of the relationship between brand and consumer. However, it is not infrequently translated into other languages as something equivalent to 'mildly hot'.

There are two main options:

1 **The initial translation** is carried out by people who understand the research process and the importance of capturing the sentiment rather than a literal translation. Oppenheim (1992) notes that whether a house had 'running water', when translated literally into other languages, was taken in some to mean having a stream or river running through the house. Wright and Crimp (2000) note how the phrase, 'out of sight, out of mind' becomes 'invisible, insane' in Mandarin Chinese.

2 **A machine translator** such as Google Translate is used to make an initial translation which is then reviewed and amended by a translator who understands the research process. Some DIY survey packages offer a translation service, but these will be a machine translation.

Using native speakers

Whichever route is taken, it is preferable that the translator is a native speaker of the language.

Native speakers are the most likely to understand the nuances of the language as they are understood by other native speakers. Many multinational research companies employ multilingual research executives or other members of staff who are from other countries. Forsyth et al (2007) advocate the use of professional translators, but they should also have some knowledge of the survey process if they are to avoid mistranslation of research terms.

However, native speakers living abroad may – depending on how long they have lived there – be out of touch with changes in the language as it is spoken locally. Subtle changes of meaning can occur with fashion or with a new usage.

With the growing number of online multi-country surveys being conducted from a central location rather than from a local office, there can be a lack of opportunity for local input.

Therefore, it is always worth finding someone who resides in the country to check the translation for usage of current language.

Figure 17.1   Translation Issue

The following questionnaire was seen in the English language version of a customer satisfaction questionnaire in a German hotel:

- Please rate the following aspects of the restaurant from 1 to 5, where 1 is not at all satisfactory and 5 is very satisfactory.

	1	2	3	4	5
The quality of the food	–	–	–	–	–
The speed of the service	–	–	–	–	–
The table	–	–	–	–	–

Did they really mean the table itself? The workmanship that went into it and its position in the restaurant? Or did they mean the food upon the table? A native translator might have queried what this question really meant.

Using the client's representative

If possible, the local representative of the client in each country should also check the translation. Local representatives may have had direct or indirect input to the questionnaire writer's understanding of the structure of the market in the country. They should be aware of any variations in technical terminology in the local market that the research-led translator may not know about. It may also be important to get local representatives to 'buy-in' to the questionnaire, especially if they are going to be responsible for implementing action that arises as a result of the research project. If they are not happy with the questionnaire, they may be less willing to implement the study's findings.

Back-translation

Finally, the questionnaire should be back-translated into the original language. This can show up changes in meaning, although it must be determined whether they arise from the original translation or from the back-translation.

The process described here is what should ideally happen. However, it is quite possible for some of these steps to be omitted, depending on the ability of the translators and whether the questionnaire has been used before.

Demographic data

One area that often causes difficulty is the classification of demographic data. Many countries subscribe to a social-grade classification system that uses a grouping system described as A, B, etc. There, the similarity often ends, with the number of groups and their definitions differing widely:

- The UK has a six-grade system (A, B, C1, C2, D, E).
- Ireland has a seven-grade system (A, B, C1, C2, D, E, F).
- India has an eight-grade system (A1, A2, B1, B2, C, D, E1, E2).

Many developing countries have no commonly acknowledged system of social-grade classification, and local researchers may all have their own approach. Level of education may be used as a surrogate for social grading or to complement it, but education systems also vary between countries. Terminal education age is something that can be measured in a consistent way between countries, but its implications are likely to be very different.

Alternatively, a measurement of living standards can be obtained by asking about ownership of durables. That too must be tailored to the local situation. Ownership of a moped, fridge or TV may indicate a very different level of social grade in, say, Vietnam and Germany.

Cultural response differences

In some cultures, people are less prepared to criticize than in others. In India, for example, it is often considered rude to be critical of someone else's work. Responses to rating scales therefore tend to be more positive than in many other countries. Within Europe, as a rule, people in Latin countries will tend to give higher ratings than in Nordic countries. Puleston and Eggers (2012) demonstrated high levels of acquiescence bias in India, but relatively low levels in Japan/Korea, North America and Northern Europe, with Southern and Eastern Europe in between. Similarly, they found a much stronger propensity to 'like' something in India and South America than in Japan and Northern Europe. This would be supported by the experience of most researchers.

These differences can also be shown between cultures within the same country. Savitz (2011) conducted an experiment in the Dallas area of the US in which he demonstrated that the cultural impact on ratings of products given by Hispanics was worth 5.9 points more on a 100-point scale on average than by non-Hispanics. This is not a universal correction factor that can be applied to all markets but is an indication of the effect.

Some researchers address the issue in the questionnaire, particularly where there are strong differences because the study includes both Western and Asiatic countries. One way is to use scales that have positive responses only. Thus, a scale might run from 'very good' to 'fair'. Alternatively, scales can be extended to 10 or 11 points with five positive responses to increase the discrimination, or extended numeric scales can be used to try to minimize the sense of criticizing by avoiding negative words.

Roster et al (2006) showed that the use of extreme points on scales can also vary between countries. This means that although the same question may be asked in several countries, the resulting data may not be directly comparable. Puleston and Eggers (2012) demonstrated that in their online surveys, respondents in India, China and South America were about twice as likely to agree to Likert scale questions as were respondents in Northern Europe and Japan.

> Tip: Always expect that Latin countries and those where 'face' is important will give you more positive results.

The extent of the bias will vary depending on the types of questions being asked, and the researcher must be careful not to rule out real differences between markets as being caused by cultural response differences. It may be possible to calculate compensation factors within a survey by asking questions with known responses, such as whether respondents were born in a particular month and estimating the amount of acquiescence bias overclaim from that. Such questions will need careful consideration at the time of questionnaire writing.

Another approach, cited by Wable and Pall (1998), is to use a 'warm-up' statement that distances the researcher from the product or advertisement being researched, allowing the respondent to feel more able to criticize. This is a technique commonly used in qualitative research that they have transferred to quantitative questionnaires. They quote a typical warm-up as:

'I would like your frank opinion about this ad. You don't necessarily have to say nice things about it. Please feel free to give us any positive or negative opinions. We have not made this ad, so we will not feel bad if you don't have nice things to say about it.'

They have shown that in India this has a measurable effect in reducing the level of positive comment, although it is not known whether it is sufficient to make the results directly comparable with all other countries.

Laying out the questionnaire

With online questionnaires administered by a central coordinator, the questionnaire layout, question numbering etc would be consistent across all language versions and all territories, diverging only for questions or issues specific to one country or region. Where interviewers are used, there may be differences in their training between countries or in the conventions used within questionnaires. These differences may be particularly acute where paper questionnaires are being used. The question then arises of how differences between the layouts can be minimized.

Layout conventions

However, it is also important that local agencies use their own layout conventions where these differ. Mistakes are more likely to be made by interviewers if they are presented with an unfamiliar layout. It may be necessary to instruct the local agency staff to lay it out in their own format. This will also encourage the local agency executives to become more familiar with the questionnaire themselves and increase the likelihood of them spotting unsuitable wording or being able to answer questions that may arise in the field.

Question numbering

A common question numbering scheme helps comparisons to be made easily for the same questions across countries. When the same question is being referred to, there is a potential source of error if that question has a different number in each country. Checking of routing instructions is also more straightforward if the same question numbers are used. However, a common question numbering scheme can mean that some question numbers are not used in some versions of the questionnaire. For example, where an additional question needs to be asked in one country only, that question number will not appear on questionnaires for all the other countries in the study. This must be clearly marked on the questionnaires, or it can cause confusion among interviewers. If there are so many missing question numbers that it creates difficulties for the interviewers to follow instructions, then consideration must be given to abandoning common question numbering for the sake of minimizing interviewer error.

CASE STUDY   Whisky usage and attitude

International considerations

Our whisky advertising and brand study has been designed for a survey of the UK market. However, the client, Crianlarich, now wants to extend it to the following countries:

- France;
- Belgium;
- US;
- Japan;
- China.

First, we must examine whether it is appropriate for these other markets. Issues may arise as follows:

- Screening QB: The set of competitive drinks used to disguise our interest in whisky is unlikely to be appropriate in these other countries. Drinks such as 'ale' and 'stout' may not be understood.

- Screening QC: We probably want to keep a common definition of a whisky drinker as someone who drinks it at least once every three months, but is this realistic in all these countries? Is the penetration of whisky drinkers, or the frequency of drinking whisky, too low to be able to obtain a reasonable sample size with this definition? Alternatively, if the penetration is so low, will respondents be sufficiently knowledgeable to be able to answer all of the questions?

As a general point, we have defined the market as being whisky drinkers without distinguishing between drinkers of Scotch whisky, Irish whiskey or bourbon, because in the UK Scotch is dominant. However, in other countries – in particular the United States – other forms of whisky have larger market shares. We therefore need to decide for these countries whether our research universe should be all whisky drinkers, including bourbon drinkers who may not drink Scotch, or to restrict it to Scotch drinkers. This is a matter of matching the research to the marketing objectives and tailoring that to the strategy within each country. It may mean though, that the sample definition is different between countries, making comparison of data between countries less straightforward. This decision will affect the screening questions and the brand lists as follows:

- Q3, Q4 and all subsequent questions with the longer brand list: these response codes need to cover the main brands in the market of interest. This will be different between markets.

- Q7: Here we have defined 'Grand Prix' as the competitor of specific interest. Is this the case for all countries? Is Grand Prix sold in all of these countries – or in the competitive set if it is? If not, what is the competitor of principal interest?

- Q9: Here we have used the UK concept of 'off-licence' and 'on-licence' drinking, which are generally understood with only minimal explanation. Are these terms appropriate in other countries? Do we need to distinguish between 'at home drinking' and 'drinking in a public place' – such as a bar or restaurant? Here we need to tap into local knowledge regarding the appropriate terminology.

- Q23: This uses a set of attributes that have been developed for the UK market. Are they appropriate for all other countries, or are there other more important attributes? For example, in some countries is it customary or common to smell the aroma of a whisky before buying? If that is important in a market, that would need to be included at the expense of something less important.

- Q24: This has a reduced brand list, comprising the competitive set to Crianlarich as defined within the marketing strategy. This will differ between countries.

- Q25: We must check that the advertisement for Crianlarich is the correct one for each country. There will often be variations between countries.

- Q27: What is the key competitor brand advertising that we wish to be measured against in each country?

Finally, we need to check the legal drinking age within each country and amend our sample definition and questionnaire to reflect that.

Translation

Because there are a number of areas of difference between countries, and some nuances in image attributes, our preferred method is for the translation to be initially carried out by an expert translator rather than to use machine translation. Then translations for each country are to be checked by the local Crianlarich office, who can also advise on any local issues that we have overlooked.

We must remember that for Belgium we will require translation into two languages!

Key take aways: designing questionnaires for multi-country surveys

- The key decision is whether to try to create a common 'master' questionnaire – with only minimal country tailoring – or whether to take a country-by-country approach. Many factors will influence this:
  - consistency in the survey objectives by country;
  - the extent of underlying structural differences between countries (eg cultural influences);
  - the extent of market and marketing differences between countries.
- Keeping the questionnaire largely consistent has many practical advantages but if important differences are not reflected then the survey will only have the illusion of producing comparability.
- Sufficient time must be built into the schedule for accurate and sensitive translations so that meaning and shades of meaning are accurately retained while working within the conventions for that language.
- It's important to get the questionnaire reviewed by native language speakers who are residents in the country and have some understanding of the challenges of creating good questions.

APPENDIX 1

Case study: whisky usage and attitude study

The questionnaire

We now have the final questionnaire. On the following pages, it will be shown as it will appear to respondents. Notes beneath each screen show the filtering or logic that that follows from each question.

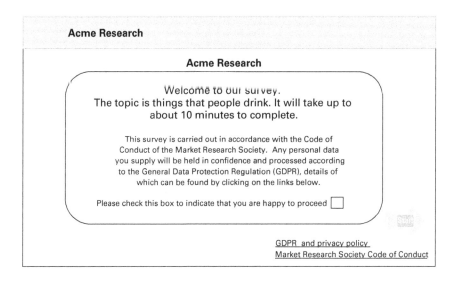

Screen 1. The welcome screen. Here we need to tell the respondent the broad nature of the subject matter – we do not want to reveal that it is about Scotch whisky at this point. We also say how long it is likely to take. For people who do not pass the screening questions it will take a lot less, which is why we say '*up to* about 10 minutes'.

Our Data Protection responsibilities are taken care of through the link to 'Data Protection and Privacy Policy'.

Acme Research

First things first.
Are you...?

- ○ 12 years or under
- ○ 13 to 17
- ○ 18 to 24
- ○ 25 to 34
- ○ 35 to 44
- ○ 45 to 54
- ○ 55 or over

Next

Screen 2. Because survey is about an alcoholic drink we need to screen out anyone below the legal drinking age, in this case 18 years. We disguise that this is what we are doing by having a range of age bands both above and below the 18 years. This makes it more difficult to guess that this is what we are doing and lie about their age.

Anyone under 18 is routed to Screen 33, the closure screen for those who do not qualify.

Others to QA.

Acme Research

Do you or any of your family work in the following industries?

- ☐ Accountancy
- ☐ Advertising
- ☐ Information technology
- ☐ Marketing/market research
- ☐ Alcoholic drinks
- ☐ Grocery retailing
- ☐ None of these

Next

Screen 3. QA. Security screener. Here we identify people who work in, or have close relatives who work in, professions which would skew the representivity of the sample. People who work for competitors to Crianlarich could also deduce the Crianlarich strategy from some of the questions.

The other answers are included as blinds, to give everyone a chance of providing an answer.

Anyone who answers Advertising, Marketing/Market Research or Alcoholic drinks goes to Screen 33.

Others to QB.

Acme Research

Which of these have you drunk in the last three months?

- ☐ Ale
- ☐ Lager
- ☐ Stout
- ☐ Wine
- ☐ Gin
- ☐ Scotch whisky
- ☐ Irish whiskey
- ☐ None of these

Next

Screen 4. QB. This identifies those who drink Scotch whisky. Again, a set of blind answers are provided to allow everyone to answer something, and not be 'helpful' by claiming to drink Scotch which might happen if it were the only option available. This also provides valuable information about what other drinks are used by Scotch whisky drinkers.

Those who do not drink Scotch whisky, go to Screen 33.

Others to QC.

Acme Research

How often do you drink Scotch whisky?

○ Most days
○ At least once a week
○ At least once a month
○ At least once every three months
○ At least once every six months
○ Less often

Next

Screen 5. QC. We want to identify people who drink Scotch whisky at least once every three months. The inclusion of other answers is partly to disguise where out cut off is, but also provides valuable information about frequency of drinking amongst the sample. In a tracking study, this, taken together with the penetration of Scotch whisky drinkers from QB, can provide valuable information about whether the market as a whole is in growth or decline.

Those who drink Scotch whisky less often than every three months go to Screen 33. Everyone else constitutes the sample definition that we are looking for, and continues to Q1.

Acme Research

Can you name eight brands of Scotch whisky?

Brand 1
Brand 2
Brand 3
Brand 4
Brand 5
Brand 6
Brand 7
Brand 8

Next

Screen 6. Q1. Spontaneous brand awareness. A key question. This is our challenge question to see if they can name eight brands. This is likely to elicit more brand names than if simply asked to name brands of Scotch whisky. We can see from the order in which the boxes are completed whether Crianlarich moves up in people's consciousness above other brands over time.

Continue with Q2.

Acme Research

Which brands of whisky have you seen or heard advertising for recently?
Enter names below

First

Second

Third

Fourth

Fifth

Sixth

Seventh

Eighth

Next

Screen 7. Q2. Spontaneous advertising awareness. A key question. No challenge here, because we want respondents to think of recent advertising, and not go back too far simply to meet the challenge.

Continue with Q3.

Acme Research

Which of these brands of Scotch whisky have you heard of?

- Bell's
- Chivas Regal
- Crianlarich
- Famous Grouse
- Glenfiddich
- Glenmorangie
- Grand Prix
- Johnnie Walker
- Teacher's
- Whyte & Mackay
- None of these

Next

Screen 8. Q3. Prompted brand awareness. Here we have a list of the major brands and those we believe to be the closest competitors to Crianlarich. This is about brand recognition, and our concern here is mostly with the proportion of people who do *not* recognize the name Crianlarich. That tells us whether the job of the advertising should be primarily to raise awareness if that is very low, to reinforce brand positioning for an already well-known brand, or if there is more scope to create a brand positioning for a brand that is known but not well known.

Acme Research

Which of these brands have you seen or heard advertising for recently?

- [ ] Bell's
- [ ] Chivas Regal
- [ ] Crianlarich
- [ ] Famous Grouse
- [ ] Glenfiddich
- [ ] Glenmorangie
- [ ] Grand Prix
- [ ] Johnnie Walker
- [ ] Teacher's
- [ ] Whyte & Mackay
- [ ] None of these

Next

Screen 9. Q4. Prompted advertising awareness. What we are looking for here is whether the Crianlarich advertising has cut through into people's consciousness. This is not as core as Q2, spontaneous advertising awareness, but allows us to identify respondents for Q5. Note that there is no 'Other' response code. We are only interested in our key brands which act as our reference set.

If Crianlarich is clicked go to Q5.
If Grand Prix is clicked go to Q7.
If neither mentioned go to Q9.
If both Crianlarich and Grand Prix mentioned the order of showing the block Q5 and Q6 about Crianlarich, and the block Q7 and Q8 about Grand Prix, should be randomized or rotated between respondents.

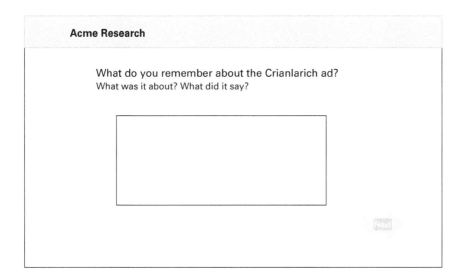

Acme Research

Where did you see or hear advertising for Crianlarich?

- Cinema
- Direct mail
- Online/internet
- Magazine
- Newspaper
- Radio
- Television
- Other (please enter) [_____]
- Can't remember/Don't know

[Next]

Screen 10. Q5. Source of Crianlarich advertising. This question is to channel recollections of the Crianlarich advertising prior to Q6. It also assists in identifying any spurious recollections in media that Crianlarich is thought to have used for advertising.

Continue with Q6.

Acme Research

What do you remember about the Crianlarich ad?
What was it about? What did it say?

[_____]

[Next]

Screen 11. Q6. Recall of Crianlarich advertising. This is to tells us a) whether the recall can be identified as genuinely Crianlarich or if there is confusion with advertising for another brand, and b) where it is confirmed as genuine, what are the salient points of the advertising that are sticking in people's minds.

These salient points may help to explain shifts in perceived brand positioning. They may also be built upon in later advertising, knowing that they cut through.

If Grand Prix was mentioned at Q4 continue with Q7.

Others go to Q9.

Acme Research

Where did you see or hear advertising for Grand Prix?
- ☐ Cinema
- ☐ Direct mail
- ☐ Online/internet
- ☐ Magazine
- ☐ Newspaper
- ☐ Radio
- ☐ Television
- ☐ Other (please enter) _____
- ☐ Can't remember/Don't know   Next

Screen 12. Q7. Source of Grand Prix advertising. This repeats Q5, but for Grand Prix, because we need to monitor the performance of our closest competitor.

Continue to Q8.

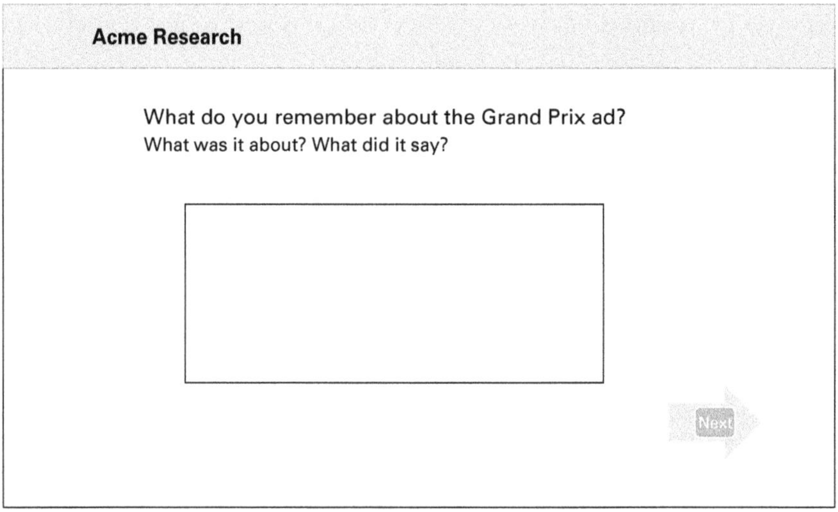

Acme Research

What do you remember about the Grand Prix ad?
What was it about? What did it say?

[text entry box]

Next

Screen 13. Q8. Recall of Grand Prix advertising. This repeats Q6 for Grand Prix. As well as giving us diagnostic information about the performance of Grand Prix, is also provides benchmark data against which we can assess Crianlarich's performance against a brand with a similar sized advertising budget.

Continue to Q9.

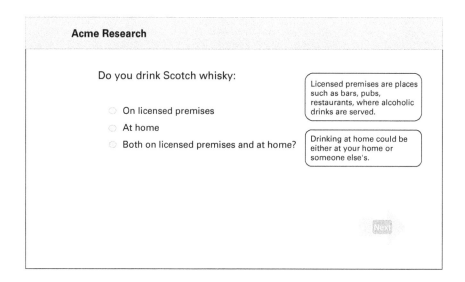

Screen 14. Q9. Where Scotch whisky drunk. Here we begin the set of questions with complex routing logic, designed to determine where Scotch whisky is drunk, which brands are chosen and by whom. This will assist in targeting decision makers, who may not always be the same as the drinkers. This question determines whether the respondent is an 'on-licence' of 'off-licence' drinker of Scotch, or both.

In order to minimize the number of words in the question, and to reduce repetition, the answer codes are used as part of the question.

Note that the definitions of terms used in the question are given in boxes well away from the question itself. This is to avoid the appearance of the question being as a large block of text, which will inhibit it being read properly. The definition could also be programmed to appear when the cursor is 'rolled over' the terms in the answer codes.

If Scotch whisky is drunk on licensed premises at all, continue with Q10.

If Scotch whisky is drunk only in off-licensed premises, ie at home, go to Q11.

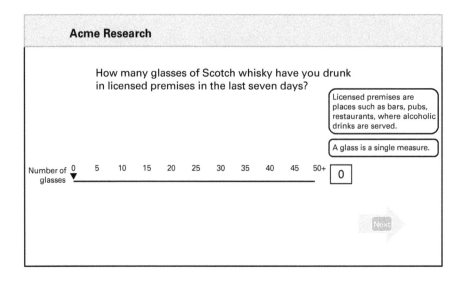

Screen 15. Q10. Consumption on licensed premises in past week. We wish to gain a measure of the weight of the respondents drinking in licensed premises. Crianlarich is primarily aimed at the off-licence market, but we need to know whether heavy in-home drinkers are also heavy drinkers in licensed premises.

We have opted for a numbered slider scale with a high top end in order to counter socially desirable responding (see Chapter 16).

If Scotch whisky is also drunk at home, off-licensed premises, at Q9, continue with Q11.

Others to Q21.

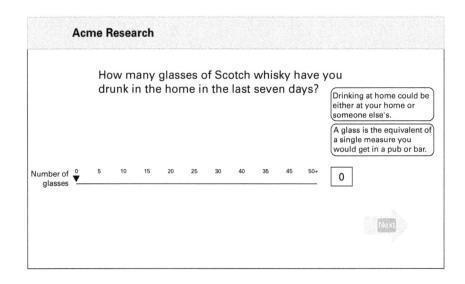

Screen 16. Q11. Consumption off licensed premises, in the home, in past week. Here we gain a measure of weight of drinking in the respondent's own home or someone else's, which accounts for the bulk of off licence drinking. We use the same scale and slider technique as a Q10. Many respondents will answer both questions and to vary the technique or to use a different length scale would invite confusion.

The size of a glass and how much is served in one is likely to vary between homes, so an instruction as to what our definition of 'a glass' is has been included. Note that again this is kept away from the question so as to avoid a large block of text.

Acme Research

Do you drink Scotch whisky:

○ Only on your own home
○ Only at someone else's home
○ Both at your home and someone else's?

Next

Screen 17. Q12. Now we want to ask only about drinking in their own home and not someone else's where they would have no choice of brand, so this funnelling question is required.

If they drink in their own home, continue with Q13.

If they only drink in someone else's home, go to Q21.

Acme Research

Who usually buys the Scotch to drink in your own home?

- ○ I do
- ○ Someone else does
- ○ Sometimes me, sometimes someone else
- ○ Given as a gift
- ○ Other answer

Next

Screen 18. Q13. We want to find out who is the brand decision maker in the home, so first we must ask who is the purchaser. Another funnelling question.

If respondent always or sometimes buys the Scotch, go to Q19.

If someone else always buys the Scotch, go to Q14.

If it was given as a gift or there is another answer, go to Q21.

Acme Research

Do you have a say in which brand is bought?

- ○ Yes I do
- ○ No, they decide
- ○ Its always the same brand

Next

Screen 19. Q14. Another funnelling question. If someone else buys it, does the respondent have an input to brand choice?

If respondent has input, go to Q19.

If respondent has no input, go to Q17.

If it is always the same brand, continue with Q15.

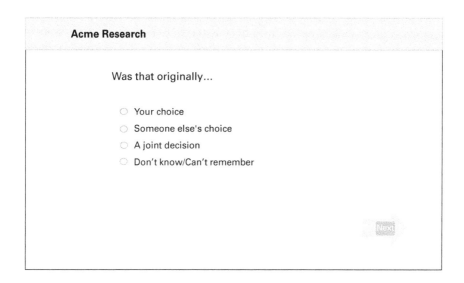

Acme Research

Which brand do they buy?

○ Bell's
○ Chivas Regal
○ Crianlarich
○ Famous Grouse
○ Glenfiddich
○ Glenmorangie
○ Grand Prix
○ Johnnie Walker
○ Supermarket's own brand
○ Teacher's
○ Whyte & Mackay
○ Other brand
○ Don't know/Can't remember

Screen 20. Q15. It is possible that the same brand of whisky is always bought for the household, and we need to allow for this possibility with this and the following question. This asks which brands this is.

If the brand is not known, go to Q21.

Others continue with Q16.

Acme Research

Was that originally...

○ Your choice
○ Someone else's choice
○ A joint decision
○ Don't know/Can't remember

Screen 21. Q16. We now want the respondent to think back to who decided that this brand should be the regular one, to discover who is or was the decision maker.

All go to Q21. This particular behavioural question route is complete.

Acme Research

Which brands do they buy?
- ☐ Bell's
- ☐ Chivas Regal
- ☐ Crianlarich
- ☐ Famous Grouse
- ☐ Glenfiddich
- ☐ Glenmorangie
- ☐ Grand Prix
- ☐ Johnnie Walker
- ☐ Supermarket's own brand
- ☐ Teacher's
- ☐ Whyte & Mackay
- ☐ None of these/Other brand
- ☐ Don't know/Can't remember

[Next]

Screen 22. Q17. This is being asked of in home drinkers for whom someone else decides the brands of Scotch whisky that are bought. Here we ask which brand or brands are bought.

If more than one brand is mentioned, continue with Q18.

Others go to Q21.

Acme Research

Which brand do they buy most often?
- ○ Bell's
- ○ Chivas Regal
- ○ Crianlarich
- ○ Famous Grouse
- ○ Glenfiddich
- ○ Glenmorangie
- ○ Grand Prix
- ○ Johnnie Walker
- ○ Supermarket's own brand
- ○ Teacher's
- ○ Whyte & Mackay
- ○ None of these/Other brand
- ○ No most often brand

[Next]

Screen 23. Q18. If there is a repertoire of brands mentioned at the previous question, we want to know if one brand is more frequently bought than others.

All go to Q21. This particular behavioural question route is complete.

Acme Research

Which brands do you buy or ask to be bought?
- ☐ Bell's
- ☐ Chivas Regal
- ☐ Crianlarich
- ☐ Famous Grouse
- ☐ Glenfiddich
- ☐ Glenmorangie
- ☐ Grand Prix
- ☐ Johnnie Walker
- ☐ Supermarket's own brand
- ☐ Teacher's
- ☐ Whyte & Mackay
- ☐ None of these/Other brand
- ☐ Don't know/Can't remember

`Next`

Screen 24. Q19. This question is addressed to in-home drinkers who are also decision makers either solely or jointly, and asks what they buy or what they ask for.

If more than one brand is mentioned, continue with Q20.

Others go to Q21.

Acme Research

Which brand do you buy most often?
- ○ Bell's
- ○ Chivas Regal
- ○ Crianlarich
- ○ Famous Grouse
- ○ Glenfiddich
- ○ Glenmorangie
- ○ Grand Prix
- ○ Johnnie Walker
- ○ Supermarket's own brand
- ○ Teacher's
- ○ Whyte & Mackay
- ○ None of these/Other brand
- ○ No most often brand

`Next`

Screen 25. Q20. If there is a repertoire of brands mentioned at the previous question, we want to know if one brand is more frequently bought than others.

All go to Q21. This particular behavioural question route is complete.

Acme Research

For each pair of phrases, show which is the more important to you when choosing a brand of whisky.

	Much more important	About the same	Much more important	
Richness of the colour		▼		Smoothness of the taste
Tradition of the brand		▼		Smoothness of the taste
Smoothness of the taste		▼		Whether it's drunk in Scotland
Richness of the colour		▼		The price
Whether it's drunk in Scotland		▼		Tradition of the brand
Tradition of the brand		▼		The price
Whether it's drunk in Scotland		▼		Richness of the colour
The price		▼		Whether it's drunk in Scotland

Screen 26. Q21. This is asked of all respondents. This is the attitude question to help us determine what are the key drivers in brand choice. With a relatively small number of attributes, here five, we can ask for choice between each pair, there being 10 pairs in all. We have chosen to use a slider scale rather than radio buttons (see Chapter 6). The order in which the pairs are shown is randomized between respondents and we make sure that each attribute appears at either end of the scale roughly the same number of times so as to minimize left-handed bias. To remove positional bias of the slider start point, it always starts in the middle of the scale.

Note that this is the only screen where the respondent on a PC should have to scroll down to complete the question.

Continue with Q22.

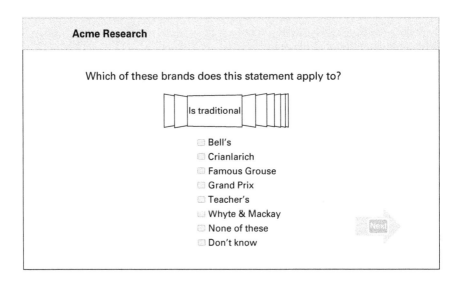

Acme Research

Which of these brands does this statement apply to?

Is traditional

☐ Bell's
☐ Crianlarich
☐ Famous Grouse
☐ Grand Prix
☐ Teacher's
☐ Whyte & Mackay
☐ None of these
☐ Don't know

Next

Screen 27. Q22. Here we are measuring perceived brand image based on a set of image attributes and a defined competitive set consisting of our closest competitors and major brands as reference points. This is a 'pick any' approach using a dynamic grid, in which the image dimensions appear one by one (see Chapter 8).

The order in which brand names are shown is randomized between respondents. We do not show pack shots or brand logos because these would influence responses by suggesting brand attributes.

With data from this question we shall be able to produce brand maps using correspondence analysis so that we can see image strengths of each brand and which brands cluster together because they are seen to be similar and which have an image that is distinct from the other brands. In this way we can see how successful we are with our advertising in positioning the Crianlarich image where we want it to be.

Continue with Q23.

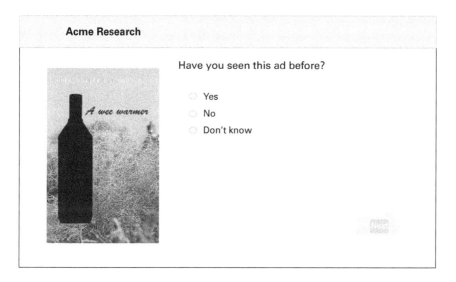

Screen 28. Q23. Here we show an ad for Crianlarich, from which the brand has been removed. We want to know whether it is recognized. This will help us to assess the reach that the advertising has had, which may reflect on the efficacy of the media placement of it. We must be careful, though, about correlating recognition of the ad with purchase of Crianlarich and attributing purchasing to the advertising. It is as likely that purchase of the brand and familiarity with it, leads in part to recognition of the ad, as it is that knowing the ad has led to the purchase. (Brand users generally have higher advertising awareness for 'their' brand.)

If ad has been seen continue to Q24.

Others to Q25.

Screen 29. Q24. Because the ad has been seen does not mean that it is known that it is for Crianlarich. This question is a measure of the success of the branding in the ad. If there is high recognition of the ad but a low level of associating it with the correct brand, this may mean that the ad needs to be re-thought and the impact of the branding improved.

The order in which the brands are shown should be randomized between respondents.

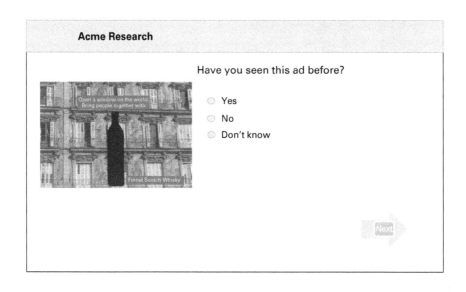

Screen 30. Q25. This repeats Q23 with a recent Grand Prix ad. This provides us both with a measure of our main competitor's performance and a benchmark against which to measure our own results.

If ad has been seen continue to Q26.

Others to Screen 32.

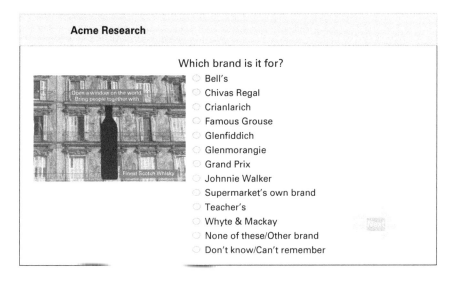

Screen 31. Q26. This repeats Q24 for Grand Prix, to provide us with a measure of how well branded their advertising is.

The brand list should be presented in the same order as it appears for Q24 for each respondent.

The blocks of questions 23, 24 (Crianlarich) and 25,26 (Grand Prix) should be rotated between respondents (see Chapter 10).

Continue to Screen 32.

Acme Research

Acme Research

Thank you for taking part in this survey.
Any personal data you have supplied will be held in confidence according to the Data Protection Act.
Acme Research hope that you will be happy to take another of our surveys if asked in the future.

Privacy policy

Screen 32. Closure screen for survey participants. It is important to thank respondents for their time and reassurance regarding the security of their data is worthwhile.

Close.

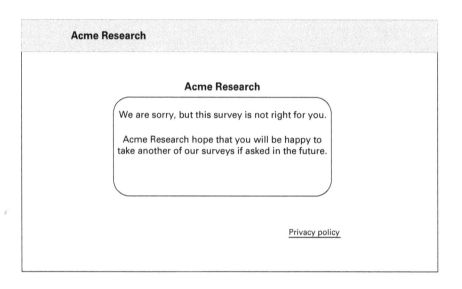

Screen 33. Closure screen for those who failed the screening questions. It is located here in the screen order to avoid disrupting the flow of questions. It is our fault that the survey is not the right one for them, rather than their fault for not meeting our qualifying criteria.

Close.

APPENDIX 2

Market research associations and codes of conduct

Market Research Society (**www.mrs.org.uk**)
    Code of Conduct: **http://www.mrs.org.uk/standards/code_of_conduct/**
ICC (**www.iccwbo.org**) and ICC/ESOMAR (**www.esomar.org**)
Australia AMSRS **www.mrsa.com.au**
    Code of Professional Behaviour: **https://researchsociety.com.au/documents/item/2796**
MRIA (Canada) **www.mria-arim.ca**
    Code of Conduct and Good Practice: **http://www.mria-arim.ca/STANDARDS/CODE2007.asp**
Declaration for the Territory of the Federal Republic of Germany concerning the ICC/ESOMAR International Code on Market and Social Research **www.adm-ev.de**
ASSIRM (Italy) Code of Professional Ethics **www.assirm.it**
JMRA (Japan) Code of Marketing Research **www.jmra-net.or.jp**
Insights Association (United States) **http://www.insightsassociation.org**
EphMRA (European pharmaceutical market research)
    http://www.ephmra.org/

REFERENCES

Albaum, G (1997) The Likert scale revisited, *Journal of the Market Research Society*, **39** (2), pp 331–48

Albaum, G, Roster, C, Yu, J H and Rogers, R D (2007) Simple rating scale formats: exploring extreme responses, *International Journal of Market Research*, **49** (5), pp 633–50

Albaum, G, Wiley, J, Roster, C, and Smith, S M (2011) Visiting item non-responses in internet survey data collection, *International Journal of Market Research*, **53** (5)

Alwin, D F and Krosnick, J (1985) The measurement of values in surveys: a comparison of ratings and rankings, *Public Opinion Quarterly*, **49** (4), pp 535–52

Anderson, K, Wright, M and Wheeler, M (2011) Snap judgement polling: street interviews enabled by new technology, *International Journal of Market Research*, **53** (4)

Antoun, C, Couper, M, Conrad, F (2017) Effects of mobile versus PC web on survey response quality: a crossover experiment in probability web panel. *Public Opinion Quarterly* **81** (S1), pp 280–306

Artingstall, R (1978) Some random thoughts on non-sampling error, *European Research*, **6** (6)

Bailey, P, Pritchard G and Kernohan, H (2015) Gamification in market research: increasing enjoyment, participant engagement and richness of data, but what of data validity?, *International Journal of Market Research,* **57** (1), pp 17–28

Baker, R and Downes-Le-Guin, T (2011) All fun and games? Myths and realities of respondent engagement in online surveys, ESOMAR Congress, Amsterdam

Basi, R K (1999) WWW response rates to socio-demographic items, *Journal of the Market Research Society*, **41** (4), pp 397–401

Bearden, W O and Netermeyer, R G (1999) *Handbook of Marketing Scales*, Sage, Thousand Oaks, CA

Behling, O and Law, K S (2000) *Translating Questionnaires and Other Research Instruments: Problems and solutions*, Sage, Thousand Oaks, CA

Brace, I and Nancarrow, C (2008) Let's get ethical: dealing with socially desirable responding online, Market Research Society Annual Conference

Brace, I, Nancarrow, C and McCloskey, J (1999) MR confidential: a help or a hindrance in the new marketing era? *The Journal of Database Marketing*, **7** (2), pp 173–85

Bradley, N (1999) Sampling for internet surveys: an examination of respondent selection for internet research, *Journal of the Market Research Society*, **41** (4), pp 387–95

Bronner, F and Kuijlen, T (2007) The live or digital interviewer: a comparison between CASI, CAPI and CATI with respect to differences in response behaviour, *International Journal of Market Research*, **49** (2), pp 167–90

Brown, G, Copeland, T and Millward, M (1973) Monadic testing of new products: an old problem and some partial solutions, *Journal of the Market Research Society*, **15** (2), pp 112–31

Brüggen, E, Wetzels, M, de Ruyter, K, Schillewaert, N (2011) Individual differences in motivation to participate in online panels: the effect on response rate and response quality perceptions. International Journal of Market Research, **53** (3), pp 369–90

Brunel, F, Tietje, B, Greenwald, A (2004) Is the Implicit Association Test a valid and valuable measure of implicit consumer social cognition?, *Journal of Consumer Psychology*, **14** (4), pp 385–404

Cape, P (2009) Slider scales in online surveys. CASRO Panel Conference, February 2–3, 2009, New Orleans, LA. Retrieved from, http://www.surveysampling.com/ssi-media/Corporate/white_papers/SSI-Sliders-White-Pape.image (archived at https://perma.cc/E92X-H5F7)

Cape, P (2015) Questionnaire length and fatigue effects: what 10 years have taught us Webinar 28/05/2015, "http://www.surveysampling.com/ssi-media/webinars/ (archived at https://perma.cc/TN62-GNT6)" www.surveysampling.com/ssi-media/webinars/ (archived at https://perma.cc/BX2E-4T3P) [Last accessed 05.08.2017]

Cape, P, Lorch, J and Piekarski, L (2007) A tale of two questionnaires, *Proceedings of the ESOMAR Panel Research Conference*, Orlando, pp 136–49

Cechanowicz, J, Gutwin, C, Brownell, B, and Goodfellow, L, (2013) Effects of gamification on participation and data quality in a real-world market research domain. *Proceedings of the First International Conference on Gameful Design, Research, and Applications, Gamification* 13, October, Stratford, Ontario

Chang, L C and Krosnick, J A (2003) Measuring the frequency of regular behaviors: comparing the 'typical week' to the 'past week', *Sociological Methodology*, **33**, pp 55–80

Christian, L M and Dillman, D A (2004) The influence of graphical and symbolic language manipulations on responses to self-administered questions, *Public Opinion Quarterly*, **68** (1) pp 57–80

Christian, L M, Dillman, D A and Smyth, J D (2007) Helping respondents get it right the first time: the influence of words, symbols, and graphics in web surveys, *Public Opinion Quarterly*, **71** (1), pp 113–25

Chrzan, K and Golovashkina, N (2006) An empirical test of stated importance measures, *International Journal of Market Research*, **48** (6), pp 717–40

Cobanoglu, C, Warde, B, and Moreo, P J (2001) A comparison of mail, fax and web-based survey methods, *International Journal of Market Research*, **43** (4), pp 441–52

Coelho, P and Esteves, S (2007) The choice between a five-point and a ten-point scale in the framework of customer satisfaction measurement, *International Journal of Market Research*, **49** (3), pp 313–39

Conrad, F, Couper, M, Tourangeau, R and Peytchev, A (2005) Impact of progress feedback on task completion: first impressions matter, Association for Computing Machinery, Conference on Human Factors in Computing Systems

Converse, J M and Presser, S (1986) *Handcrafting the Standardized Questionnaire*, Sage, Thousand Oaks, CA

Cooke, M (2010) The Engagement Agenda, Association of Survey Computing Conference, Bristol

Couper, M, Traugott, M and Lamias, M (2001) Web survey design and administration, *Public Opinion Quarterly*, **65**, pp 230–53

Cox, E (1980) The optimal number of response alternatives for a scale: a review, *Journal of Marketing Research*, **17**, pp 407–22

Crowne, D P and Marlowe, D (1960) A new scale of social desirability independent of psychopathology, *Journal of Consulting Psychology*, **24**, pp 349–54

Diamantopolous, A, Schlegelmilch, B and Reynolds, N (1994) Pre-testing in questionnaire design: the impact of respondent characteristics on error detection, *Journal of the Market Research Society*, **36** (4), pp 295–311

Dillman, D (2000) *Mail and Internet Surveys, 2nd edn, The Tailored Design Method*, John Wiley, New York

Dillman, D A, Singer, E, Clark, J R and Treat, J B (1996) Effects of benefits appeals and variations in statements of confidentiality on completion rate for census questionnaires, *Public Opinion Quarterly*, **60** (3)

Dolnicar, S, Grun, B and Leisch, F (2011) Quick, simple and reliable: forced binary survey questions, *International Journal of Market Research*, **53** (2)

Dolnicar, S, Rossiter, J and Grun, B (2012) 'Pick any' measures contaminate brand image studies, *International Journal of Market Research*, **56** (6)

Duffy, B (2003) Response order effects: how do people read?, *International Journal of Market Research*, **45** (4), pp 457–66

Duffy, B, Smith, K, Terhanian, G and Bremer, J (2005) Comparing data from online and face-to-face surveys, *International Journal of Market Research*, **47** (6), pp 615–40

Edwards, A L (1957) *The Social Desirability Variable in Personality Assessment*, Dryden, New York

Eisenhower, D, Mathiowetz, N A and Morganstein, D (1991) Recall error: sources and bias reduction techniques, in (eds) P Biemer, S Sudman, and R M Groves, *Measurement Error in Surveys*, Wiley, New York

Esuli, A and Sebastiani, F (2010) Machines that learn how to code open-ended questions, *International Journal of Market Research*, **52** (6)

Findlay, K and Alberts, K (2011) Gamification – the reality of what it is ... and what it isn't, ESOMAR Congress, Amsterdam

Flores, L (2007) Customer Satisfaction, in *Market Research Handbook*, 5th edn, ESOMAR, pp 347–63

Forsyth, B H, Kudela, M S, Levin, K, Lawrence, D and Willis, G B (2007) Methods for translating an English-language questionnaire on tobacco use into Mandarin, Cantonese, Korean and Vietnamese, *Field Methods*, **19** (3), pp 264–83

Funke, F (2016) A web experiment showing negative effects of slider compared to visual analogue scales and radio button scales, *Social Science Computer Review*, **34** (2), pp 244–254

Goodyear, M (1996) Divided by a common language, *International Journal of Market Research*, **38** (2)

Greenleaf, E A (1992) Measuring extreme response style, *The Public Opinion Quarterly*, **56** (3), pp 328–51

Greenwald, H J and Satow, Y (1970) A short social desirability scale, *Psychology Rep*, **27**, pp 131–35

Gregg, A, Klymowsky, J, Owens, D, and Perryman, A (2013) Let their fingers do the talking? Using the implicit association test in market research, *International Journal of Market Research*, **55** (4)

Harms, J, Biegler, S, Wimmer, C, Kappel, K and Grechenig, T, (2014) 'Gamification of online surveys: design process, case study, and evaluation', NordiCHI '14: proceedings of the 8th Nordic Conference on Human-Computer Interaction: Fun, Fast, Foundational, Association for Survey Computing, Berkeley, England

Harms, J, Seitz, D, Wimmer, C, Kappel, K, and Grechenig, T (2015) Low-Cost Gamification of Online Surveys: Improving the User Experience through Achievement Badges, CHI PLAY 2015, October 03–07, 2015, London

Hogg, A and Masztal, J J (2001) A practical learning about online research, *Advertising Research Foundation Workshop*, October

Holbrook, A L and Krosnick, J A (2010) Social desirability bias in voter turnout reports *Public Opinion Quarterly* **74** (1), pp 37–67

Holbrook, A L, Green, M C and Krosnick, J A (2003) Telephone versus face-to-face interviewing of national probability samples with long questionnaires, *Public Opinion Quarterly*, **67**, pp 79–125

Holtgraves, T, Eck, J and Lasky, B (1997) Face management, question wording and social desirability, *Journal of Applied Psychology*, **27**, pp 1650–71

Hubert, M, Kenning, P (2008) A current overview of consumer neuroscience, *Journal of Consumer Behaviour*, 7, pp 272–92

Johnson, A and Rolfe, G (2011) Engagement, consistency, reach – why the technology landscape precludes all three, Association of Survey Computing Conference, Bristol

Kalton, G and Schuman, H (1982) The effect of the question on survey responses: a review, *Journal of the Royal Statistical Society, Series A*, **145** (1), pp 42–73

Kalton, G, Roberts, J and Holt, D (1980) The effects of offering a middle response option with opinion questions, *Statistician*, **29**, pp 65–78

Katz, L (2006) *Rethinking and Remodelling Customer Satisfaction, Working Paper,* quoted in *Market Research Handbook*, Fifth Edition, ESOMAR, 2007.

Kellner, P (2004) Can online polls produce accurate findings?, *International Journal of Marketing Research*, **46** (1), pp 3–21

Keusch, F, and Zhang, C (2014) A review of issues in gamified survey design, *Annual Conference of the Midwest Association for Public Opinion Research*, November 21–22, Chicago

Krosnick, J A and Alwin, D F (1987) An evaluation of a cognitive theory of response order effects in survey measurement, *Public Opinion Quarterly*, **51** (2), pp 201–19

Krosnick, J and Fabrigar, L (1997) Designing rating scales for effective measurement in surveys, in (eds) L Lyberg, P Biemer, M Collins, E De Leeuw, C Dippo, N Schwarz and D Trewin, *Survey Measurement and Process Quality*, John Wiley, New York

Laflin, L and Hanson, M (2006) https://www.quirks.com/articles/satisfaction-study-is-vehicle-for-minnesota-departmentof-transportation-to-test-question-order (archived at https://perma.cc/HN7P-TV4H) Accessed 23 August 2017

Likert, R (1932) A technique for the measurement of attitudes, *Archives of Psychology*, **140**, pp 5–55

Macer, T and Wilson S (2013) https://www.quirks.com/articles/a-report-on-the-confirmit-market-research-software-survey-1 (archived at https://perma.cc/663F-N79R). Accessed 20 September 2017

McDaniel, C Jr and Gates, R (1993) *Contemporary Marketing Research*, West Publishing Company, St Paul, MN, Chs 11/12

McFarland, S G (1981) Effects of question order on survey responses, *Public Opinion Quarterly*, **45**, pp 208–15

McKay, R and de la Puente, M (1996) Cognitive testing of racial and ethnic questions for the CPS supplement, *Monthly Labor Review*, September, pp 8–12

Malinoff, B and Puleston, J (2011) How far is too far: traditional, flash and gamification interfaces for the future of market research online survey design, ESOMAR 3D Digital Dimensions Conference, Miami

Nancarrow, C, Brace, I and Wright, L T (2000) Tell me lies, tell me sweet little lies: dealing with socially desirable responses in market research, *The Marketing Review*, **2** (1), pp 55–69

Nancarrow, C, Pallister, J and Brace, I (2001) A new research medium, new research populations and seven deadly sins for internet researchers, *Qualitative Market Research*, **4** (3), pp 136–49

Nunan, D and Knox, S (2011) Can search engine advertising help access rare samples?, *International Journal of Market Research*, **53** (4)

Oppenheim, A N (1992) *Questionnaire Design, Interviewing and Attitude Measurement*, 2nd edn, Continuum, London

Osgood, C E, Suci, G J and Tannenbaum, P (1957) *The Measurement of Meaning*, University of Illinois Press, Urbana, IL

Paulhus, D L and Reid, D B (1991) Enhancement and denial in socially desirable responding, *Journal of Personality and Social Psychology*, **60** (2), pp 307–17

Peterson, R A (2000) *Constructing Effective Questionnaires*, Sage, Thousand Oaks, CA

Phillips, D L and Clancy, K J (1972) Some effects of 'social desirability' in survey studies, *American Journal of Sociology*, **77** (5), pp 921–38

Poynter, R and Comley, P (2003) Beyond online panels, *Proceedings of ESOMAR Technovate Conference*, Cannes

Presser, S and Schuman, H (1980) The measurement of a middle position in attitude studies, *Public Opinion Quarterly*, **44**, pp 70–85

Puleston, J and Eggers, M (2012) Dimensions of online survey data quality: What really matters?, *Proceedings of the ESOMAR Congress*, Atlanta

Puleston, J and Sleep, D (2008) Measuring the value of respondent engagement – innovative techniques to improve panel quality, ESOMAR Panel Research, Dublin, October

Puleston, J and Sleep, D (2011) The game experiments – researching how gaming techniques can be used to improve the quality of feedback from online research, ESOMAR Congress, Amsterdam

Reichheld, F (2003) The one number you need to grow, *Harvard Business Review*, December

Reid, J, Morden, M and Reid, A (2007) Maximizing respondent engagement: the use of rich media, *Proceedings of the ESOMAR Congress*, Berlin

Ring, E (1975) Asymmetrical rotation, *European Research*, **3** (3), pp 111–19

Roster, C, Albaum, G and Rogers, R (2006) Can cross-national/cultural studies presume etic equivalency in respondents' use of extreme categories of Likert rating scales?, *International Journal of Market Research*, **48** (6), pp 741–59

Roster, C, Lucianetti, L, and Albaum, G. (2015). Exploring slider vs. categorical response formats in web-based surveys, *Journal of Research Practice*, **11** (1), Article D1. Retrieved from http://jrp.icaap.org/index.php/jrp/article/view/509/413 (archived at https://perma.cc/22PC-4TU9)

Rungie, C, Laurent, G, Dall'Olmo Riley, F, Morrison, D G and Roy, T (2005) Measuring and modeling the (limited) reliability of free choice attitude questions, *International Journal of Research in Marketing*, **22** (3), pp 309–18

Saris, W E and Gallhofer, I N (2007) *Design, Evaluation, and Analysis of Questionnaires for Survey Research*, John Wiley, Hoboken

Saris, W E, Krosnick, J A and Schaeffer, E M (2005) Comparing questions with agree/disagree options to questions with construct-specific response options, http://comm.stanford.edu/faculty/krosnick (archived at https://perma.cc/L3Z4-UQUX). Accessed October 2012

Savitz, J (2011) https://www.quirks.com/articles/data-use-reconciling-hispanic-product-evaluation-ratings (archived at https://perma.cc/PR9V-UU5K). Accessed 23 August 2017

Schaeffer, E M, Krosnick, J A, Langer, G E and Merkle, D M (2005) Comparing the quality of data obtained by minimally balanced and fully balanced attitude questions, *Public Opinion Quarterly*, **69** (3), pp 417–28

Schuman, H and Presser, S (1981) *Questions and Answers in Attitude Surveys*, Sage, Thousand Oaks, CA

Schwarz, N, Hippler, H and Noelle-Neumann, E (1991) A cognitive model of response-order effects in survey measurement, in (eds) N Schwarz and S Sudman, *Context Effects in Social and Psychological Research*, pp 187–201, Springer Verlag, New York

Singer, E, Hippler, H-J and Schwarz, N (1992) Confidentiality assurances in surveys: reassurance or threat, *International Journal of Public Opinion Research*, **4** (34), pp 256–68

Singer, E, Von Thurn, D R and Miller, E R (1995) Confidentiality assurances and response: a quantitative review of the experimental literature, *Public Opinion Quarterly*, **59** (1), pp 67–77

Smyth, J D, Dillman, D A, Christian, L M and Stern, M J (2006) Comparing check-all and forced-choice question formats in web surveys, *Public Opinion Quarterly*, **70** (1), pp 66–77

Stern, M J, Smyth, J D and Mendez, J (2012) The effects of item saliency and question design on measurement error in a self-administered survey, *Field Methods*, **24** (1), pp 3–27

Strahan, R and Gerbasi, K C (1972) Short homogeneous versions of the Marlowe-Crowne social desirability scale, *Journal of Clinical Psychology*, **28**, pp 191–3

Suchman, L and Jordan, B (1990) Interactional troubles in face-to-face survey interviews, *Journal of the American Statistical Association*, **85** (409), pp 232–41

Sudman, S and Bradburn, N (1973) Effects of time and memory factors on response in surveys, *Journal of the American Statistical Association*, **68**, pp 805–15

Sudman, S and Bradburn, N (1982) *Asking Questions: A practical guide to questionnaire design*, Jossey-Bass, San Francisco, CA

Sullivan, O and Gershuny, J (2017) Speed up society? Evidence from the UK 2000 and 2015 time use diary surveys. *Oxford University Research Archive* https://ora.ox.ac.uk/objects/uuid:9a837e21-7e86-4d77-ab66-60c14dea8b97 (archived at https://perma.cc/4VL4-LUW8) Accessed 24 August 2017

Thomas, R, Couper, M P, Bremer, J and Terhanian, G (2007) Truth in measurement: comparing web-based interviewing techniques, *Proceedings of the ESOMAR Congress*, Berlin, pp 195–206

Toepoel, V and Dillman, D A (2010) Words, numbers and visual heuristics in web surveys: is there a hierarchy of importance? *Social Science Computer Review*, **29**, pp 193–207

Toepoel, V, Das, M and Van Soest, A (2008) Effects of design in web surveys – comparing trained and fresh respondents, *Public Opinion Quarterly*, **72** (5), pp 985–1007

Tourangeau, R (1984) Cognitive science and survey methods, in (eds) T Jabine, M Straf, J Tanur and R Tourangeau, *Cognitive Aspects of Survey Methodology: Building a bridge between disciplines*, National Academy Press, Washington, DC

Tourangeau, R, Couper, M and Conrad, F (2004) Spacing, position, and order: interpretive heuristics for visual features of survey questions, *Public Opinion Quarterly*, **68** (3), pp 368–93

Tourangeau, R, Couper, M and Conrad, F (2007) Color, labels and interpretative heuristics for response scales, *Public Opinion Quarterly*, **71** (1), pp 91–112

Tourangeau, R, Rips, L J and Rasinski, K (2000) *The Psychology of Survey Response*, Cambridge University Press, Cambridge

Van Schaik, P and Ling, J (2007) Design parameters of rating scales for web sites, *ACM Transactions on Computer–Human Interaction*, **14**

Vercruyssen, A, van de Putte, B, and Stoop, I, (2011) Are they really too busy for survey participation? The evolution of busyness and busyness claims in Flanders, *Journal of Official Statistics*, 27 (4), pp 619–632

Wable, N and Pall, S (1998) You just do not understand! More and more respondents are saying this to market researchers today, ESOMAR Congress

Warner, S L (1965) Randomized response: a survey technique for eliminating evasive answer bias, *Journal of the American Statistical Association*, 60, pp 63–9

Weijters, B, Geuens, M and Schillewaert, N (2010) The individual consistency of acquiescence and exteme response style in self-report questionnaires, *Applied Psychological Measurement*, **34** (2), pp 105–21

Wood, O (2007) Using faces: measuring emotional engagement for early stage creative, *Proceedings of the ESOMAR Congress*, Berlin, pp 412–37

Worcester, R and Downham, J (1978) *Consumer Market Research Handbook*, 2nd edn, Van Nostrand Reinhold, Wokingham

Wright, L T and Crimp, M (2000) *The Marketing Research Process*, 5th edn, Pearson Education, Harlow

Yang, M-L and Yu, R-R (2011) Effects of identifiers in mail surveys, *Field Methods*, **23** (3), pp 243–65

Zaichkowsky, J L (1999) Personal involvement inventory for advertising, in (eds) W O Bearden and R G Netemeyer, *Handbook of Marketing Scales*, Sage Publications, Thousand Oaks, CA

Zaltman, G (1997) Rethinking market research: putting people back in, *Journal of Marketing Research*, **34** (4), pp 424–437

INDEX

Printed in the USA
CPSIA information can be obtained
at www.ICGtesting.com
JSHW071409211123
52497JS00019B/383

9 781398 604124